CASENOTE® Legal Briefs®

TORTS

Keyed to Courses Using

Epstein and Sharkey's
Cases and Materials on Torts
Thirteenth Edition

Authored by: Publisher's Editorial Staff

ASPEN PUBLISHING

To contact Customer Service, e-mail customer.service@aspenpublishing.com, call 1-800-950-5259, or mail correspondence to:

Aspen Publishing
Attn: Order Department
1 Wall Street
Burlington, MA 01803

Printed in the United States of America.

1 2 3 4 5 6 7 8 9 0

ISBN 979-8-8890-6966-9

SUSTAINABLE FORESTRY INITIATIVE Certified Sourcing
www.forests.org
SFI-00756

DEFAMATION

DEFAMATION

Restatement (Second) of Torts § 559

1. Defamatory language.
2. "Of or concerning" the plaintiff.
3. Publication.
4. Damage to plaintiff's reputation.

DEFAMATORY LANGUAGE

1. Defamatory language must adversely affect plaintiff's reputation. "Inducement and innuendo": Plaintiff may plead additional facts to establish defamatory meaning by innuendo.
2. The person being defamed must be alive.
3. Opinions are permissible.

"OF OR CONCERNING" THE PLAINTIFF

Colloquium: If a statement does not refer to plaintiff on its face, extrinsic evidence may be introduced to establish a connection.

PUBLICATION

1. To be actionable, a defamatory statement must be "published" to third parties.
2. One who republishes defamatory statements made by another is held to be a publisher of defamatory material.

DAMAGE TO PLAINTIFF'S REPUTATION

1. Libel is written or printed.
2. Slander is spoken defamation.
3. Special damages are required for slander, unless it is slander per se.
4. Slander per se are statements that:
   - **a.** Adversely affect one's business.
   - **b.** One has a loathsome disease.
   - **c.** One is guilty of a crime involving moral turpitude.
   - **d.** A woman is unchaste.

CONSTITUTIONAL CONCERNS

When defamation involves a matter of public concern, plaintiff must prove:

1. Falsity of defamatory language; AND
2. Fault on the part of the defendant.

FALSITY

Plaintiff must prove falsity of statement. Thus, if a statement concerning a matter of public concern is true, plaintiff has no cause of action.

FAULT

1. If the plaintiff is a public figure/official, she must prove malice.
2. Malice–*New York Times Co. v. Sullivan*, 376 U.S. 254 (1964).
   - **a.** Knowledge that the statement was false.
   - **b.** Reckless disregard as to whether it was false.
3. Therefore, a private person defendant is not required to prove malice, although the plaintiff must still prove falsity on the matter of public concern. *Gertz v. Robert Welch, Inc.*, 418 U.S. 323 (1974).

DEFENSES TO DEFAMATION

DEFENSES

1. Consent is a complete defense.
2. Truth: If constitutional concerns (*see* box above) are not triggered, then defendant may use truth as a complete defense.
3. Absolute Privilege:
   Defendant may invoke an absolute privilege as a defense when the defamation concerns:
   - **a.** Statements made during judicial proceedings. Restatement (Second) of Torts §§ 585–589.
   - **b.** Statements made by legislators during debate. Restatement (Second) of Torts § 590–590A.
   - **c.** Statements made by government officials in official capacity.
   - **d.** Statements made between spouses. Restatement (Second) of Torts § 592.
4. Qualified Privilege:
   Defendant has the burden of establishing qualified privilege. Privilege may be lost if statements exceed scope of privilege or are made with malice. Examples:
   - **a.** Statements made in defense of speaker's interests. Restatement (Second) of Torts § 594.
   - **b.** Statements made in the interest of the speaker. Restatement (Second) of Torts § 595(1)(b).
   - **c.** Statements made to protect common interests or those of third parties. Restatement (Second) of Torts § 596.
   - **d.** Reports of official proceedings/meetings (must be accurate). Restatement (Second) of Torts § 598.

PRIVACY

FOUR TYPES OF INVASION

1. Commercial Appropriation: Plaintiff must show:
   - **a.** An unauthorized use of plaintiff's picture or name.
   - **b.** Used for defendant's commercial advantage.
2. Intrusion Upon Plaintiff's Solitude:
   - **a.** The act of prying or intruding must be objectionable to a "reasonable person."
   - **b.** Intrusion must take place in a private area (photographs in public are permissible).
3. False Light:
   - **a.** Defendant attributes to plaintiff views she does not hold or actions she did not take.
   - **b.** The false light must be objectionable to a reasonable person under the circumstances.
   - **c.** There must be publicity.
   - **d.** If the false light involves a matter of public concern, malice must be found (*see* Defamation: Fault, point 2).
4. Public Disclosure of Embarrassing Private Facts:
   - **a.** Public disclosure of private information about plaintiff.
   - **b.** The disclosure must be objectionable to a reasonable person of ordinary sensibilities.

VICARIOUS LIABILITY

SITUATIONS WHERE VICARIOUS LIABILITY MAY ARISE

In certain situations, the tortious actions of one party to a third party will be imposed upon another.

1. Principal/Agent–Employer/Employee (*Respondeat Superior*)
   - **a.** An employer is liable for tortious acts committed by an employee, if the act occurs within the scope of employment. **Frolic and Detour**–If an employee substantially deviates from her duties, the employer is not liable.
   - **b.** An employer is usually not liable for intentional torts of an employee, unless the employer authorized the tortious act.
   - **c.** Generally, an employer will not be held liable for the tortious actions of independent contractors, unless:
     - **i.** Independent contractor is engaged in a nondelegable duty (i.e., an abnormally dangerous activity).
     - **ii.** Independent contractor is acting with the apparent authority of the principal.
2. Business Partners/Joint Venturers: Partners and those engaged in the joint venture are liable for the partnership-related torts of each other.
3. Bailors/Bailees:
   - **a.** Generally, a bailor is not vicariously liable for the tortious conduct of his bailee. **Negligent Entrustment**–A bailor may be liable for negligent entrustment as this is not vicarious liability.
   - **b.** Automobile owner will not be held vicariously liable for the driver's tortious conduct.
     - **i.** The car owner may be liable for negligent entrustment to an incompetent driver, which is not vicarious liability.
     - **ii.** **Family Car Doctrine**–In certain jurisdictions, vicarious liability may be found if tortfeasor is an immediate family member of the owner.
4. Parents/Children:
   - **a.** Generally, parents are not vicariously liable for the torts of their children.
   - **b.** Beware of statutes that impose vicarious liability.
   - **c.** Liability may be based on the negligence of the parent to supervise, rather than on the conduct of the child, which is not vicarious liability.

"INTENTIONAL INFLICTION" v. "NEGLIGENT INFLICTION" OF EMOTIONAL DISTRESS

	IIED	NIED
Type of Conduct	Extreme and outrageous conduct	Negligent conduct
Intent	Actual intent or recklessness	No intent, but defendant must be in "zone of danger"
Harm	Extreme emotional distress.	Physical injury or illness required Split authority
Transferred Intent	No	Yes
Punitives	Yes	No

NUISANCE

PUBLIC NUISANCE

Restatement (Second) of Torts § 821(B)(1)

1. Public nuisance is an act that unreasonably interferes with the health, safety, or property rights of the community.
2. A private party may recover only if the private party suffered unique damage not suffered by the public at large.

PRIVATE NUISANCE

Restatement (Second) of Torts § 822
Private nuisance is a substantial, unreasonable interference of another individual's "use and enjoyment" of land. *Jost v. Dairyland Power Cooperative*, 172 N.W.2d 647 (Wisc. 1970).

1. Substantial interference is interference that is offensive to the average person in the community.
   a. The plaintiff's hypersensitivity or specialized use of the property should NOT be taken into account.
2. To establish unreasonable interference, there must be a balancing test between the severity of the nuisance and the utility of the defendant's activity.

Note: Distinguish private nuisance from trespass to land: The latter is an interference with the owner's exclusive possession, while the former is an interference with "use and enjoyment."

REMEDIES

1. Damages: The plaintiff will usually be awarded monetary damages. *Boomer v. Atlantic Cement Co.*, 257 N.E.2d 870 (N.Y. 1970).
2. Injunctive Relief: If the nuisance will cause irreparable injury, and money damages are insufficient, injunctive relief will be granted.
3. Abatement by Self-Help:
   a. In private nuisance cases, self-help abatement is available after notice to defendant and her subsequent refusal to act.
   b. Only necessary force may be used.
   c. In a public nuisance case, only a public authority or a plaintiff suffering from a unique harm may engage in abatement.

DEFENSES TO NUISANCE

DEFENSES

1. Legislative authority: A zoning ordinance permitting nuisance activity is not an absolute defense, but it is persuasive.
2. Conduct of others: When no one actor is liable for all damage, rather the damage is caused by a concurrence of her act and others.
3. "Coming to the nuisance": Plaintiff purchased land next to an existing nuisance for the sole purpose of bringing a harassing lawsuit. *Spur Industries, Inc. v. Del E. Webb Development Co.*, 494 P.2d 700 (Ariz. 1972).

INTENTIONAL INTERFERENCE WITH BUSINESS CONTRACT

TO ESTABLISH A PRIMA FACIE CASE

1. Existence of a valid contractual relationship or business expectancy between plaintiff and a third party.
2. Defendant's knowledge of the relationship or expectancy.
3. Intentional interference by defendant inducing a breach or termination of the expectancy or relationship.
4. Damages.

PRODUCTS LIABILITY

PLAINTIFF MUST FIND

1. A defect.
2. Existence of the defect when the product left the defendant's control.

Note: Be certain to study both Restatement (Second) and Restatement (Third) of Torts: Product Liability, especially in Strict Liability, unless the professor focuses on one Restatement's position.

FOUR TYPES OF DEFECTS

1. Manufacturing defects. Restatement (Third) of Torts: Products Liability § 3
2. Design defects. Restatement (Third) of Torts: Products Liability §§ 2, 16
3. Failure to warn adequately. *Cf.* Restatement (Third) of Torts: Products Liability § 2, cmt. j.
4. Misrepresentation regarding the character or quality of the product.

TO RECOVER ON A DEFECTIVE PRODUCT

Once a plaintiff finds a defective product, she may recover on the following legal theories:

1. Negligence.
2. Strict Liability.
3. Implied Warranties.

NEGLIGENCE THEORY

As in other negligence cases, the plaintiff must show:

1. Duty: Owed to any foreseeable plaintiff (e.g., user, consumer, bystander). *MacPherson v. Buick Motor Co.*, 111 N.E. 1050 (1916).
2. Breach
   a. Standard is the same as in other negligence cases.
   b. Generally, retailers and wholesalers escape negligence liability as long as they satisfy their duty through cursory inspection.
3. Actual and proximate cause.
4. Damages: Physical injury or property damage must be shown. Pure economic loss is not sufficient.

DEFENSES: Same as in negligence cases; disclaimers are irrelevant.

STRICT TORT LIABILITY

To Establish a Prima Facie Case [Restatement (Second) of Torts § 402A; *cf.* Restatement (Third) of Torts: Products Liability § 2(a) (1998)]:

1. Duty: Strict duty is owed by a commercial supplier of a product.
   a. Duty extends to any user and consumer of the product as well as to bystanders.
   b. Product must NOT have been substantially altered when it reaches the plaintiff.
2. Breach:
   a. Defect must make product unreasonably dangerous.
   b. Retailers may be liable even if they had no opportunity to inspect the product.
3. Actual and Proximate Cause:
   a. Actual cause is shown when it is proven that the defect existed when the product left defendant's control; this is inferred if the product moved through the normal channels of distribution.
   b. Proximate cause must be shown as in other negligence cases.
4. Damages: Physical injury or property damage must be shown. Pure economic loss is insufficient.

DEFENSES: Comparative negligence may apply in states that apply it. Contributory negligence is NOT a defense. Disclaimers are irrelevant.

Note: The Restatement (Third) of Torts: Products Liability significantly amended the Restatement (Second) of Torts stance on strict liability. Pay close attention to the differences and to which school of thought the professor subscribes.

IMPLIED WARRANTIES

1. Implied Warranty of Merchantability: Goods of acceptable quality are fit for the ordinary purpose for which the goods are intended.
2. Fitness for a Particular Purpose: Seller has reason to know that the buyer is relying on the seller's skill or judgment to select or furnish goods suitable for a particular purpose.
3. There must be some sort of privity of contract between plaintiff and defendant. Thus, only the buyer, her family, household, and guests can sue for personal injury.
4. Pure economic loss, personal injury, and property damage may be recovered.
5. Disclaimers will be effective against pure economic loss.

DEFENSES: Assumption of risk and comparative negligence are available as defenses. Also, failure to give notice of breach to defendant is a defense under the UCC.

MISUSE OF PROCESS

MALICIOUS PROSECUTION

To Establish a Prima Facie Case:

1. Institution of criminal proceedings against plaintiff.
2. Termination in plaintiff's favor.
3. Absence of probable cause.
4. Improper purpose.
5. Damages.

Note: Prosecutors are immune from liability.

ABUSE OF PROCESS

1. Wrongful use of process (civil or criminal) for an ulterior purpose.
2. Definite act or threat against plaintiff in order to accomplish an ulterior purpose.

About Aspen Publishing

Aspen Publishing is a leading provider of educational content and digital learning solutions to law schools in the U.S. and around the world. Aspen provides best-in-class solutions for legal education through authoritative textbooks, written by renowned authors, and breakthrough products such as Connected eBooks, Connected Quizzing, and PracticePerfect.

The Aspen Casebook Series (famously known among law faculty and students as the "red and black" casebooks) encompasses hundreds of highly regarded textbooks in more than eighty disciplines, from large enrollment courses such as Torts and Contracts to emerging electives such as Sustainability and the Law of Policing. Study aids such as the *Examples & Explanations* and the *Emanuel Law Outlines* series, both highly popular collections, help law students master complex subject matter.

Major products, programs, and initiatives include:

- **Connected eBooks** are enhanced digital textbooks and study aids that come with a suite of online content and learning tools designed to maximize student success. Designed in collaboration with hundreds of faculty and students, the Connected eBook is a significant leap forward in the legal education learning tools available to students.
- **Connected Quizzing** is an easy-to-use formative assessment tool that tests law students' understanding and provides timely feedback to improve learning outcomes. Delivered through CasebookConnect.com, the learning platform already used by students to access their Aspen casebooks, Connected Quizzing is simple to implement and integrates seamlessly with law school course curricula.
- **PracticePerfect** is a visually engaging, interactive study aid to explain commonly encountered legal doctrines through easy-to-understand animated videos, illustrative examples, and numerous practice questions. Developed by a team of experts, PracticePerfect is the ideal study companion for today's law students.
- The **Aspen Learning Library** enables law schools to provide their students with access to the most popular study aids on the market across all of their courses. Available through an annual subscription, the online library consists of study aids in e-book, audio, and video formats with full text search, note-taking, and highlighting capabilities.
- Aspen's **Digital Bookshelf** is an institutional-level online education bookshelf, consolidating everything students and professors need to ensure success. This program ensures that every student has access to affordable course materials from day one.
- **Leading Edge** is a community centered on thinking differently about legal education and putting those thoughts into actionable strategies. At the core of the program is the Leading Edge Conference, an annual gathering of legal education thought leaders looking to pool ideas and identify promising directions of exploration.

Format for the Casenote® Legal Brief

Nature of Case: This section identifies the form of action (e.g., breach of contract, negligence, battery), the type of proceeding (e.g., demurrer, appeal from trial court's jury instructions) or the relief sought (e.g., damages, injunction, criminal sanctions).

Fact Summary: This is included to refresh your memory and can be used as a quick reminder of the facts.

Rule of Law: Summarizes the general principle of law that the case illustrates. It may be used for instant recall of the court's holding and for classroom discussion or home review.

Facts: This section contains all relevant facts of the case, including the contentions of the parties and the lower court holdings. It is written in a logical order to give you a clear understanding of the case. The plaintiff and defendant are identified by their proper names throughout and are always labeled with a (P) or (D).

Issue: The issue is a concise question that brings out the essence of the opinion as it relates to the section of the casebook in which the case appears. Both substantive and procedural issues are included if relevant to the decision.

Palsgraf v. Long Island R.R. Co.

Injured bystander (P) v. Railroad company (D)

N.Y. Ct. App., 248 N.Y. 339, 162 N.E. 99 (1928).

NATURE OF CASE: Appeal from judgment affirming verdict for plaintiff seeking damages for personal injury.

FACT SUMMARY: Helen Palsgraf (P) was injured on R.R.'s (D) train platform when R.R.'s (D) guard helped a passenger aboard a moving train, causing his package to fall on the tracks. The package contained fireworks which exploded, creating a shock that tipped a scale onto Palsgraf (P).

RULE OF LAW
The risk reasonably to be perceived defines the duty to be obeyed.

FACTS: Helen Palsgraf (P) purchased a ticket to Rockaway Beach from R.R. (D) and was waiting on the train platform. As she waited, two men ran to catch a train that was pulling out from the platform. The first man jumped aboard, but the second man, who appeared as if he might fall, was helped aboard by the guard on the train who had kept the door open so they could jump aboard. A guard on the platform also helped by pushing him onto the train. The man was carrying a package wrapped in newspaper. In the process, the man dropped his package, which fell on the tracks. The package contained fireworks and exploded. The shock of the explosion was apparently of great enough strength to tip over some scales at the other end of the platform, which fell on Palsgraf (P) and injured her. A jury awarded her damages, and R.R. (D) appealed.

ISSUE: Does the risk reasonably to be perceived define the duty to be obeyed?

HOLDING AND DECISION: (Cardozo, C.J.) Yes. The risk reasonably to be perceived defines the duty to be obeyed. If there is no foreseeable hazard to the injured party as the result of a seemingly innocent act, the act does not become a tort because it happened to be a wrong as to another. If the wrong was not willful, the plaintiff must show that the act as to her had such great and apparent possibilities of danger as to entitle her to protection. Negligence in the abstract is not enough upon which to base liability. Negligence is a relative concept, evolving out of the common law doctrine of trespass on the case. To establish liability, the defendant must owe a legal duty of reasonable care to the injured party. A cause of action in tort will lie where harm, though unintended, could have been averted or avoided by observance of such a duty. The scope of the duty is limited by the range of danger that a reasonable person could foresee. In this case, there was nothing to suggest from the appearance of the parcel or otherwise that the parcel contained fireworks. The guard could not reasonably have had any warning of a threat to Palsgraf (P), and R.R. (D) therefore cannot be held liable. Judgment is reversed in favor of R.R. (D).

DISSENT: (Andrews, J.) The concept that there is no negligence unless R.R. (D) owes a legal duty to take care as to Palsgraf (P) herself is too narrow. Everyone owes to the world at large the duty of refraining from those acts that may unreasonably threaten the safety of others. If the guard's action was negligent as to those nearby, it was also negligent as to those outside what might be termed the "danger zone." For Palsgraf (P) to recover, R.R.'s (D) negligence must have been the proximate cause of her injury, a question of fact for the jury.

ANALYSIS

The majority defined the limit of the defendant's liability in terms of the danger that a reasonable person in defendant's situation would have perceived. The dissent argued that the limitation should not be placed on liability, but rather on damages. Judge Andrews suggested that only injuries that would not have happened but for R.R.'s (D) negligence should be compensable. Both the majority and dissent recognized the policy-driven need to limit liability for negligent acts, seeking, in the words of Judge Andrews, to define a framework "that will be practical and in keeping with the general understanding of mankind." The Restatement (Second) of Torts has accepted Judge Cardozo's view.

Quicknotes

FORESEEABILITY A reasonable expectation that change is the probable result of certain acts or omissions.

NEGLIGENCE Conduct falling below the standard of care that a reasonable person would demonstrate under similar conditions.

PROXIMATE CAUSE The natural sequence of events without which an injury would not have been sustained.

Party ID: Quick identification of the relationship between the parties.

Concurrence/Dissent: All concurrences and dissents are briefed whenever they are included by the casebook author.

Analysis: This last paragraph gives you a broad understanding of where the case "fits in" with other cases in the section of the book and with the entire course. It is a hornbook-style discussion indicating whether the case is a majority or minority opinion and comparing the principal case with other cases in the casebook. It may also provide analysis from restatements, uniform codes, and law review articles.

Holding and Decision: This section offers a clear and in-depth discussion of the rule of the case and the court's rationale. It is written in easy-to-understand language and answers the issue presented by applying the law to the facts of the case. When relevant, it includes a thorough discussion of the exceptions to the case as listed by the court, any major cites to the other cases on point, and the names of the judges who wrote the decisions.

Quicknotes: Conveniently defines legal terms found in the case.

Note to Students

Aspen Publishing is proud to offer *Casenote® Legal Briefs*—continuing thirty years of publishing America's best-selling legal briefs.

Casenote® Legal Briefs are designed to help you save time when briefing assigned cases. Organized under convenient headings, they show you how to abstract the basic facts and holdings from the text of the actual opinions handed down by the courts. Used as part of a rigorous study regimen, they can help you spend more time analyzing and critiquing points of law than on copying bits and pieces of judicial opinions into your notebook or outline.

Casenote® Legal Briefs should never be used as a substitute for assigned casebook readings. They work best when read as a follow-up to reviewing the underlying opinions themselves. Students who try to avoid reading and digesting the judicial opinions in their casebooks or online sources will end up shortchanging themselves in the long run. The ability to absorb, critique, and restate the dynamic and complex elements of case law decisions is crucial to your success in law school and beyond. It cannot be developed vicariously.

In addition to *Casenote® Legal Briefs*, Aspen Publishing offers the following study aids:

- *Casenote® Legal Briefs*
- *Emanuel® Law Outlines*
- Emanuel® *Law in a Flash Flash Cards*
- Emanuel® *CrunchTime® Series*

Each of these series is designed to provide you with easy-to-understand explanations of complex points of law. Each volume offers guidance on the principles of legal analysis and, consulted regularly, will hone your ability to spot relevant issues. We have titles that will help you prepare for class, prepare for your exams, and enhance your general comprehension of the law along the way.

To find out more about our law school tools for success, visit us at *www.AspenPublishing.com* or e-mail us at *customer.service@aspenpublishing.com*. We'll be happy to assist you.

How to Brief a Case

A. Decide on a Format and Stick to It

Structure is essential to a good brief. It enables you to arrange systematically the related parts that are scattered throughout most cases, thus making manageable and understandable what might otherwise seem to be an endless and unfathomable sea of information. There are, of course, an unlimited number of formats that can be utilized. However, it is best to find one that suits your needs and stick to it. Consistency breeds both efficiency and the security that when called upon you will know where to look in your brief for the information you are asked to give.

Any format, as long as it presents the essential elements of a case in an organized fashion, can be used. Experience, however, has led *Casenote® Legal Briefs* to develop and utilize the following format because of its logical flow and universal applicability.

NATURE OF CASE: This is a brief statement of the legal character and procedural status of the case (e.g., "Appeal of a burglary conviction").

There are many different alternatives open to a litigant dissatisfied with a court ruling. The key to determining which one has been used is to discover *who is asking this court for what.*

This first entry in the brief should be kept as *short as possible.* Use the court's terminology if you understand it. But since jurisdictions vary as to the titles of pleadings, the best entry is the one that addresses who wants what in this proceeding, not the one that sounds most like the court's language.

RULE OF LAW: A statement of the general principle of law that the case illustrates (e.g., "An acceptance that varies any term of the offer is considered a rejection and counteroffer").

Determining the rule of law of a case is a procedure similar to determining the issue of the case. Avoid being fooled by red herrings; there may be a few rules of law mentioned in the case excerpt, but usually only one is *the* rule with which the casebook editor is concerned. The techniques used to locate the issue, described below, may also be utilized to find the rule of law. Generally, your best guide is simply the chapter heading. It is a clue to the point the casebook editor seeks to make and should be kept in mind when reading every case in the respective section.

FACTS: A synopsis of only the essential facts of the case, i.e., those bearing upon or leading up to the issue.

The facts entry should be a short statement of the events and transactions that led one party to initiate legal proceedings against another in the first place. While some cases conveniently state the salient facts at the beginning of the decision, in other instances they will have to be culled from hiding places throughout the text, even from concurring and dissenting opinions. Some of the "facts" will often be in dispute and should be so noted. Conflicting evidence may be briefly pointed up. "Hard" facts must be included. Both must be *relevant* in order to be listed in the facts entry. It is impossible to tell what is relevant until the entire case is read, as the ultimate determination of the rights and liabilities of the parties may turn on something buried deep in the opinion.

Generally, the facts entry should not be longer than three to five *short* sentences.

It is often helpful to identify the role played by a party in a given context. For example, in a construction contract case the identification of a party as the "contractor" or "builder" alleviates the need to tell that that party was the one who was supposed to have built the house.

It is always helpful, and a good general practice, to identify the "plaintiff" and the "defendant." This may seem elementary and uncomplicated, but, especially in view of the creative editing practiced by some casebook editors, it is sometimes a difficult or even impossible task. Bear in mind that the *party presently* seeking something from this court may not be the plaintiff, and that sometimes only the cross-claim of a defendant is treated in the excerpt. Confusing or misaligning the parties can ruin your analysis and understanding of the case.

ISSUE: A statement of the general legal question answered by or illustrated in the case. For clarity, the issue is best put in the form of a question capable of a "yes" or "no" answer. In reality, the issue is simply the Rule of Law put in the form of a question (e.g., "May an offer be accepted by performance?").

The major problem presented in discerning what is *the* issue in the case is that an opinion usually purports to raise and answer several questions. However, except for rare cases, only one such question is really the issue in the case. Collateral issues not necessary to the resolution of the matter in controversy are handled by the court by language known as *"obiter dictum"* or merely *"dictum."* While dicta may be included later in the brief, they have no place under the issue heading.

To find the issue, ask *who wants what* and then go on to ask *why did that party succeed or fail in getting it.*

Once this is determined, the "why" should be turned into a question.

The complexity of the issues in the cases will vary, but in all cases a single-sentence question should sum up the issue. *In a few cases,* there will be two, or even more rarely, three issues of equal importance to the resolution of the case. Each should be expressed in a single-sentence question.

Since many issues are resolved by a court in coming to a final disposition of a case, the casebook editor will reproduce the portion of the opinion containing the issue or issues most relevant to the area of law under scrutiny. A noted law professor gave this advice: "Close the book; look at the title on the cover." Chances are, if it is Property, you need not concern yourself with whether, for example, the federal government's treatment of the plaintiff's land really raises a federal question sufficient to support jurisdiction on this ground in federal court.

The same rule applies to chapter headings designating sub-areas within the subjects. They tip you off as to what the text is designed to teach. The cases are arranged in a casebook to show a progression or development of the law, so that the preceding cases may also help.

It is also most important to remember to *read the notes and questions* at the end of a case to determine what the editors wanted you to have gleaned from it.

HOLDING AND DECISION: This section should succinctly explain the rationale of the court in arriving at its decision. In capsulizing the "reasoning" of the court, it should always include an application of the general rule or rules of law to the specific facts of the case. Hidden justifications come to light in this entry: the reasons for the state of the law, the public policies, the biases and prejudices, those considerations that influence the justices' thinking and, ultimately, the outcome of the case. At the end, there should be a short indication of thedisposition or procedural resolution of the case (e.g., "Decision of the trial court for Mr. Smith (P) reversed").

The foregoing format is designed to help you "digest" the reams of case material with which you will be faced in your law school career. Once mastered by practice, it will place at your fingertips the information the authors of your casebooks have sought to impart to you in case-by-case illustration and analysis.

B. Be as Economical as Possible in Briefing Cases

Once armed with a format that encourages succinctness, it is as important to be economical with regard to the time spent on the actual reading of the case as it is to be economical in the writing of the brief itself. This does not mean "skimming" a case. Rather, it means reading the case with an "eye" trained to recognize into which "section" of your brief a particular passage or line fits and having a system for quickly and precisely marking the case so that the passages fitting any one particular part of the brief can be easily identified and brought together in a concise and accurate manner when the brief is actually written.

It is of no use to simply repeat everything in the opinion of the court; record only enough information to trigger your recollection of what the court said. Nevertheless, an accurate statement of the "law of the case," i.e., the legal principle applied to the facts, is absolutely essential to class preparation and to learning the law under the case method.

To that end, it is important to develop a "shorthand" that you can use to make marginal notations. These notations will tell you at a glance in which section of the brief you will be placing that particular passage or portion of the opinion.

Some students prefer to underline all the salient portions of the opinion (with a pencil or colored underliner marker), making marginal notations as they go along. Others prefer the color-coded method of underlining, utilizing different colors of markers to underline the salient portions of the case, each separate color being used to represent a different section of the brief. For example, blue underlining could be used for passages relating to the rule of law, yellow for those relating to the issue, and green for those relating to the holding and decision, etc. While it has its advocates, thecolor-coded method can be confusing and time-consuming (all that time spent on changing colored markers). Furthermore, it can interfere with the continuity and concentration many students deem essential to the reading of a case for maximum comprehension. In the end, however, it is a matter of personal preference and style. Just remember, whatever method you use, underlining must be used sparingly or its value is lost.

If you take the marginal notation route, an efficient and easy method is to go along underlining the key portions of the case and placing in the margin alongside them the following "markers" to indicate where a particular passage or line "belongs" in the brief you will write:

N (NATURE OF CASE)
RL (RULE OF LAW)
I (ISSUE)
HL (HOLDING AND DECISION, relates to the RULE OF LAW behind the decision)
HR (HOLDING AND DECISION, gives the RATIONALE or reasoning behind the decision)
HA (HOLDING AND DECISION, applies the general principle(s) of law to the facts of the case to arrive at the decision)

Remember that a particular passage may well contain information necessary to more than one part of your brief, in which case you simply note that in the margin. If you are using the color-coded underlining method instead of marginal notation, simply make asterisks or checks in the margin next to the passage in question in the colors that indicate the additional sections of the brief where it might be utilized.

The economy of utilizing "shorthand" in marking cases for briefing can be maintained in the actual brief writing process itself by utilizing "law student shorthand" within the brief. There are many commonly used words and phrases for which abbreviations can be substituted in your briefs (and in your class notes also). You can develop abbreviations that are personal to you and which will save you a lot of time. A reference list of briefing abbreviations can be found on page x of this book.

C. Use Both the Briefing Process and the Brief as a Learning Tool

Now that you have a format and the tools for briefing cases efficiently, the most important thing is to make the time spent in briefing profitable to you and to make the most advantageous use of the briefs you create. Of course, the briefs are invaluable for classroom reference when you are called upon to explain or analyze a particular case. However, they are also useful in reviewing for exams. A quick glance at the fact summary should bring the case to mind, and a rereading of the rule of law should enable you to go over the underlying legal concept in your mind, how it was applied in that particular case, and how it might apply in other factual settings.

As to the value to be derived from engaging in the briefing process itself, there is an immediate benefit that arises from being forced to sift through the essential facts and reasoning from the court's opinion and to succinctly express them in your own words in your brief. The process ensures that you understand the case and the point that it illustrates, and that means you will be ready to absorb further analysis and information brought forth in class. It also ensures you will have something to say when called upon in class. The briefing process helps develop a mental agility for getting to the *gist* of a case and for identifying, expounding on, and applying the legal concepts and issues found there. The briefing process is the mental process on which you must rely in taking law school examinations; it is also the mental process upon which lawyers rely in serving their clients and in making a living.

Abbreviations for Briefs

acceptance . . . acp
affirmed . . . aff
answer . . . ans
assumption of risk . . . a/r
attorney . . . atty
beyond a reasonable doubt . . . b/r/d
bona fide purchaser . . . BFP
breach of contract . . . br/k
cause of action . . . c/a
common law . . . c/l
Constitution . . . Con
constitutional . . . con
contract . . . K
contributory negligence . . . c/n
cross . . . x
cross-complaint . . . x/c
cross-examination . . . x/ex
cruel and unusual punishment . . . c/u/p
defendant . . . D
dismissed . . . dis
double jeopardy . . . d/j
due process . . . d/p
equal protection . . . e/p
equity . . . eq
evidence . . . ev
exclude . . . exc
exclusionary rule . . . exc/r
felony . . . f/n
freedom of speech . . . f/s
good faith . . . g/f
habeas corpus . . . h/c
hearsay . . . hr
husband . . . H
injunction . . . inj
in loco parentis . . . ILP
inter vivos . . . I/v
joint tenancy . . . j/t
judgment . . . judgt
jurisdiction . . . jur
last clear chance . . . LCC
long-arm statute . . . LAS
majority view . . . maj
meeting of minds . . . MOM
minority view . . . min
Miranda rule . . . Mir/r
Miranda warnings . . . Mir/w
negligence . . . neg
notice . . . ntc
nuisance . . . nus
obligation . . . ob
obscene . . . obs
offer . . . O
offeree . . . OE
offeror . . . OR
ordinance . . . ord
pain and suffering . . . p/s
parol evidence . . . p/e
plaintiff . . . P
prima facie . . . p/f
probable cause . . . p/c
proximate cause . . . px/c
real property . . . r/p
reasonable doubt . . . r/d
reasonable man . . . r/m
rebuttable presumption . . . rb/p
remanded . . . rem
res ipsa loquitur . . . RIL
respondeat superior . . . r/s
Restatement . . . RS
reversed . . . rev
Rule Against Perpetuities . . . RAP
search and seizure . . . s/s
search warrant . . . s/w
self-defense . . . s/d
specific performance . . . s/p
statute . . . S
statute of frauds . . . S/F
statute of limitations . . . S/L
summary judgment . . . s/j
tenancy at will . . . t/w
tenancy in common . . . t/c
tenant . . . t
third party . . . TP
third party beneficiary . . . TPB
transferred intent . . . TI
unconscionable . . . uncon
unconstitutional . . . unconst
undue influence . . . u/e
Uniform Commercial Code . . . UCC
unilateral . . . uni
vendee . . . VE
vendor . . . VR
versus . . . v
void for vagueness . . . VFV
weight of authority . . . w/a
weight of the evidence . . . w/e
wife . . . W
with . . . w/
within . . . w/i
without . . . w/o
without prejudice . . . w/o/p
wrongful death . . . wr/d

Table of Cases

CHAPTER 1

Intentional Harms: The Prima Facie Case and Defenses

Quick Reference Rules of Law

Vosburg v. Putney

Student (P) v. Student (D)

Wis. Sup. Ct., 50 N.W. 403 (1891)

NATURE OF CASE: Appeal from award of damages for a battery.

FACT SUMMARY: While at school, 11-year-old Putney (D) kicked 14-year-old Vosburg (P) in the leg, and, as a result, Vosburg (P) later lost the use of that leg.

RULE OF LAW

In an action to recover damages for an alleged assault and battery, the victim must only show either that the alleged wrongdoer had an unlawful intention to produce harm (i.e., an unlawful intention in committing the act which occurred) or that he committed an unlawful act.

FACTS: Vosburg (P), 14 years old, and Putney (D), 11 years old, were both students at the high school in Waukesha. On February 20, 1889, while school was in session, Putney (D) lightly kicked Vosburg (P) in the leg. Since Vosburg's (P) leg was in a weakened condition from a previous injury which was still healing, the kick caused Vosburg (P) to permanently lose the use of that leg (i.e., infection destroyed the bone). Thereafter, Vosburg (P) sued Putney (D) for damages resulting from the kick. The jury found the kick was the exciting cause of Vosburg's (P) injury, Putney (D) did not intend harm, and Vosburg (P) was entitled to $2,500 damages. Thereupon, judgment was entered for Vosburg (P) and this appeal followed.

ISSUE: In an action to recover damages for an alleged assault and battery, must the victim only show either that the alleged wrongdoer had an unlawful intention to produce harm (i.e., an unlawful intention in committing the act which occurred) or that he committed an unlawful act?

HOLDING AND DECISION: (Lyon, J.) Yes. In an action to recover damages for an alleged assault and battery, the victim must only show either that the alleged wrongdoer had an unlawful intention to produce harm (i.e., an unlawful intention in committing the act which occurred) or that he committed an unlawful act. This rule is based upon the rationale that "if the intended act is unlawful, the intention to commit it must necessarily be unlawful." Of course, once it is established that the wrongdoer committed an assault and battery, he is liable for all injuries resulting directly from the wrongful act, whether or not the injuries could have been foreseen by him. Here, since the kick occurred after regular school exercises had commenced (i.e., when there was no "implied license of the playgrounds" allowing for boyish sports, etc.), it was unlawful. As such, Putney (D) committed an assault and battery and he is liable for all damages that resulted, even though Vosburg's (P) leg was in a weakened condition from a previous injury. Since certain testimony, though, was erroneously admitted at trial, judgment is reversed, and the case remanded.

ANALYSIS

Any intent to do an act that is wrong is sufficient. Malice is not necessary. Note tha t the intent may be to "do" the wrongful act or to do an act which is "substantially certain" to cause a result which is wrongful. Note, also, that this case demonstrates the well-settled proposition that "the tortfeasor must take his victim as he finds him." Referred to in negligence as the "thin skull" doctrine, it essentially means the fact that a plaintiff, such as Vosburg (P), is particularly susceptible to serious injury will not mitigate the tortfeasor's liability whatsoever.

Quicknotes

ASSAULT The intentional placing of another in fear of immediate bodily injury.

BATTERY Unlawful contact with the body of another person.

INTENT The state of mind that exists when one's purpose is to commit an act.

THIN SKULL DOCTRINE Doctrine holding the defendant is liable in tort for the aggravation of a plaintiff's existing injury or condition, regardless of whether the magnitude of the injury was foreseeable.

Dougherty v. Stepp

Landowner (P) v. Adverse possession claimant (D)

N.C. Sup. Ct., 18 N.C. 371 (1835)

NATURE OF CASE: Appeal from judgment for defendant in action to recover damages for trespass.

FACT SUMMARY: Stepp (D) entered the unenclosed property of Dougherty (P) without permission for the purpose of surveying Dougherty's (P) property and claiming a portion of it as his own.

RULE OF LAW

Every unprivileged entry onto the land of another is a trespass regardless of the amount of actual damages.

FACTS: Stepp (D) entered the unenclosed property of Dougherty (P) without consent. While on the property, Stepp (D) surveyed the land and claimed part of it as his own. However, the surveying techniques involved no marking of trees or cutting of bushes. The jury found for Stepp (D), and Dougherty (P) appealed. The state's highest court granted review.

ISSUE: Is every unprivileged entry onto the land of another a trespass regardless of the amount of actual damages?

HOLDING AND DECISION: (Ruffin, C.J.) Yes. Every unprivileged entry onto the land of another is a trespass regardless of the amount of actual damages. An action for trespass can be maintained without proof of any actual damage. From every entry against the will of the landowner, the law implies some damage; "if nothing more, the treading down the grass or herbage." Reversed.

ANALYSIS

At common law the trespass action was a safeguard against the *repeated* trespasser. Without the deterrent of legal liability for *mere entry* on the land without damage, the trespasser could after numerous entries onto the land claim an easement by prescription. The case also presents the old rule that a person is strictly liable for trespass, i.e., if he enters the land of another without permission, he is liable regardless of his intent or negligence in doing so. The present rule is that liability for trespass exists only if there is intentional or negligent intrusion.

Quicknotes

PRESCRIPTIVE EASEMENT A manner of acquiring an easement in another's property by continuous and uninterrupted use in satisfaction of the statutory requirements of adverse possession.

TRESPASS QUARE CLAUSUM FREGIT Action for damages sustained as a result of the defendant's illegal entry onto plaintiff's property.

Mohr v. Williams

Patient (P) v. Surgeon (D)

Minn. Sup. Ct., 104 N.W. 12 (1905)

NATURE OF CASE: Action to recover damages for battery.

FACT SUMMARY: Without permission, either in writing or orally, the defendant operated on plaintiff's ear.

RULE OF LAW

If a defendant's actions exceed the consent given and defendant does a substantially different act than the one authorized, defendant is liable.

FACTS: Mohr (P) was admitted to surgery so that defendant could operate on her right ear. When Mohr (P) was unconscious, Williams (D) discovered the issue with the right ear was not that serious, but that the left ear was infected. Thus, without awakening Mohr (P), Williams (D) operated on the left ear. Williams (D) did this despite only having permission to operate on the right ear. The operation was successful, but Mohr (P) nevertheless brought an action for battery. The verdict was for the plaintiff, but the court ordered a new trial to reset the damages.

ISSUE: If a defendant's actions exceed the consent given and defendant does a substantially different act than the one authorized, is defendant liable?

HOLDING AND DECISION: (Brown, J.) Yes. If defendant's actions exceed the consent given and defendant does a substantially different act than the one authorized, defendant is liable. Unless the defendant discovers a condition that endangers the life of the plaintiff patient during the operation to which the plaintiff consented, there is no consent to a different operation. In this case, the diseased condition was not discovered in the course of the authorized operation but by independent examination before the operation, and, further, it was not an imminently dangerous condition. Affirmed.

ANALYSIS

The case falls into the majority view. However, doctors have circumvented the problem of this decision by requiring the patient to give blanket consent to any remedy the physician thinks best.

Quicknotes

BATTERY Unlawful contact with the body of another person.

Hudson v. Craft

Boxer (P) v. Fight organizer (D)

Cal. Sup. Ct., 204 P.2d 1 (1949)

NATURE OF CASE: Appeal from dismissal of an action for damages for assault and battery.

FACT SUMMARY: Hudson (P) was injured in an unlicensed carnival boxing match for which he was promised $5, but his complaint for damages against Craft (D), the concessionaire, was dismissed on the ground that Hudson (P) consented to his injury.

RULE OF LAW

A promoter is liable where he conducts boxing matches or prize fights without a license and in violation of the statutory provisions regardless of the rights as between the contestants. The consent of the combatants does not relieve the promoter of that liability.

FACTS: Hudson (P), an 18-year-old boy, attended a carnival where he paid a separate admission to enter a boxing concession. Craft (D), the operator of the concession, had no license from the state athletic commission to stage prize fights. Hudson (P) was promised $5 prize money to participate in a boxing match. Hudson (P) fought and was struck, suffering injuries for which he sought damages. Hudson's (P) complaint was dismissed on the ground that he had consented to risk of injury. Hudson (P) appealed, arguing that his consent was ineffective as a matter of policy.

ISSUE: Is a promoter liable where he conducts boxing matches or prize fights without a license and in violation of the statutory provisions regardless of the rights as between the contestants?

HOLDING AND DECISION: (Carter, J.) Yes. A promoter is liable where he conducts boxing matches or prize fights without a license and in violation of the statutory provisions regardless of the rights as between the contestants. The consent of the combatants does not relieve the promoter of that liability. Reversed.

ANALYSIS

The minority rule stated in the decision is followed by Restatement (Second) of Torts §60, while the exception (the concise rule) is found in §61. The majority rule holds that where persons consent to fight, each may sue the other for his injuries. This being contrary to the maxim, "one is not legally injured if he has consented to the act complained of or was willing that it should occur," the courts have attempted to rationalize the majority rule on the basis of the state's being a party to a breach of the peace to which breach no one may consent.

Quicknotes

BATTERY Unlawful contact with the body of another person.

PROMOTER LIABILITY A finding of liability on the part of a promoter where the corporation has not expressly assumed the acts of the promoter.

McGuire v. Almy

Nurse (P) v. Insane patient (D)

Mass. Sup. Jud. Ct., 8 N.E.2d 760 (1937)

NATURE OF CASE: Action for damages for assault and battery.

FACT SUMMARY: Almy (D), an insane ward, injured her nurse, McGuire (P), during a rage.

RULE OF LAW

An insane person may be capable of entertaining the intent to commit a battery.

FACTS: McGuire (P), a registered nurse, had been hired to give 24-hour care to Almy (D), an insane person. Almy (D) had a violent attack during which she broke furniture and warned McGuire (P) not to enter her room or she would be killed. After entering, McGuire (P) approached Almy (D), who stood in striking position with a piece of furniture raised above her head. When McGuire (P) grabbed for the hand with the weapon, Almy (D) struck her. There was a jury verdict for McGuire (P). Almy (D) appealed the denial of her motion for a directed verdict.

ISSUE: May an insane person be capable of entertaining the intent to commit a battery?

HOLDING AND DECISION: (Qua, J.) Yes. An insane person may be capable of entertaining the intent to commit a battery. An insane person is to be judged by the same standards as a normal person. Intent to do the act is the key to a battery, not the intent to harm. If an insane person can entertain that intent, then he can be liable for battery. The standard applies even though an insane person's act may be uncontrollable. The loss is placed on the insane actor rather than on the innocent victim. Judgment for the plaintiff on the verdict.

ANALYSIS

This case represents a basic policy decision that is generally accepted. The policy reasons are (1) the loss is better borne by the actor than the victim; (2) liability will encourage closer surveillance by custodians; and (3) insanity is easily feigned. The counterargument is that one should not be liable for acts not within his control. This is not generally accepted.

Quicknotes

BATTERY Unlawful contact with the body of another person.

INSANITY DEFENSE A defense which negates liability or culpability by alleging that the defendant is inflicted with a psychological condition preventing him from controlling his actions or comprehending the nature and consequences of his conduct.

INTENT The existence of a particular state of mind whereby an individual seeks to achieve a particular result by his action.

Courvoisier v. Raymond

Shop owner (D) v. Sheriff (P)

Colo. Sup. Ct., 47 P. 284 (1896)

NATURE OF CASE: Appeal from award of damages.

FACT SUMMARY: Courvoisier (D) believed that Raymond (P), a policeman, was one of the rioters outside of his home and shot him as he approached.

RULE OF LAW

An action of force is justified by self-defense whenever the circumstances are such as to cause a reasonable man to believe that his life is in danger or that he is in danger of receiving great bodily harm and that it is necessary to use such force for protection.

FACTS: On June 12, 1892, Courvoisier (D) was asleep in a room he occupied over his jewelry store when two men invaded his house. Presuming these men to be burglars, Courvoisier (D) took his revolver and ejected them. Once outside, the men were joined by others who assaulted Courvoisier (D) with stones. In order to frighten the men away, Courvoisier (D) fired several shots in the air. The shots attracted the attention of deputy sheriff Raymond (P) and two other deputy sheriffs. As the other two officers approached the men in the street, Raymond (P) approached Courvoisier (D) from the direction of the rioting men. As Raymond (P) approached, Courvoisier (D) shot him. Thereafter, Raymond (P) sued Courvoisier (D) for damages. As a defense, Courvoisier (D) claimed that he believed his life was in danger, that Raymond (P) was one of the rioters, and that the shooting was necessary for his self-defense. After a verdict for Raymond (P), this appeal followed.

ISSUE: Is an action of force justified by self-defense whenever the circumstances are such as to cause a reasonable man to believe that his life is in danger or that he is in danger of receiving great bodily harm and that it is necessary to use such force for protection?

HOLDING AND DECISION: (Hayt, C.J.) Yes. An act of force is justified by self-defense whenever the circumstances are such as to cause a reasonable man to believe that his life is in danger or that he is in danger of receiving great bodily harm and that it is necessary to use such force for protection. Under this rule, a person using force does not actually have to be in danger as long as he reasonably believes that he is and that force is necessary for his self-defense. Here, though, the trial court instructed the jury that the shooting was only justified if Raymond (P) was actually attacking Courvoisier (D). Since this instruction was in error, the judgment must be reversed.

ANALYSIS

This case illustrates the general view. Note, also, that under the general rule there is no duty to retreat, rather than use force, whenever a person reasonably believes that he is in danger and that force is necessary for self-defense. Under the minority view, though, a person must retreat rather than use deadly force, unless (1) retreating would be dangerous to oneself or a third person, or (2) he is in his own home, or (3) he is attempting a "valid arrest." Note, finally, that there is no privilege of self-defense when the danger has passed or when excessive force is used.

Quicknotes

SELF-DEFENSE A justification doctrine that permits one to respond to a threatened injury with a corresponding degree of physical force, while negating any corresponding legal consequence for the results of his defensive act.

Bird v. Holbrook

Trespasser (P) v. Landowner (D)

C.P., 130 Eng. Rep. 911 (1825)

NATURE OF CASE: Action for damages resulting from an assault.

FACT SUMMARY: Bird (P) was injured by a spring gun on Holbrook's (D) property.

RULE OF LAW
Deadly force in the nature of traps may not be used without notice to protect property.

FACTS: Holbrook's (D) garden had been robbed of valuable flowers. Holbrook (D) set a spring gun to injure the thief if he tried to steal more flowers. No notices were posted. Bird (P) entered Holbrook's (D) property to recover a peafowl that had flown onto the property. Bird (P) did not see the wires to the spring gun and was shot. Holbrook (D) alleged self-defense and that a party should not profit from his own wrongs (trespass). Damages were awarded Bird (P) on the grounds the force used was excessive and was designed to injure rather than deter.

ISSUE: May deadly force in the nature of traps be used without notice to protect property?

HOLDING AND DECISION: (Best, C.J.) No. Deadly force in the nature of traps may not be used without notice to protect property. Here, Holbrook's (D) sole purpose was to injure the thief. Barbed wire or glass on a wall is meant to deter. It is noticeable and is not calculated to cause severe injury. A spring gun is for the purpose of killing or maiming. Its use is not privileged. If notices are posted all around the property that deadly traps are present, and with knowledge of this fact a party enters, no suit may be maintained. However, where no notice of such traps is present, liability is predicated on the assumption that human life is more important than property. Even a thief could recover. Affirmed.

CONCURRENCE: (Burrough, J.) Not only should Holbrook (D) have given notice of the spring guns, but had he (D) just wanted to protect his property from thieves, he would have set the guns only at night. Furthermore, if Holbrook (D) had been present when Bird (P) intruded, Holbrook (D) could not have lawfully taken Bird (P) into custody.

ANALYSIS

One is not privileged to spread poison on land for the purpose of killing trespassing animals. Cases have split over whether a felon can recover for injury caused to him by traps. The use of dangerous animals is also prohibited unless their presence is well posted. If injury occurs to those who rightfully enter on to the land of another, posting of notices will not normally save a defendant from liability unless contributory negligence or assumption of the risk can be established.

Quicknotes

DEADLY FORCE Physical force used in the defense of oneself or others that carries with it the potential for causing death.

Ploof v. Putnam

Sailor (P) v. Dock owner (D)

Vt. Sup. Ct., 71 A. 188 (1908)

NATURE OF CASE: Damages for battery.

FACT SUMMARY: Ploof (P) sued for damages caused when Putnam (D) denied him the use of a safe mooring for his boat during a storm.

RULE OF LAW

Necessity justifies the entry upon the land of another.

FACTS: Ploof (P) was sailing upon a lake with his wife and children. A storm arose and Ploof (P) attempted to moor his boat to Putnam's (D) dock. Putnam's servant unmoored the boat, causing the storm to drive the boat into the shore. Ploof (P), his wife, and children were injured and the boat was destroyed. Ploof (P) sued Putnam (D) in trespass and also for not permitting the boat to be anchored to the dock during the storm. The lower court held for Ploof (P).

ISSUE: Does necessity justify the entry upon the land of another?

HOLDING AND DECISION: (Munson, J.) Yes. Necessity justifies the entry upon the land of another. Many cases have established the rule that necessity, and an inability to control movements inaugurated in the proper exercise of a strict right, will justify entries upon land and interferences with personal property that would otherwise have been trespasses. The doctrine of necessity applies with special force to the preservation of human life. One may sacrifice the personal property of another to save his life or the lives of his fellows. The evidence showed that there was a necessity to preserve human life. However, the allegations of Ploof (P) do not show that there were no natural objects to which he could have moored the boat with equal safety. The lower court judgment, finding a necessity, is affirmed and the cause remanded.

ANALYSIS

This rule follows the great weight of authority which gives a private individual a privilege to enter another's land if the emergency is sufficiently great, if one enters to save his own life, the life of another, or his own property. The scope of this privilege is narrower than the privilege that allows an individual to act for a public goal. For example, an individual who dynamites a house to prevent the spread of fire or who destroys property that during wartime should not reach enemy hands is not liable to the true owner. The rule is found in Restatement (Second) of Torts § 197. Note that one acting under the private privilege must reimburse the true owner for the cost of repairing any damage that he has caused.

Quicknotes

BATTERY Unlawful contact with the body of another person.

NECESSITY A defense to liability for unlawful activity where the conduct is unavoidable and is justified by preventing the injury to life or health.

Vincent v. Lake Erie Transportation Co.

Wharf owner (P) v. Transportation company (D)

Minn. Sup. Ct., 124 N.W. 221 (1910)

NATURE OF CASE: Damages for injury to property.

FACT SUMMARY: Vincent (P) sued for damages to its wharf, caused by Lake Erie Transportation Co. (D) negligently keeping its boat tied to the wharf.

RULE OF LAW

Public necessity may require the taking of private property for public purposes, but our system of jurisprudence requires that compensation be made.

FACTS: Lake Erie Transportation Co. (D) moored their boat to Vincent's (P) wharf at the place and in the manner designated by Vincent (P). Cargo consigned to Vincent (P) was unloaded. By the time the cargo was unloaded a storm had arisen which prevented the boat from leaving the wharf. Vincent (P) sued for damages caused to the wharf by the boat's hitting it during the storm. The trial court rendered a judgment for Vincent (P). The defendant appealed.

ISSUE: Does our system of jurisprudence require that compensation be made when public necessity requires the taking of private property for public purposes?

HOLDING AND DECISION: (O'Brien, J.) Yes. Public necessity may require the taking of private property for public purposes, but our system of jurisprudence requires that compensation be made. The ship's master was required to use ordinary prudence and care. The evidence showed that it would have been imprudent for the ship's master to have attempted to leave the dock. However, this was not a case in which, because of an act of God or an unavoidable accident, the infliction of injury was beyond the control of the defendant. Here, the defendant prudently and advisedly availed itself of the plaintiff's property for the purpose of preserving its own more valuable property. Having thus preserved the ship at the expense of the dock, the defendant must compensate the owner of the dock for the injury inflicted. The judgment for the plaintiff is affirmed.

DISSENT: (Lewis, J.) The damage was caused by an unavoidable accident. Therefore, the defendant is not liable for damages.

ANALYSIS

The few cases in this area appear to agree with *Vincent*. The same liability apparently attaches to the infliction of personal injury in cases of private necessity. The Restatement (Second) of Torts combines the principles of *Ploof v. Putnam*, 71 A. 188 (1908), and *Vincent* in § 197, and creates a privilege in favor of an actor to enter the land of another in order to avoid serious harm, coupled with an obligation on the part of the actor to pay for whatever he damages.

Quicknotes

PUBLIC NECESSITY The defense of necessity, alleging that the harm caused by the defendant was less than the harm sought to be prevented against the public; since the public interest is involved, defendant is not required to pay for any damage caused.

I. de S. and Wife v. W. de S.

Tavern owner (P) v. Patron (D)

At the Assizes, 1348 [or 1349] Year Book, Liber Assisarum, f. 99, pl. 60

NATURE OF CASE: Action to recover damages for trespass because of an assault made upon the plaintiff.

FACT SUMMARY: W (D) struck at I's wife M (P) with a hatchet but missed her.

RULE OF LAW

An act that causes another to be fearful of a harmful or offensive contact is known as an assault, and the plaintiff may recover damages, even though there is no actual physical contact or physical harm.

FACTS: W (D) was beating with a hatchet upon the door of I's tavern, which was closed for the night. When I's wife M (P) put her head out the window and ordered W (D) to stop, he struck at her with the hatchet. W (D) claimed there was no trespass for which the woman (P) could recover, since he did not actually harm her.

ISSUE: Is there a wrong and a trespass for which a plaintiff may recover damages, when the plaintiff is caused to fear for her safety, but is not actually harmed?

HOLDING AND DECISION: (Thorpe, C.J.) Yes. An assault—making another fearful of a harmful contact—is a harm for which a plaintiff may recover. In this case, W (D) struck at I's wife M (P) with a hatchet, thereby frightening her. The harm was in the assault itself, and she is entitled to recover damages from W (D).

ANALYSIS

This case was one of the earliest decisions to recognize a mental, as opposed to physical, injury, and the need to compensate the plaintiff for such an injury. Thus, the law of assault developed to protect a person's interest in freedom from being fearful of a harmful or offensive contact upon his person, as opposed to battery, which protected a person from the injury itself.

Quicknotes

ASSAULT The intentional placing of another in fear of immediate bodily injury.

Tuberville v. Savage

[Parties not identified.]

K.B., 86 Eng. Rep. 684 (1669)

NATURE OF CASE: Action for damages for assault and battery.

FACT SUMMARY: Savage (D) struck at Tuberville (P), claiming Tuberville (P) had assaulted him first.

RULE OF LAW

A threatening gesture will not constitute an assault when there are accompanying words that clearly negate the gesture's threat.

FACTS: Savage's (D) evidence of an assault committed upon him was that Tuberville (P) put his hand on his sword and said, "If it were not assize-time, I would not take such language from you."

ISSUE: Will a threatening gesture constitute an assault when there are accompanying words that clearly negate the gesture's threat?

HOLDING AND DECISION: [Judge not stated in casebook excerpt.] No. A threatening gesture will not constitute an assault when there are accompanying words that clearly negate the gesture's threat. This is because there can be no assault without an intent to cause apprehension of a harmful contact. In this case, Tuberville (P), although he put his hand on his sword, clearly indicated by his words that he had no intent to harm Savage (D). Savage's (D) claim that he was acting in self-defense to Tuberville's (P) assault therefore failed because there was no assault.

ANALYSIS

The holding of this case represents the current view that for an assault, there must be an overt act, together with an apparent ability and intent to carry out the threat immediately. When there is an overt act that is threatening but is accompanied by words that clearly negate its threat, a reasonable person would not be fearful of any immediate harm. On the other hand, it is possible for the words to make an assault out of an act that is itself not sufficient for an assault, as where the defendant has been making verbal threats and then suddenly reaches into his pocket. Where the words state a conditional threat, so that the plaintiff reasonably believes no harm will occur if he meets that condition, there may still be an assault. A robber holding a gun who says, "Your money or your life," has committed an assault even if it is clear he will not harm the victim if he is given the money.

Quicknotes

ASSAULT The intentional placing of another in fear of immediate bodily injury.

COURT OF ASSIZE A medieval English court that preceded the circuit courts. The assizes were circuit courts distributed throughout the country that sat with juries four times yearly to hear criminal causes and certain private actions dealing primarily with claims to lands and estates." *The Wolters Kluwer Bouvier Law Dictionary, Compact Edition,* 271 (Stephen Michael Sheppard, gen'l ed., 2011).

Alcorn v. Mitchell

Trespass victim (D) v. Trespasser (P)

Ill. Sup. Ct., 63 Ill. 553 (1872)

NATURE OF CASE: Action in damages for insult and emotional distress.

FACT SUMMARY: At the conclusion of a trial, Alcorn (D) spit in Mitchell's (P) face.

RULE OF LAW

Punitive damages may be assessed for highly offensive conduct to provide an alternative redress to physical retribution.

FACTS: After the conclusion of an action for trespass, Alcorn (D) spit in Mitchell's (P) face. Mitchell (P) recovered punitive damages of $1,000 for the offensive battery. Alcorn (D) appealed, alleging the award was excessive.

ISSUE: May punitive damages be assessed for highly offensive conduct to provide an alternative redress to physical retribution?

HOLDING AND DECISION: (Sheldon, J.) Yes. Punitive damages may be assessed for highly offensive conduct to provide an alternative redress to physical retribution. Highly egregious antisocial actions provoke physical retribution, and an alternative method of redress/satisfaction must be provided by the law in order to discourage future misconduct of this nature. Spitting in the face of another in courtroom is such an action. Severe punitive awards are encouraged by the law to give a party an adequate redress and to punish the other for his misconduct. Affirmed.

ANALYSIS

Any offensive touching of clothes or a cane may be prosecuted as a battery and/or the intentional infliction of emotional distress, *Republica v. De Longchamps*, 1 U.S. 111 (Pa. 1784). An offensive kiss will also be deemed a battery for which damages may be recovered for injured feelings, *Craker v. Chicago & N.W. Ry.*, 36 Wis. 657 (1875). Seizing an object from a person's hand will also be deemed a battery because of its close connection to the plaintiff's body and the concomitant shock/embarrassment, *Morgan v. Loyacomo*, 1 So. 2d 510 (Miss. 1941).

Quicknotes

PUNITIVE DAMAGES Damages exceeding the actual injury suffered for the purposes of punishment, deterrence, and comfort to plaintiff.

Coblyn v. Kennedy's, Inc.

Shopper (P) v. Store (D)

Mass. Sup. Jud. Ct., 268 N.E. 2d 860 (1971)

NATURE OF CASE: Action for false imprisonment.

FACT SUMMARY: An employee of Kennedy's, Inc. (D) detained Coblyn (P) on suspicion of shoplifting.

RULES OF LAW

(1) If a person is restrained in his or her personal liberty by fear of a personal difficulty, it amounts to fa lse imprisonment.

(2) If a shopkeeper has reasonable grounds to believe a person has committed or is attempting to commit larceny of goods for sale on the premises, the shopkeeper may detain that person in a reasonable manner for a reasonable length of time.

FACTS: Coblyn (P), a small, elderly man, was leaving Kennedy's, Inc. (D) store when an employee stopped him, grasped his arm, and accused him of shoplifting. Coblyn (P) went inside where another clerk confirmed that the item in question belonged to Coblyn (P). Coblyn (P) became sick from the excitement and was hospitalized with a "myocardial infraction." Coblyn brought suit for false imprisonment and Kennedy's (D) asserted that no imprisonment had taken place and that it was protected by the "shopkeeper's privilege" to detain suspected shoplifters.

ISSUE:

(1) If a person is restrained in his or her personal liberty by fear of a personal difficulty, does it amount to false imprisonment?

(2) If a shopkeeper has reasonable grounds to believe a person has committed or is attempting to commit larceny of goods for sale on the premises, may the shopkeeper detain that person in a reasonable manner for a reasonable length of time?

HOLDING AND DECISION: (Spiegel, J.)

(1) Yes. If a person is restrained of his or her personal liberty by fear of a personal difficulty, it amounts to false imprisonment. A genuine restraint is sufficient to be imprisonment, and any demonstration of physical power which, it appears can be avoided only by submission, operates to constitute imprisonment. Considering Coblyn's (P) age and health, Kennedy's (D) employee's grasp on Coblyn's (P) arm gave Coblyn (P) no choice other than to comply with their request.

(2) Yes. If a shopkeeper has reasonable grounds to believe a person has committed or is attempting to commit larceny of goods for sale on the premises, the shopkeeper may detain that person in a reasonable manner for a reasonable length of time. The court held that there were no reasonable grounds to believe that Coblyn (P) was shoplifting. Exceptions overruled.

ANALYSIS

The "shopkeeper's privilege" allows the storeowner to retain the suspect for an investigation only. There is no privilege to arrest or to demand that the suspect sign a confession.

Quicknotes

FALSE IMPRISONMENT Intentional confinement to a bounded area from which one cannot reasonably leave, for an appreciable length of time, however short.

PROBABLE CAUSE A reasonable basis for believing that a crime has been committed.

Wilkinson v. Downton

Wife of supposed accident victim (P) v. Storyteller (D)

Q.B., 2 Q.B. 57 (1897)

NATURE OF CASE: Appeal by Downton (D) from judgment for Wilkinson (P) for injuries caused by nervous shock.

FACT SUMMARY: As part of a practical joke, Downton (D) told Wilkinson (P) that her husband had been severely injured in an accident.

RULE OF LAW

Extreme and outrageous conduct that causes physical harm or mental distress creates a valid cause of action.

FACTS: Downton (D) represented to Wilkinson (P) that Wilkinson's (P) husband had been seriously injured in an accident and was lying at The Elms in Leytonstone with two broken legs. Downton (D) requested that she get a cab and two pillows and go to her husband. All of this was untrue. The effect of the statement was a severe mental shock that threatened Wilkinson's (P) reason and entailed weeks of suffering. There was no evidence that Wilkinson (P) was predisposed to ill health or weakness of constitution. Downton (D) contended that damage caused by nervous shock is not actionable.

ISSUE: Does extreme and outrageous conduct that causes physical harm or mental distress create a valid cause of action?

HOLDING AND DECISION: (Wright, J.) Yes. Extreme and outrageous conduct that causes physical harm or mental distress creates a valid cause of action. Where a person willfully does an act that is calculated to cause physical harm and in fact does cause physical harm, there is a good cause of action. Here, Downton (D) suddenly appeared before Wilkinson (P) and with apparent seriousness advised that her husband had been injured. This is an act that could not fail to produce grave effects under the circumstances, and therefore an intention to produce such an effect must be imputed. Affirmed.

ANALYSIS

This case set the precedent on which the new tort of intentional infliction of emotional distress was founded. In it, the court recognized that there are some special situations where recovery must be allowed even though the established rule of law held otherwise. Justice Wright imposed liability simply because he believed that Downton's (D) conduct was beyond the realm of common decency. The rule that has since evolved is that there is liability for conduct that is calculated to cause, and does cause, severe mental distress.

Quicknotes

INTENTIONAL INFLICTION OF EMOTIONAL DISTRESS Intentional and extreme behavior on the part of the wrongdoer with the intent to cause the victim to suffer severe emotional distress, or with reckless indifference, resulting in the victim's suffering severe emotional distress.

CHAPTER 2

Strict Liability and Negligence: Historic and Analytic Foundations

Quick Reference Rules of Law

The Thorns Case (Hull v. Orange)

[Parties not identified.]

Y.B. Mich. 6 Ed. 4, f. 7, pl. 18 (1466)

NATURE OF CASE: Action for damages due to a trespass.

FACT SUMMARY: Defendant alleged that the injury done to plaintiff's land was caused while recovering thorn bushes that had inadvertently fallen on the land.

RULE OF LAW

Even an innocent trespass on land is actionable.

FACTS: Defendant had land adjacent to plaintiff. Defendant cut some thorn bushes on his land that, through no fault of his own, fell on plaintiff's land. Defendant entered plaintiff's land to recover the thorn bushes. Plaintiff brought suit for the trespass, alleging damage to crops. Defendant alleged that his actions were privileged, since the loss occurred without any fault on his part and the entry was to recover his property.

ISSUE: Is even an innocent trespass on land actionable?

HOLDING AND DECISION: (Littleton, J.) Yes. Even an innocent trespass on land is actionable. Fault is not required for liability. If the land or person of another is invaded to his detriment, it is actionable regardless of whether the defendant acted legally or was totally without fault. The defendant's actions caused the loss. Defendant will be deemed liable.

CONCURRENCE: (Choke, C.J.) The falling of the thorn bushes onto the plaintiff's land was not lawful and the coming to take them away was thus unlawful. If on the other hand, the wind had caused the thorns to fall, then the defendant could have lawfully gone onto the plaintiff's land to recover them.

CONCURRENCE: (Pigot, J.) Where there is damage to the plaintiff's land, an action in trespass will lie, notwithstanding that the defendant's action was lawful and the result of that action was not intentional, as where a defendant cuts willows and they stop water from flowing to the plaintiff's mill, or where a defendant's draining of a pond to take the fish therein floods the plaintiff's land.

CONCURRENCE: (Brian, J.) Where a person acts, he is bound to act so as not to injure others, and, even if the act is lawful (as it was here), and the consequence of his act is against his will (as it was here), a party injured by the act will have an action against the person committing the act. For example, if a defendant is building a house and a timber falls and damages the defendant's neighbor's house, the neighbor has an action in trespass against the defendant, notwithstanding that the building of the house was lawful and the falling of the timber was against the defendant's will. This is also the case where a defendant, acting in self-defense, harms a third party. The defendant's self-defense is lawful, and the harm to the third party is unintended. Nevertheless, the third party will have an action against the defendant.

DISSENT: (Yonge, J.) Where the plaintiff suffers no legal injury, no action for trespass will lie. Here, the defendant's entry onto the plaintiff's land to recover his thorns, which were his property, was not tortious, so even if the plaintiff suffered damages, he did not suffer a tort, and, therefore, he has no action against defendant.

ANALYSIS

It has been held that, without justification, the trampling of a single blade of grass is actionable in trespass, i.e., nominal damages may be awarded for every unjustified trespass. Every unwarranted invasion of property is actionable. Nominal damages are generally not awarded where no injury was caused and the entry was to recover property. The entry must be intentional or caused by the defendant's actions. One who is pushed onto the property of another is not liable. However, the pusher would be liable, since he caused the entry.

Quicknotes

TRESPASS Unlawful interference with, or damage to, the real or personal property of another.

Weaver v. Ward

Injured soldier (P) v. Soldier whose weapon accidentally discharged (D)

K.B., 80 Eng. Rep. 284 (1616)

NATURE OF CASE: Action to recover damages for assault and battery.

FACT SUMMARY: During a military exercise Ward's (D) musket accidentally discharged, injuring Weaver (P).

RULE OF LAW

An actor is liable for injury directly caused by his act unless he can prove himself utterly without fault.

FACTS: Ward (D) and Weaver (P) were participants in a military exercise. During the exercise, Ward's (D) musket accidentally discharged, injuring Weaver (P). Ward (D) contended that the accidental nature of his action should be a defense. The lower court held, as a matter of law, that a showing of accident alone is not a defense to an injury caused by Ward (D). The court gave judgment for Weaver (P) by sustaining his demurrer to the answer.

ISSUE: Is an actor liable for injury directly caused by his act if he can prove himself utterly without fault?

HOLDING AND DECISION: [Judge not stated in casebook excerpt.] No. An actor is liable for injury directly caused by his act unless he can prove himself utterly without fault. Ward (D), however, voluntarily fired the musket and therefore was at fault. Affirmed.

ANALYSIS

This is one of the first cases clearly recognizing that some form of fault may be necessary for imposition of liability upon an actor. Modernly, the test for imposition of liability under a fault-based negligence theory is whether a reasonable man might have taken the defendant's (Ward's) action. If so, then there is no negligence, no fault, and consequently no liability.

Quicknotes

ASSAULT AND BATTERY Illegal bodily contact.

NEGLIGENCE Conduct falling below the standard of care that a reasonable person would demonstrate under similar conditions.

TRESPASS Unlawful interference with, or damage to, the real or personal property of another.

Scott v. Shepherd

Blinded stall owner (P) v. Squib thrower (D)

K.B., 96 Eng. Rep. 525 (1773)

NATURE OF CASE: Action in damages for trespass.

FACT SUMMARY: Shepherd (D) threw a lighted squib into a marketplace where, to avoid injury, it was thrown by others until it finally burned Scott (P).

RULE OF LAW

A party will be liable for setting forces in motion that are likely to cause injury of a sort and do cause injury even though the force is diverted by another.

FACTS: Shepherd (D) threw a lighted squib (made of gunpowder, etc.) into a marketplace. The squib landed on Yates's stall. Willis threw it away to prevent injury to Yates's stall and person. It landed on Ryal's stall and he threw it away for the same reason. It then landed on Scott (P) and blinded him in one eye. Scott (P) sued Shepherd (D) for trespass. The jury found for Scott (P) subject to this court's opinion.

ISSUE: Will a party be liable for setting forces in motion that are likely to cause injury of a sort and do cause injury even though the force is diverted by another?

HOLDING AND DECISION: (Nares, J.) Yes. A party will be liable for setting forces in motion that are likely to cause injury of a sort and do cause injury even though the force is diverted by another. The action of trespass is maintainable. The natural and probable consequence of the act done by the defendant was injury to somebody and therefore was unlawful. The defendant must answer for his actions whether the injury caused is immediate or not. Judgment for Scott (P).

CONCURRENCE: (De Grey, C.J.) Yes. Throwing a lighted squib into a crowded marketplace can obviously cause injury to someone. The force unleashed was designed to indiscriminately cause injury. The injury is a direct and immediate act of Shepherd (D). The throwing of the squib was an unlawful act, and whatever follows, Shepherd (D) is responsible for it. Everything done after the original throwing was a continuation of the first throw. Any innocent person removing the danger from oneself to another is justifiable and the blame lies upon the first thrower.

DISSENT: (Blackstone, J.) Trespass only lies for immediate actions. Consequential damages of the sort herein are not actionable as a trespass but must be brought as a trespass on the case. The intervention of third parties destroys the immediate nature of the force. The original act was, as against Yates, a trespass not as against Ryal, or Scott (P). The tortuous act was complete when the squib lay at rest upon Yates's stall. Shepherd (D) is not responsible for what Willis or Ryal did with the squib.

ANALYSIS

A trespass will lie where one throws a stone at another and inadvertently hits a third party. An action will also lie where one throws a bomb into a crowded area killing and injuring a number of people including the person against whom it was directed. Where a specific injury was intended or was likely to occur, intent to injure a specific party or property is not required. The general intent to cause injury is sufficient to establish the trespass or assault.

Quicknotes

TRESPASS Unlawful interference with, or damage to, the real or personal property of another.

TRESPASS ON THE CASE Action at common law in early England granting a remedy to a person who sustains injury to his person or property as a result of the defendant's conduct.

Brown v. Kendall

Injured dog owner (P) v. Stick-wielding dog owner (D)

Mass. Sup. Jud. Ct., 60 Mass. 292 (1850)

NATURE OF CASE: Trespass for assault and battery.

FACT SUMMARY: Kendall (D), while attempting to separate his dog from Brown's (P) dog when the two dogs were fighting, accidentally struck Brown (P) with a stick.

RULE OF LAW

If in the prosecution of a lawful act, a casualty purely accidental arises, i.e., the injury was unavoidable, and the conduct of the defendant was free from blame, no action can be supported for an injury arising therefrom.

FACTS: Two dogs, owned by Brown (P) and Kendall (D), respectively, were fighting. Kendall (D) attempted to separate the dogs with a stick. When he raised the stick to strike the dogs, Kendall (D) stepped back to avoid the dogs as they approached him, and he accidentally struck Brown (P), who was behind him, in the eye, inflicting a serious injury. Brown (P) brought an action in trespass for assault and battery. The trial court instructed the jury that if it was not a necessary act, and Kendall (D) was not in duty bound to part the dogs, he was responsible for the consequences of the blow, unless it appeared he exercised extraordinary care, so the accident was inevitable. It further instructed that if Kendall (D) had no duty to separate the dogs, then the burden of proving extraordinary care was on him, as well as showing alternatively lack of ordinary care on the part of Brown (P). Following Kendall's (D) death, his executrix (D) was summoned in.

ISSUE: If in the prosecution of a lawful act, a casualty purely accidental arises, i.e., the injury was unavoidable, and the conduct of the defendant was free from blame, can action be supported for an injury arising therefrom?

HOLDING AND DECISION: (Shaw, C.J.) No. If in the prosecution of a lawful act, a casualty purely accidental arises, i.e., the injury was unavoidable, and the conduct of the defendant was free from blame, no action can be supposed for an injury arising therefrom. The instructions that should have been given are to the effect that Brown (P) could not recover (1) if at the time of the accident both Kendall (D) and Brown (P) were using ordinary care; (2) if Kendall (D) was using ordinary care and Brown (P) was not; or (3) if neither were using ordinary care. What constitutes ordinary care will vary with the circumstances, but generally it means that kind and degree of care which prudent and cautious people would use. Such is required under the circumstances and is necessary to guard against probable danger. An inevitable accident is one the defendant could not avoid by the use of kind and degree of care necessary under the circumstances. Because the instructions to the jury placed the burden on Kendall (D) to show that he used extraordinary care or that Brown (P) failed to use ordinary care, rather than having placed the burden of proof on Brown (P) to prove his case, a new trial must be ordered.

ANALYSIS

This case established that some form of fault, negligent or intentional, must form the basis of liability. Consequently, the loss from an unavoidable accident will stay where it falls. This case is also interesting because its discussion includes the concept of contributory negligence, which was fully accepted by the Massachusetts court, but which is losing favor to the concept of comparative negligence today.

Quicknotes

ASSAULT The intentional placing of another in fear of immediate bodily injury.

BATTERY Unlawful contact with the body of another person.

NEGLIGENCE Conduct falling below the standard of care that a reasonable person would demonstrate under similar conditions.

ORDINARY CARE The degree of care exercised by a reasonable person when conducting everyday activities or under similar circumstances; synonymous with due care.

TRESPASS Unlawful interference with, or damage to, the real or personal property of another.

Fletcher v. Rylands

Flooded landowner (P) v. Reservoir owner (D)

Ex., 159 Eng. Rep. 737 (1865)

NATURE OF CASE: Action in strict liability for damages.

FACT SUMMARY: Fletcher's (P) land was flooded when Rylands's (D) reservoir leaked through an unknown, abandoned mine.

RULE OF LAW

Where a party's actions unwittingly cause damage to the land of another, he is liable regardless of negligence.

FACTS: Rylands (D) constructed a dam on his property. Fletcher's (P) land and mines were flooded when water seeped through old abandoned mine shafts on Rylands's (D) property. Rylands (D) did not know of these shafts and the reservoir had been competently built. Fletcher (P) sued for damages. Rylands (D) defended on the ground that he was totally without negligence.

ISSUE: Where a party's actions unwittingly cause damage to the land of another, is he liable regardless of negligence?

HOLDING AND DECISION: (Baron Bramwell, J.) Yes. Where a party's actions unwittingly cause damage to the land of another, he is liable regardless of negligence. If Rylands (D) had intentionally caused the flooding he would be liable. We perceive no difference where the injury was unintentional. The damage was the same. Rylands's (D) acts caused the flooding and, regardless of fault, Fletcher (P) should be compensated.

DISSENT: (Baron Martin, J.) Injury to personal property is not actionable without fault/negligence. There is no difference between damage to personal or real property.

ANALYSIS

Most modern jurisdictions would not follow the above decision. Injuries sustained through no one's fault must be borne by the injured party as a cost of living in our modern society. Injury neither to real nor to personal property is actionable without fault except where the particular activity is deemed "hazardous." These activities are subject to a strict liability in tort theory and no negligence need be shown.

Quicknotes

NEGLIGENCE Conduct falling below the standard of care that a reasonable person would demonstrate under similar conditions.

TRESPASS Unlawful interference with, or damage to, the real or personal property of another.

Fletcher v. Rylands

Flooded landowner (P) v. Reservoir owner (D)

Ex., L.R. 1 Ex. 265 (1866)

NATURE OF CASE: Appeal from decision in an action for damages to property.

FACT SUMMARY: Fletcher (P) contended that Rylands (D) was responsible for damage to Fletcher's (P) mining property caused by the breakage of Rylands's (D) reservoir, which flooded Fletcher's (P) property.

RULE OF LAW

If a person brings anything onto his property that, if it escapes, might damage his neighbor's property, the person is responsible for all the damage that is the natural consequence of the escape.

FACTS: Fletcher (P) sued Rylands (D) after Rylands (D) built a reservoir on his own property, the reservoir leaked, and Fletcher's (P) mining property was flooded and damaged. The lower court held that Rylands (D) was responsible for causing the damage to Fletcher's (P) mines. Rylands (D) appealed on the basis that his duty was to take all reasonable and prudent precautions to keep the reservoir from damaging a neighbor's property but no more.

ISSUE: If a person brings anything onto his property that, if it escapes, might damage his neighbor's property, is the person responsible for all the damage that is the natural consequence of the escape?

HOLDING AND DECISION: (Baron Blackburn, J.) Yes. If a person brings anything onto his property that, if it escapes, might damage his neighbor's property, the person is responsible for all the damage that is the natural consequence of the escape. Someone who has brought something on his property that was not naturally there and that is harmless to others as long as it is confined to his own property, but which he knows will be damaging if it should escape to his neighbor's property, should be responsible for any damage caused his neighbor if it escapes. There is no ground here for saying that Fletcher (P) took upon himself any risk arising from uses to which Rylands (D) chose to apply to his land. Fletcher (P) neither knew nor could stop Rylands (D) from building his reservoir and storing water, so long as that water remained on Rylands's (D) property and did not escape onto Fletcher's (P) property. Affirmed.

ANALYSIS

Dam failures in England in the 1800s were frequent and considered great disasters. Before the landmark case of *Fletcher v. Rylands* was tried, several dam failures had already occurred with great loss of life and property. The decision in *Fletcher* no doubt was meant to be a cure for what had become extremely costly events. However, the rule of strict liability set forth in *Fletcher* was rarely, if ever, followed, and later decisions instead applied a standard that was somewhere between negligence and strict liability.

Quicknotes

STRICT LIABILITY Liability for all injuries proximately caused by a party's conducting of certain inherently dangerous activities without regard to negligence or fault.

Rylands v. Fletcher

Reservoir owner (D) v. Flooded landowner (P)

H.L., L.R. 3 H.L. 330 (1868)

NATURE OF CASE: Appeal from an award of damages for injury to land.

FACT SUMMARY: Rylands (D) built a reservoir on his land, but the water escaped through an abandoned mine shaft and flooded an adjoining mine owned by Fletcher (P).

RULE OF LAW

A person using his land for a dangerous, nonnatural use is strictly liable for damage to another's property resulting from such nonnatural use.

FACTS: Rylands (D) built a water reservoir on his land. The water escaped through an abandoned coal mine shaft and flooded an adjoining coal mine owned by Fletcher (P). Fletcher (P) sued for damages to his land caused by the water.

ISSUE: Is a person who uses his land for a dangerous, nonnatural use strictly liable for damage to another's property resulting from such nonnatural use?

HOLDING AND DECISION: (Lord Cairns, C.) Yes. A person using his land for a dangerous, nonnatural use is strictly liable for damage to another's property resulting from such nonnatural use. If water had naturally accumulated upon the land and, by the laws of nature, had run off on to adjoining land, there would be no liability. But if water, not being a natural condition of the land, is introduced upon it, any water that escapes does so at the landowner's peril, for which any damage to adjoining land he is strictly liable. Judgment of the Court of Exchequer Chamber affirmed.

CONCURRENCE: (Lord Cranworth, C.) No matter how cautious a person is, he will be liable if he brings upon his land something that causes damage to his neighbor's land. The determinative factor is not whether the defendant has acted with due care but rather if his actions caused the damage. Rylands (D) brought onto his land water and stored it in a reservoir that ended up harming Fletcher (P) and, therefore, Rylands (D) is liable.

ANALYSIS

This is the leading case from which was developed the doctrine of strict liability for abnormally dangerous activities or conditions. In determining whether a certain activity is a nonnatural use, the court looks to the place where the activity occurs, the customs of the community, and the natural fitness or adaptation of the premises for the purpose. The Restatement, while accepting the principle of the case, has limited it to ultrahazardous activities.

Quicknotes

DUE CARE The degree of care that can be expected from a reasonably prudent person under similar circumstances; synonymous with ordinary care.

STRICT LIABILITY Liability for all injuries proximately caused by a party's conducting of certain inherently dangerous activities without regard to negligence or fault.

Brown v. Collins

Landowner (P) v. Runaway horse owner (D)

N.H. Sup. Ct., 53 N.H. 442 (1873)

NATURE OF CASE: Action for damages to property.

FACT SUMMARY: Brown (P) sued Collins (D) on strict liability grounds after Collins's (D) horses were frightened, became unmanageable, broke from Collins's (D) control, went onto Brown's (P) land, and broke a post there.

RULE OF LAW

Property owners should not be held strictly liable for the natural consequences of the escape of things they bring on their land.

FACTS: Collins (D), who generally exercised ordinary care and skill in managing his horses, lost that control when the horses became frightened. The horses then became unmanageable and ran against and broke a post on Brown's (P) land. Brown (P) sued Collins (D) for the damage caused by the runaway horses, arguing that Collins (D) should be held strictly liable pursuant to *Rylands v. Fletcher*, L.R. 3 H.L. 330 (1868).

ISSUE: Should property owners be held strictly liable for the natural consequences of the escape of things they bring on their land?

HOLDING AND DECISION: (Doe, J.) No. Property owners should not be held strictly liable for the natural consequences of the escape of things they bring on their land. Most of the rights of property, as well as of person, in the social state are not absolute but relative. Everything that a person can bring upon his land is capable of escaping against his will, without his fault, with or without his assistance, in some form, solid, liquid, or gaseous—and of doing damage after its escape. Even if an arbitrary test were applied only to the things a man brings on his land, it would still recognize the peculiar rights of savage life in a wilderness, ignore the rights growing out of a civilized state of society, and make a distinction not warranted by the enlightened spirit of common law. It would impose a penalty upon efforts, made in a reasonable, skillful, and careful manner, to rise above a condition of barbarism. Legal principles should not throw so serious an obstacle in the way of progress and improvement. Judgment for Collins (D).

ANALYSIS

As reflected in the above case, the standard of strict liability set forth in *Rylands v. Fletcher*, L.R. 3 H.L. 330 (1868), was not initially popular in courts. Current cases have adhered to the *Rylands* standard more closely, and in 1984, it was reported that thirty of the states accepted *Rylands's* strict liability principles while only seven rejected them. Other state courts continue to move in support of the *Rylands* standard.

Quicknotes

STRICT LIABILITY Liability for all injuries proximately caused by a party's conducting of certain inherently dangerous activities without regard to negligence or fault.

Powell v. Fall

Farmer (P) v. Tractor driver (D)

Q.B., 5 Q.B. 597 (1880)

NATURE OF CASE: Appeal of strict liability judgment.

FACT SUMMARY: Fall (D) contended he was not liable for damages to Powell's (P) haystack caused by a spark from Fall's (D) tractor because the tractor complied with all laws regulating its construction and use.

RULE OF LAW

A person who operates a potentially dangerous machine is liable for injuries resulting therefrom even if the operator is not negligent.

FACTS: Powell (P) owned a farm adjoining a public highway. Fall (D) drove his steam propelled tractor in a reasonably prudent manner on the highway, and a spark from the engine escaped, igniting Powell's (P) haystack. Powell (P) sued for damages. The lower court found for Powell (P) reasoning that a person who operates a potentially dangerous machine is liable for injuries resulting therefrom even if the operator is not negligent. It also found that the statutes, while authorizing the use of tractors, did not abrogate any cause of action against the operator for damages caused by their use. Fall (D) appealed.

ISSUE: Is a person who operates a potentially dangerous machine liable for injuries resulting therefrom even if the operator is not negligent?

HOLDING AND DECISION: (Sir John Mellor, J.) Yes. A person who operates a potentially dangerous machine is liable for injuries resulting therefrom even if the operator is not negligent. The statutes, while authorizing the use of tractors, did not abrogate any cause of action against the operator for damages caused by their use. Therefore, despite the fact there was no negligence, responsibility for the damage to the hay must rest with Fall (D). Judgment for Powell (P).

CONCURRENCE: (Lord Bramwell, J.) Yes. A person who operates a potentially dangerous machine is liable for injuries resulting therefrom even if the operator is not negligent because one who keeps a dangerous thing on his property is strictly liable if it escapes and injures his neighbor. The statutes have no effect on the common-law rule.

ANALYSIS

The lower court specifically relied upon *Rylands v. Fletcher*, L.R. 3H.L. 330 (1868). This case was appealed and affirmed, and specifically overruled *Vaughn v. Taff Vale Ry. Co.*, 5 H & N. 679, 29 L.J. (Ex.) 247 (1860), which held that the operator of a railroad was not to be held liable for injuries without proof of negligence.

Quicknotes

ABNORMALLY DANGEROUS ACTIVITY An activity, as set forth in Restatement (Second) of Torts § 520, giving rise to strict liability on the part of the actor for damages caused thereby.

NEGLIGENCE Conduct falling below the standard of care that a reasonable person would demonstrate under similar conditions.

STRICT LIABILITY Liability for all injuries proximately caused by a party's conducting of certain inherently dangerous activities without regard to negligence or fault.

Stone v. Bolton

Injured woman (P) v. Cricket club (D)

Ct. App., 1 K.B. 201 (1950)

NATURE OF CASE: Action for damages for personal injury caused by negligence.

FACT SUMMARY: Stone (P) was injured when a cricket ball was hit over a fence and struck her.

RULE OF LAW

A known risk, even if extremely slight, is actionable if it occurs and leads to a foreseeable injury.

FACTS: Stone (P) was struck and injured by a cricket ball that was hit over a high wall onto a public street. Stone (P) brought suit for negligence against the home cricket club (D), but not against the batsman or the batsman's club. The cricket club (D) defended on the ground that over the last 30 years only six balls had been hit over the wall. The cricket club (D) alleged that the risk was so slight that injury was unforeseeable.

ISSUE: Is a known risk, even if extremely slight, actionable if it occurs and leads to a foreseeable injury?

HOLDING AND DECISION: [Judge not stated in casebook excerpt.] Yes. A known risk, even if extremely slight, is actionable if it occurs and leads to a foreseeable injury. The cricket club (D) knew that balls could be hit over the wall. The cricket club (D) knew that if the ball cleared the wall it could strike and injure a passerby. Regardless of how unlikely the possibility of injury, the cricket club (D) owed a duty to protect the public against a known risk. The wall was never made higher and the cricket field was never moved even though the risk was known. This was negligence and Stone (P) may recover.

ANALYSIS

The decision herein is akin to a theory of strict liability, i.e., any risk, however slight, must be guarded against to avoid a finding of negligence. The law of negligence elaborated in *Bolton v. Stone*, A.C. 850 (1951), is not quite so strict. However, where the activity is inherently dangerous to life or property, e.g., blasting, strict liability rules generally apply and negligence need not be established. A policy decision has been made that while the activity is socially acceptable, the risk of harm is so potentially great that people and property must be protected.

Quicknotes

FORESEEABILITY A reasonable expectation that an act or omission would result in injury.

NEGLIGENCE Conduct falling below the standard of care that a reasonable person would demonstrate under similar conditions.

Bolton v. Stone

Cricket club (D) v. Injured woman (P)

H.L., A.C. 850 (1951)

NATURE OF CASE: Appeal of damages award for negligence.

FACT SUMMARY: Stone (P) was struck by a cricket ball. Defendant, the cricket club (D), appealed the lower courts finding of negligence.

RULE OF LAW

If a party takes reasonable care to prevent a known risk, or its chance of occurrence is extremely slight, no negligence exists.

FACTS: Stone (P) was struck and injured by a cricket ball that was hit over a wall onto a public street. Only six balls in 30 years had cleared that wall. The cricket club (D) was held guilty of negligence in not protecting passersby from a known risk. The cricket club (D) maintained that the chance of injury was so slight that it was not negligent in failing to protect against a recurrence.

ISSUE: If a party takes reasonable care to prevent a known risk, or its chance of occurrence is extremely slight, does negligence exist?

HOLDING AND DECISION: (Lord Reid, J.) No. If a party takes reasonable care to prevent a known risk, or its chance of occurrence is extremely slight, no negligence exists. In a modern society it is virtually impossible to guard against the creation of all risks. People must expect to be exposed to occasional risks. Property owners may use their premises in any reasonable manner even if it creates a slight risk to passersby. Only the creation of substantial risks is actionable. Here, only six balls had been hit over the wall in 30 years. The court of appeals held that if such a risk of injury could not be guarded against, the use of the property should have been discontinued. This is an application of a strict liability theory. Once the risk occurs it is foreseeable and must be guarded against. Negligence law, which is applicable herein, is less strict. Reasonable risks of a slight nature are permitted where one uses one's property in a reasonable manner. While I personally feel sorry for Stone (P), the law of negligence will not permit recovery for the occurrence of such a slight risk of injury. Reversed.

CONCURRENCE: (Lord Radcliffe, J.) The cricket club (D) is not guilty of any culpable act or omission. The cricket club's (D) actions did not fall below the standard of conduct that a reasonable person would set for himself. A reasonable person would not have abandoned the use of the ground for cricket or increased the height of the surrounding fences.

ANALYSIS

Many courts might disagree with the decision herein if the known risk could have easily and inexpensively been prevented. Strict liability is normally imposed against antisocial activities, such as nuisances, on the grounds that a person should not have to suffer known risks associated with such conduct. Occasionally, certain conduct is made unlawful and private damage actions are allowed for previously acceptable risks, e.g. modern pollution laws.

Quicknotes

FORESEEABILITY A reasonable expectation that an act or omission would result in injury.

NEGLIGENCE Conduct falling below the standard of care that a reasonable person would demonstrate under similar conditions.

REASONABLE CARE The degree of care observed by a reasonably prudent person under similar circumstances; synonymous with due care or ordinary care.

Hammontree v. Jenner

Car accident victim (P) v. Epileptic driver (D)

Cal. Ct. App., 97 Cal. Rptr. 739 (1971)

NATURE OF CASE: Action for damages based on negligence and strict liability.

FACT SUMMARY: Jenner (D) had an epileptic seizure while driving and injured Hammontree (P).

RULE OF LAW

A sudden illness that renders a driver unconscious will not be grounds for an action in negligence or strict liability.

FACTS: Jenner (D) had a history of epileptic seizures. Jenner (D) had been under a doctor's care and medication since 1951. Jenner's (D) last seizure was in 1953. In 1967, Jenner (D) apparently had a seizure while driving and while unconscious he crashed into Hammontree's (P) store causing personal injuries and property damage. Hammontree (P) brought suit for negligence and strict liability in tort. The judge refused to instruct the jury on strict liability on the ground that the theory was not applicable to sudden illnesses that strike a driver rendering him unconscious. The jury found no negligence.

ISSUE: Will a sudden illness that renders a driver unconscious be grounds for an action in negligence or strict liability?

HOLDING AND DECISION: (Lillie, J.) No. A sudden illness that renders a driver unconscious will not be grounds for an action in negligence or strict liability. The court declined to superimpose absolute liability in such situations. This was not akin to a products liability case, where a manufacturer put out a defective product. Here, Jenner (D) had not had a seizure for 14 years, was under a doctor's care, and was receiving medication to control his condition. The jury properly found Jenner (D) had no notice of the onset of the seizure or any grounds to suspect it was likely to occur. Since there were no grounds for a finding of negligence, Hammontree (P) could not recover. Affirmed.

ANALYSIS

Where the driver has constructive or actual notice of the onset of a serious illness that might make driving dangerous, negligence may be found. Where an outside force beyond the driver's control, e.g., a swarm of bees enters the car and causes the accident, no liability will normally be found. These cases are all decided on a fault/negligence issue. Sudden heart attack is not grounds for liability. *Tannyhill v. Pacific Motor Transport Co.*, 227 Cal. App. 2d 512 (1964).

Quicknotes

FORESEEABILITY A reasonable expectation that an act or omission would result in injury.

NEGLIGENCE Conduct falling below the standard of care that a reasonable person would demonstrate under similar conditions.

STRICT LIABILITY Liability for all injuries proximately caused by a party's conducting of certain inherently dangerous activities without regard to negligence or fault.

CHAPTER 3

Negligence

Quick Reference Rules of Law

CHAPTER 3

Vaughan v. Menlove

Neighboring cottage owner (P) v. Farmer (D)

C.P., 132 Eng. Rep. 490 (1837)

NATURE OF CASE: Action for damages for negligence.

FACT SUMMARY: Menlove's (D) hayrick burst into flames and the fire spread to Vaughan's (P) cottages.

RULE OF LAW

The level of care is determined by what a reasonably prudent man would do in similar circumstances.

FACTS: Menlove (D) stored a hayrick on his land near Vaughan's (P) land. The rick was very dry and Menlove (D) was repeatedly warned that it should be moved or unloaded. The rick burst into flames by spontaneous combustion. The fire spread and burned Vaughan's (P) cottages. The trial judge (Patteson, J.) charged the jury that it should decide if Menlove (D) was grossly negligent by applying a standard of care owed by a reasonably prudent man in similar circumstances. From an adverse verdict, Menlove (D) appealed on the grounds that he owed no duty of care to Vaughan (P) and the proper standard of care should be whether, in his eyes, his conduct was proper. The lawyers for Vaughan (P) (Talfourd and Whately) argued that even if this was a case of first impression, the principles to be applied to it were well established, and that the correct standard to be applied was that of the reasonably prudent man. They also argued that applying any other standard would create greater uncertainties and difficulties. Arguing for Menlove (D), his lawyer (Richards) contended that Menlove's (D) actions were lawful, as he had the right to place his hayrick wherever he wanted on his own property, and that his actions should be judged against his own best judgment under the circumstances, since different people have different levels of judgment and faculties. Thus, Richards argued that a determination of gross negligence should be judged against Menlove's (D) faculties, and not those of others, since the measure of prudence varies with the variation in people's faculties.

ISSUE: Is the level of care determined by what a reasonably prudent man would do in similar circumstances?

HOLDING AND DECISION: (Tindal, C.J.) Yes. The level of care is determined by what a reasonably prudent man would do in similar circumstances. While the reasonable, prudent man standard is inexact, attempting to determine the standard of care based on the thoughts of an individual is more difficult. Menlove (D) may use his property in any manner he wishes. However, he owes a general duty to do so in a manner that will not endanger the property of another. The proper standard of care is determined by deciding what a reasonably prudent man would do in similar circumstances. The jury may more easily determine this than attempting to determine a defendant's subjective belief. Rule discharged.

CONCURRENCE: (Park, J.) A man must so use his own property as not to injure that of others. It was proper to let the jury decide if Menlove (D) acted like a reasonably prudent man.

CONCURRENCE: (Vaughan, J.) Everyone takes upon himself the duty of so dealing with his own property as not to injure the property of others. It is clear Menlove (D) was grossly negligent and it should not have been left to the jury to decide.

ANALYSIS

Other activities which have been deemed unreasonable are burning weeds near the land of another; cutting trees near a sidewalk or the land of another; and engaging in hazardous activities on one's land. For these and similar activities the owner of property owes a duty of care to others. All these activities may cause damage to others if not properly performed. The less likely the activity is to cause others damage, the lower the standard of care.

Quicknotes

NEGLIGENCE Conduct falling below the standard of care that a reasonable person would demonstrate under similar conditions.

REASONABLY PRUDENT PERSON A hypothetical person whose judgment represents the standard to which society requires its members to act in their private affairs and in their dealings with others.

STANDARD OF CARE A uniform degree of behavior against which a person's conduct can be measured when determining liability in negligence cases.

Roberts v. Ring

Father of 7-year-old (P) v. Elderly driver (D)

Minn. Sup. Ct., 173 N.W. 437 (1919)

NATURE OF CASE: Appeal from denial of damages for negligence.

FACT SUMMARY: Roberts's (P) son ran in front of Ring's (D) car and was injured.

RULE OF LAW

If one, by his acts or omissions, causes injury to others, his negligence is judged by the standard of care usually exercised by the ordinary prudent normal man.

FACTS: Ring (D), an infirm, 70-year-old man, was driving four or five miles per hour in blocked traffic. Roberts's (P) son, a seven-year-old, ran from behind a buggy in front of Ring's (D) car and was struck and injured. Roberts (P) sued Ring (D) for damages based on negligence. The jury instruction told the jury to take into account Ring's (D) age and infirmities. The jury found for Ring (D). Roberts (P) appealed.

ISSUE: If one, by his acts or omissions, causes injury to others, should his negligence be judged by the standard of care usually exercised by the ordinary prudent normal man?

HOLDING AND DECISION: (Hallam, J.) Yes. If one, by his acts or omissions, causes injury to others, his negligence is judged by the standard of care usually exercised by the ordinary prudent normal man. Ring (D) was driving only four or five miles per hour when he saw the boy. It is common knowledge that an auto traveling at that speed can be stopped in a very few feet. Yet, Ring's (D) car knocked the boy down and ran over him. The evidence shows Ring's (D) lack of alertness in stopping his car. Therefore, Ring (D) was negligent. Ring's (D) advanced age does not relieve him from the charge of negligence. Such infirmity, to the extent it should be considered at all, presents a reason why Ring (D) should refrain from operating an auto in a crowded street. Reversed.

ANALYSIS

A related issue concerns the proper standard of care to which to hold beginners. The general rule has been to hold the beginner to the standard of care expected of those who are reasonably skilled and practiced in the art. However, an exception arises in cases in which the plaintiff has assumed the risk that defendant will exercise a lower standard of care, such as where an experienced driver agrees to teach a beginning driver how to drive.

Quicknotes

NEGLIGENCE Conduct falling below the standard of care that a reasonable person would demonstrate under similar conditions.

REASONABLY PRUDENT PERSON A hypothetical person whose judgment represents the standard to which society requires its members to act in their private affairs and in their dealings with others.

STANDARD OF CARE A uniform degree of behavior against which a person's conduct can be measured when determining liability in negligence cases.

Daniels v. Evans

Administrator of estate of deceased motorcycle driver (P) v. Car driver (D)

N.H. Sup. Ct., 224 A.2d 63 (1966)

NATURE OF CASE: Negligence of a minor.

FACT SUMMARY: Robert E. Daniels, age 19, was killed when his motorcycle collided with Evans's (D) car. Evans (D) objected to the court's instruction to the jury that Daniels was not to be held to the same degree of care as an adult.

RULE OF LAW

When a minor undertakes an adult activity that can result in grave danger to himself and to others, he is held to the same standard of care as the average prudent adult.

FACTS: Daniels, 19 years of age, was killed when his motorcycle collided with Evans's (D) car. The trial court, instructing the jury as to the standard of care to be applied to Daniels stated, "he is not held to the same degree of care as an adult." The jury gave a verdict for the administrator of the estate of Daniels (P). Evans (D) objected to the jury instructions, arguing that a minor operating a motor vehicle must be judged by the same standard of care as an adult.

ISSUE: When a minor undertakes an adult activity that can result in grave danger to himself and to others, is he held to the same standard of care as the average prudent adult?

HOLDING AND DECISION: (Lampron, J.) Yes. When a minor undertakes an adult activity that can result in grave danger to himself and to others, he is held to the same standard of care as the average prudent adult. Although the trial court's instructions to the jury reflect this court's traditional yardstick for judging the standard of care for minors, most of the cases applying that standard dealt with minors engaged in activities commensurate with their age (e.g., riding a bicycle or horse, walking). But many recent cases hold that—especially in the operation of motor vehicles—a minor undertaking any adult activity, which can result in grave danger to himself or others, must be judged by the care a reasonable and prudent adult would use. It would be unfair to the public to require a lesser standard. Although one, observing a typical child's activity, may anticipate conduct that does not reach adult standards of care and prudence, one cannot always determine that the driver of an approaching automobile is an adult or a minor, and often could not protect himself even if warned. Further, the state statute regarding obedience to traffic laws applies to "any person." This would indicate the intent of the legislature that all drivers have a right to expect that others—regardless of age and experience—will obey traffic laws and thus exercise the adult standard of ordinary care. The same legislative intent is evident in the state's excluding application of its *parens patriae* power over minors in cases where they are charged with violations of laws regarding motor vehicles, airplanes, boating, and hunting. To apply to minors a lower standard than adults in the operation of motor vehicles is unrealistic, contrary to the intent of the legislature, and harmful to public policy. Exception sustained.

ANALYSIS

The rule is now quite generally accepted that whenever a child, whether as plaintiff or as defendant, engages in an activity which is normally one for adults only, such as driving an auto or flying an airplane, the public interest and public safety require that any consequences stemming from his incapacity shall fall on him rather than on the innocent victim, and that he must be held to an adult standard without allowance for his age.

Quicknotes

ORDINARY CARE The degree of care exercised by a reasonable person when conducting everyday activities or under similar circumstances; synonymous with due care.

PARENS PATRIAE Maxim the government as sovereign is conferred with the duty to act as guardian on behalf of those citizens under legal disability.

STANDARD OF CARE A uniform degree of behavior against which a person's conduct can be measured when determining liability in negligence cases.

Breunig v. American Family Insurance Co.

Truck driver (P) v. Insurance company (D)

Wis. Sup. Ct., 173 N.W.2d 619 (1970)

NATURE OF CASE: Action for damages for personal injury from negligence.

FACT SUMMARY: While overcome by a sudden state of insanity, Erma Veith, insured by American Family Insurance Co. (D), drove her automobile into Breunig's (P) truck.

RULE OF LAW

A person seized with a sudden mental disability for which he had no warning will be excused from the general rule holding an insane person liable for his negligence.

FACTS: A psychiatrist testified that Erma Veith, insured by American Family Insurance Co. (D), told him that while she was driving, she believed God was directing her car. She saw a truck coming and stepped on the accelerator in order to become airborne, because she knew she could fly. Instead of flying, she collided with Breunig's (P) truck. At the time of the collision, Veith's automobile was on the left side of the road. The jury found her causally negligent on the theory she "had knowledge or forewarning of her mental delusions or disability."

ISSUE: Will a person seized with a sudden mental disability for which he had no warning be excused from the general rule holding an insane person liable for his negligence?

HOLDING AND DECISION: (Hallows, C.J.) Yes. A person seized with a sudden mental disability for which he had no warning will be excused from the general rule holding an insane person liable for his negligence. Cases supporting the general rule generally involve preexisting or permanent insanity. The general rule is supported by the following policies: (1) where one of two innocent persons must suffer a loss it should be borne by the one who occasioned it; (2) to induce those interested in the insane person's estate to restrain and control him/her; and (3) the fear an insanity defense would lead to false claims of insanity to avoid liability. Sudden mental disability is equivalent to sudden physical disability such as heart attack, stroke, fainting, and epileptic seizure and should be treated alike and not under the general rule. Here, unless it is shown that Veith, insured by American Family Insurance Co. (D), had warning or knowledge that the mental disability would occur, she will not be held liable for acts she committed while suddenly mentally disabled. Affirmed.

ANALYSIS

In nearly all cases, an insane person is held liable for negligence without reference to his insanity. However, this rule has been criticized, as, in this case, a transitory, sudden mental disability is commonly regarded as a circumstance depriving the actor of control over his conduct and relieving him of liability.

Quicknotes

FORESEEABILITY A reasonable expectation that an act or omission would result in injury.

MENTAL CAPACITY The ability to comprehend the nature, terms, and effect of the act in which one is engaged.

Fletcher v. City of Aberdeen

Blind man (P) v. City (D)

Wash. Sup. Ct., 338 P.2d 743 (1959)

NATURE OF CASE: Action for damages for negligence.

FACT SUMMARY: A workman negligently removed a barrier around a ditch and Fletcher (P), who was blind, fell into it.

RULE OF LAW

A person who is infirm is held to that degree of care as would be exhibited by a reasonably prudent person suffering the same infirmity in the same situation.

FACTS: The City of Aberdeen (the City) (D) dug a ditch near a sidewalk to affect repairs. A barricade was erected. One of the workmen removed the barricade to do some work and negligently failed to replace it. Fletcher (P), who was blind, fell into the ditch. Testimony indicated that Fletcher's (P) cane would have warned him of the ditch if the barrier were in place. The judge instructed the jury that the City (D) was not an insurer and it must find negligence on its part. The judge refused to instruct the jury that the City (D) owed no greater duty to the blind than to the sighted and that the blind should be held to the same standard of care as the sighted. The City (D) appealed from a verdict for Fletcher (P).

ISSUE: Is a person who is infirm held to that degree of care as would be exhibited by a reasonably prudent person suffering the same infirmity in the same situation?

HOLDING AND DECISION: (Foster, J.) Yes. A person who is infirm is held to that degree of care as would be exhibited by a reasonably prudent person suffering the same infirmity in the same situation. The City (D) is obligated to safeguard all who travel the streets. This obligation applies to the rich and the poor, the physically well and those who are infirm. While the City (D) is not an insurer, it is liable for its negligence or that of its employees. While a sighted person would probably not have fallen into the ditch, a blind person is not held to that standard of care. If one suffering a physical infirmity is injured, he is not held to be contributorily negligent unless he has failed to act with the same degree of care that a prudent man with similar disability would have exhibited under similar circumstances. Affirmed.

ANALYSIS

A private citizen does not owe the same duty to the infirm (normally). In such situations, the plaintiff who is infirm will normally be held to a higher standard of care in determining whether the private defendant was negligent. Cases dealing with private parties who hold themselves open to the public have caused a great deal of problems in this area. To what standard of care should the private party beheld in such situations? Courts have split over the question, with most decisions being based on the factual nature of the injury.

Quicknotes

STANDARD OF CARE A uniform degree of behavior against which a person's conduct can be measured when determining liability in negligence cases.

Denver & Rio Grande R.R. v. Peterson

[Parties not identified.]

Colo. Sup. Ct., 69 P. 578 (1902)

NATURE OF CASE: [Nature of case not stated in casebook excerpt.]

FACT SUMMARY: [Facts not stated in casebook excerpt.]

RULE OF LAW

Once a party assumes a duty, he must act in a reasonable manner no matter what his station in life.

FACTS: [Facts not stated in casebook excerpt.]

ISSUE: Once a party assumes a duty, must he act in a reasonable manner no matter what his station in life?

HOLDING AND DECISION: (Campbell, C.J.) Yes. Once a party assumes a duty, he must act in a reasonable manner no matter what his station in life. Wealth is not a factor in determining whether a party has fulfilled his duty of due care and reasonable conduct. Poverty will not excuse the duty and wealth will not increase it. A warehouseman owes the same duty to those storing goods whether he is rich or poor.

ANALYSIS

An infirmity will not normally excuse a duty of care. This is especially true where it is in a commercial setting. The standard of care to be met is that of a normally prudent person under similar circumstances. Beginners are generally held to the same standard of care as more experienced people. An exception is sometimes made where the party engaging the beginner is alerted to the fact that he is a beginner. The standard then becomes the reasonable care of a prudent beginner.

Quicknotes

DUTY OF CARE A principle of negligence requiring an individual to act in such a manner as to avoid injury to a person to whom he or she owes an obligatory duty.

Blyth v. Birmingham Water Works

Landowner (P) v. Water works company (D)

Ex., 156 Eng. Rep. 1047 (1856)

NATURE OF CASE: Action to recover damages for negligence on appeal.

FACT SUMMARY: An extraordinarily severe frost caused a fireplug owned by Birmingham Water Works (D) to flood the property of Blyth (P).

RULE OF LAW

Negligence involves the creation of an "unreasonable" risk, by act or omission, that a reasonable and prudent person would not create.

FACTS: Birmingham Water Works Co. (Water Works) (D) operated the water pipes in the county of Birmingham. By statute they were also required to maintain fireplugs for the pipes in a certain manner (18" below the surface, etc.). At all times, Water Works (D) maintained the fireplugs according to the law and had for 25 years. During an extraordinarily cold frost one winter, however, one of the plugs got stopped up by ice, which caused water from the pipes to flood the property of Blyth (P), causing damage. (Note, moving water does not freeze.) Blyth (P) sued for damages, charging negligence of Water Works (D) in not taking adequate precautions to prepare for the contingency of this frost. Upon judgment for Blyth (P), Water Works (D) appealed, contending that the frost was so extraordinary and unforeseeable as to make damage resulting from it a mere accident.

ISSUE: Does negligence involve the creation of an "unreasonable" risk, by act or omission, that a reasonable and prudent person would not create?

HOLDING AND DECISION: (Baron Alderson, J.) Yes. Negligence involves the creation of an "unreasonable" risk, by act or omission, that a reasonable and prudent person would not create. A prudent person is guided upon those considerations that ordinarily regulate the conduct of human affairs. A reasonable man acts with reference to the average circumstances of ordinary times. He cannot be held, therefore, for extraordinary occurrences. Here, Water Works (D) took all necessary precautions for ordinary frost. They cannot equitably be held responsible for a frost such as the one involved here as such a frost is seldom seen south of the polar region. Negligence liability may not be imposed where damage results from a mere accident, the contingency of which was wholly extraordinary. The judgment must be reversed. The rationale here is that making Water Works (D) responsible for all harm caused, even inadvertently, would be to make them the insurers of all people with whom they deal.

CONCURRENCE: (Baron Bramwell, J.) The defendants were not bound to keep the plugs clear. It appears to me that the plaintiff was under quite as much obligation to remove the accumulated ice and snow as the defendants. However that may be, it appears to me that it would be monstrous to hold the defendants responsible because they did not foresee and prevent an accident, the cause of which was so obscure that it was not discovered until many months after the accident had happened.

ANALYSIS

This case points out the general rule for the negligence standard of care that all people owe. Basically, it is the objective "reasonable man under similar circumstances" test. Note that simply following the statutory duties required above did not determine whether this standard had been met, however. Though compliance with a statute is evidence of meeting the standard, it is not conclusive. If the conduct involved nevertheless creates an "unreasonable risk" of harm, negligence will be found. On the other hand, failure to meet a statutory standard where (1) statutory duty is clear and (2) the statute is designed to prevent the type of injury suffered or protect the class of persons of which the victim is a member, may be negligence per se. Caution must be taken, however, to avoid confusion between the foreseeability standard for standard of care (above) and the absence of this standard for proximate cause.

Quicknotes

FORESEEABILITY A reasonable expectation that an act or omission would result in injury.

NEGLIGENCE Conduct falling below the standard of care that a reasonable person would demonstrate under similar conditions.

PROXIMATE CAUSE The natural sequence of events without which an injury would not have been sustained.

REASONABLE PERSON STANDARD The standard of care exercised by a hypothetical person who possesses the intelligence, education, knowledge, attention, and judgment required by society of its members when governing behavior; the standard applied to a person's judgment when determining breach of duty under the theory of negligence.

STANDARD OF CARE A uniform degree of behavior against which a person's conduct can be measured when determining liability in negligence cases.

Osborne v. Montgomery

Bicycle errand runner (P) v. Auto owner (D)

Wis. Sup. Ct., 234 N.W. 372 (1931)

NATURE OF CASE: Action for negligence.

FACT SUMMARY: A jury instruction that gave no definition of how to determine whether a risk was reasonable was challenged.

RULE OF LAW
To determine whether a risk is acceptable, the value of the social interest involved should be balanced against the risk created.

FACTS: Osborne (P), a 13-year-old youth, was riding his bicycle when the right handlebar bar of his bicycle contacted the outside edge of an opened door of Montgomery's (D) stopped car. The bicycle subsequently tipped and Osborne (P) was thrown to the ground and injured. The jury was instructed that negligence is the want of ordinary care, and ordinary care is the degree of care that the great mass of mankind exercises under similar circumstances. The jury found Montgomery (D) negligent, and Montgomery (D) appealed.

ISSUE: To determine whether a risk is acceptable, should the value of the social interest involved be balanced against the risk created?

HOLDING AND DECISION: (Rosenberry, C.J.) Yes. To determine whether a risk is acceptable, the value of the social interest involved should be balanced against the risk created. Human beings are constantly creating situations that lead to the injury of another. To determine whether the conduct is justified based on societal demands, there must be a balancing of the social interest involved against the risk created by the conduct. If the interest justifies the risk, then the jury must be instructed to determine whether the defendant conducted himself under the situation with the same degree of care that a majority of people would exhibit under similar circumstances. Reversed and remanded on the question of damages.

ANALYSIS

Driving, even under hazardous conditions, is a socially justified risk. However, the driver must be handling his car in a reasonable, prudent manner consonant with the conditions. Observance of the speed limit where the streets are icy might not be deemed compliance with ordinary care under the above-announced rule of law. However, a fire engine speeding to a fire could justify a higher rate of speed so long as it was warranted, and the driver handled the truck with the same degree of skill other drivers would exhibit in similar circumstances.

Quicknotes

CONTRIBUTORY NEGLIGENCE Behavior on the part of an injured plaintiff falling below the standard of ordinary care that contributes to the defendant's negligence, resulting in the plaintiff's injury.

ORDINARY CARE The degree of care exercised by a reasonable person when conducting everyday activities or under similar circumstances; synonymous with due care.

Cooley v. Public Service Co.

Injured telephone user (P) v. Power company (D)

N.H. Sup. Ct., 10 A.2d 673 (1940)

NATURE OF CASE: Action for damages resulting from negligence.

FACT SUMMARY: Public Service Co. (D) hung its electrical wires over telephone lines at a right angle.

RULE OF LAW

Where danger to two classes of persons cannot be simultaneously guarded against, only the most immediate and injurious risk need be protected.

FACTS: Public Service Co. (D) hung its uninsulated power lines at right angles above telephone company (D) lines. A severe storm downed one of Public Service's (D) lines. It fell across a telephone company line, burned through it, and caused a loud screech on the line that injured Cooley (P), who was making a call. Cooley (P) sued both the telephone company (D) and Public Service (D) for negligence. The telephone company (D) was dismissed from the suit, and the jury found against Public Service (D) on the basis that certain safety devices could have been installed to protect against such an occurrence. Public Service (D) appealed a judgment against it on the ground that these devices would have caused a greater risk of electrocution to those on the streets below the lines. Public Service (D) alleged that its primary duty was to protect this class of people rather than telephone subscribers.

ISSUE: Where danger to two classes of persons cannot be simultaneously guarded against, need only the most immediate and injurious risk be protected?

HOLDING AND DECISION: (Page, J.) Yes. Where danger to two classes of persons cannot be simultaneously guarded against, only the most immediate and injurious risk need be protected. Public Service (D) owed its primary duty to pedestrians who could be electrocuted. Its safety devices were sufficient to protect that class. The safety devices suggested by Cooley (P) would have increased the risk to this class at the expense of protecting telephone subscribers from a reasonably remote and less dangerous risk. Reversed.

ANALYSIS

Where there is a danger to property versus a risk to human life, the latter is always given preference. This is one of the major justifications for burying cables, power lines, etc. Certain risks carry with them a danger to both life and property that, because of the nature of the activity, cannot be reasonably safeguarded. These activities, e.g., blasting, are subjected to a strict liability theory for any class of injury.

Quicknotes

NEGLIGENCE Conduct falling below the standard of care that a reasonable person would demonstrate under similar conditions.

STRICT LIABILITY Liability for all injuries proximately caused by a party's conducting of certain inherently dangerous activities without regard to negligence or fault.

United States v. Carroll Towing Co.

Federal government (D) v. Tugboat company (D)

159 F.2d 169 (2d Cir. 1947)

NATURE OF CASE: Action to recover damages in admiralty for the sinking of a barge.

FACT SUMMARY: The attendant of defendant's barge abandoned it for 21 hours; during this period the barge broke loose and while it was adrift struck the plaintiff's barge, causing it to sink.

RULE OF LAW

There is a duty of care to protect others from harm when the burden of taking adequate precautions is less than the product of the probability of the resulting harm and the magnitude of the harm.

FACTS: The attendant of defendant's barge left that barge unwatched for more than 21 hours during a period when the harbor was full of vessels. During the period when the attendant of defendant's barge was absent, the barge became untied and drifted away from the dock, running into another barge and sinking it.

ISSUE: Is there a duty of care to protect others from harm when the burden of taking adequate precautions is less than the product of the probability of the resulting harm and the magnitude of the harm?

HOLDING AND DECISION: (Hand, J.) Yes. There is a duty of care to protect others from harm when the burden of taking adequate precautions is less than the product of the probability of the resulting harm and the magnitude of the harm. In this case, the burden of preventing the accident was low; it only involved the watchman staying in the vicinity of the barge or recruiting someone else to stand by and watch it. The probability of the barge getting untied and striking another barge is undoubtedly a variable that changes with conditions, as is the amount of injury that will result. The existing conditions, the crowded harbor with barges constantly being moved about, made the probability of injury more than a negligible factor and made the magnitude of resulting injury an enormous figure. Thus, since the burden of preventing the collision was low and the product of the probability and the amount of injury projected is high, the fact that it occurred was a breach of duty.

ANALYSIS

This effort to formulate negligence, this "calculus of the risk," is an acceptable method of determining negligence. Behind this formula, however, is always the recognition that the measure of the reasonableness of the risk revolves around the specific circumstances of the situation. Conduct is relative to the particular occasion and need.

Quicknotes

CONTRIBUTORY NEGLIGENCE Behavior on the part of an injured plaintiff falling below the standard of ordinary care that contributes to the defendant's negligence, resulting in the plaintiff's injury.

Andrews v. United Airlines

Injured passenger (P) v. Airline company (D)

24 F.3d 39 (9th Cir. 1994)

NATURE OF CASE: Appeal from summary judgment dismissing action in negligence.

FACT SUMMARY: Andrews (P), a passenger injured on a United Airlines (United) (D) flight when a briefcase fell out of an overhead compartment and hit her, alleged that United (D) was liable for negligence because it breached its duty of care to her.

RULE OF LAW

Even a small risk of serious injury to passengers may form the basis of a common carrier's liability if that risk could be eliminated consistent with the practical operation of airline travel.

FACTS: Andrews (P) was a passenger aboard a United Airlines (United) (D) flight when a briefcase fell out of an overhead compartment and hit her in the head, causing serious injuries. Andrews (P) alleged that United (D), as a common carrier, owed Andrews (P) an utmost duty of care and that United (D) breached that duty by not doing more to prevent objects from falling out of overhead compartments. United (D) moved for summary judgment, arguing that Andrews (P) showed too little proof of United's (D) breach to be allowed to go to a jury on the issue. The district court granted summary judgment for United (D) and Andrews (P) appealed.

ISSUE: May even a small risk of serious injury to passengers form the basis of a common carrier's liability if that risk could be eliminated consistent with the practical operation of airline travel?

HOLDING AND DECISION: (Kozinski, J.) Yes. Even a small risk of serious injury to passengers may form the basis of a common carrier's liability if that risk could be eliminated consistent with the practical operation of airline travel. Andrews (P) demonstrated that United (D) was aware of the problem of items falling out of overhead bins; however, its solution was to merely warn passengers of the danger. Here, United (D), as a common carrier, owed an utmost duty of care to passenger Andrews (P). Andrews (P) presented enough proof that United (D) breached its duty to defeat summary judgment and have a jury decide the issue of breach. A reasonable jury might find that United (D) should have done more to prevent items from falling out of the overhead compartments, or it might find that United (D) did do enough. The district court, therefore, incorrectly granted summary judgment for United (D). Reversed and remanded.

ANALYSIS

Common carriers owe a higher duty to passengers than the ordinary standard of care. The ordinary standard is that of reasonable care under the circumstances. Common carriers, as this case demonstrates, are responsible for even the slightest negligence. Regardless of the standard applied, the issues of duty and breach are ones to be decided by the jury, if a reasonable jury could decide the issues either way.

Quicknotes

COMMON CARRIER An entity whose business is the transport of persons or property.

DUTY OF CARE A principle of negligence requiring an individual to act in such a manner as to avoid injury to a person to whom he or she owes an obligatory duty.

NEGLIGENCE Conduct falling below the standard of care that a reasonable person would demonstrate under similar conditions.

SUMMARY JUDGMENT Judgment rendered by a court in response to a motion by one of the parties, claiming that the lack of a question of material fact in respect to an issue warrants disposition of the issue without consideration by the jury.

Titus v. Bradford, B. & K. R. Co.

Railroad brakeman (P) v. Railroad (D)

Pa. Sup. Ct., 20 A. 517 (1890)

NATURE OF CASE: Action for negligence.

FACT SUMMARY: Titus (P) was killed when a broad-gauge boxcar that Bradford, B. & K. R. Co. (D) had set on its narrow-gauge tracks tipped off its truck when a securing block became loose.

RULE OF LAW

The unbending test of negligence in methods, machinery, and appliances is the ordinary usage of the business.

FACTS: Bradford, B. & K. R. Co. (D) (the Railroad) customarily took the broad-gauge cars used by the other carrier having standard-gauge lines and set them on its narrow-gauge tracks by means of trucks, utilizing securing blocks to eliminate the undue rocking that otherwise occurred. One of these securing blocks became loose, and Titus (P), a brakeman riding the car, was killed. In defending a suit based on negligence seeking to recover damages for his death, the Railroad (D) offered testimony that the shifting of broad-gauge or standard car bodies onto narrow-gauge trucks for transportation was a regular part and common practice of the business of narrow-gauge railroads. The jury rendered a verdict for Titus (P).

ISSUE: Is the unbending test of negligence in methods, machinery, and appliances the ordinary usage of the business?

HOLDING AND DECISION: (Mitchell, J.) Yes. The unbending test of negligence in methods, machinery, and appliances is the ordinary usage of the business. An employer is not bound to use the best and newest devices to avoid a claim that he is negligent. Rather, he performs his duty when he furnishes those of ordinary character and reasonable safety. In regard to the style of implement or nature of the mode of performance of any work, "reasonably safe" means safe according to the usage, habits, and ordinary risks of the business. Absolute safety is unattainable, and employers are not insurers. Furthermore, some jobs are essentially dangerous. The employer is liable not for the consequences of danger but for the consequences of negligence. No jury can be permitted to say that the usual and ordinary way, commonly adopted by those in the same business, is a negligent way for which liability shall be imposed. As the Railroad (D) acted in accord with his standard of care, it was not negligent. Furthermore, this was a perfectly plain case of acceptance of an employment with full knowledge of the risks. Reversed.

ANALYSIS

The use of safety codes, manuals, etc., as "pertinent and valuable aids in the resolution of the issue of negligence" was affirmed in *McComish v. DeSoi*, 42 N.J. 274, 200 A.2d 116 (1964). While warning that prevailing safety practices were not "of themselves the absolute measure of due care," the court made it clear that they have "probative force as evidence" of what would constitute reasonable care in a particular area or situation.

Quicknotes

STANDARD OF CARE A uniform degree of behavior against which a person's conduct can be measured when determining liability in negligence cases.

Mayhew v. Sullivan Mining Co.

Mineworker (P) v. Mining company (D)

Me. Sup. Jud. Ct., 76 Me. 100 (1884)

NATURE OF CASE: Appeal from verdict for plaintiff in a negligence action.

FACT SUMMARY: Sullivan Mining Co. (D) argued that it should be allowed to present evidence regarding customary industry practices in defending against Mayhew's (P) negligence suit.

RULE OF LAW

"Custom" has no proper place in the definition of what constitutes ordinary care.

FACTS: Mayhew (P), an independent contractor, was hired by Sullivan Mining Co. (Sullivan) (D) to trace new veins of ore. While working on a platform 270 feet below ground, which contained a "bucket hole" that Mayhew (P) used in his work, Mayhew (P) was injured when he fell thirty-five feet down the mineshaft. Mayhew (P) fell through a hole about three feet by twenty-six inches in size, which had been cut by one of Sullivan's (D) employees as a "ladder hole." No railing or barrier had been put around this ladder hole or any light or other warning of its existence. At trial, the court refused to allow evidence regarding whether ladder holes in mines ever had railings. The jury found Sullivan (D) negligent and awarded Mayhew (P) $2,500. Sullivan (D) appealed.

ISSUE: Does "custom" have a proper place in the definition of what constitutes ordinary care?

HOLDING AND DECISION: (Barrows, J.) No. "Custom" has no proper place in the definition of what constitutes ordinary care. Here, Sullivan (D) contends that it should have been allowed by the trial court to question its mining superintendent, who had supervised the cutting of the ladder hole, regarding whether there was any lack of "average ordinary care" on Sullivan's (D) part. These questions related to whether it was customary or feasible in the mining business to fence or put a railing around a ladder hole. These questions were properly excluded. No matter what custom or practice in the mining industry could prove, it would have no tendency to show that the act was consistent with ordinary prudence or due regard for the safety of those who were using Sullivan's (D) premises by its invitation. The gross carelessness of the act appears conclusively upon its recital. Sullivan (D) argues that if one conforms to custom, he is so far exercising ordinary care. This argument proceeds upon an erroneous idea of what constitutes ordinary care. It is no excuse that carelessness is universal. Affirmed.

ANALYSIS

In the history of negligence decisions, the *Mayhew v. Sullivan Mining Co.* case has not been frequently followed. A more recent case states a more current view. This case is *Bimberg v. Northern Pacific Ry.*, 14 N.W. 410 (Minn. 1944). In *Bimberg*, the court stated that local usage and custom, either singly or in combination, will not justify or excuse negligence. Plans of construction or uses commonly followed by years of successful operation may be evidence of due care but cannot establish as safe in law what is dangerous in fact.

Quicknotes

ORDINARY CARE The degree of care exercised by a reasonable person when conducting everyday activities or under similar circumstances; synonymous with due care.

The T.J. Hooper

Owner of cargo (P) v. Tugboat (D)

53 F.2d 107 (S.D.N.Y 1931)

NATURE OF CASE: Appeal from award of damages for negligence.

FACT SUMMARY: *The T.J. Hooper* (D), a tugboat, lost its cargo after it failed to receive warnings of an approaching storm.

RULE OF LAW

The standard of care in a negligence case changes with advances, knowledge, and new devices of demonstrated worth.

FACTS: *The T.J. Hooper* (D) was one of six tugboats hauling coal barges from Virginia to New York. *Hooper's* (D) cargo was lost in a gale. Four of the other tugboats had received storm warnings on their radios and escaped the storm by moving to calmer waters. *Hooper* (D) was not equipped with a reliable radio and therefore failed to receive the storm warnings. Ninety percent of coast side tugboats had radios. The cargo owners (P) sued *Hooper* (D) for damages based on *Hooper's* (D) operator's negligence in failing to equip the boat with a reliable radio even though the use of such radios in coastal navigation was almost universally accepted. The trial court found for the cargo owners.

ISSUE: Does the standard of care in a negligence case change with advances, knowledge, and new devices of demonstrated worth?

HOLDING AND DECISION: (Coxe, J.) Yes. The standard of care in a negligence case changes with advances, knowledge, and new devices of demonstrated worth. Radio broadcasting was not new or untried in 1928. It was utilized by almost 90 percent of coastal tugboat operators, and radio receivers were regarded as necessary equipment on every reasonably equipped tugboat. The use of the radios was so extensive it became an almost universal practice in coastal navigation. *Hooper's* (D) owner had a duty to supply effective receiving sets. Affirmed.

ANALYSIS

On appeal, 60 F.2d 737 (2d Cir. 1932), Judge Learned Hand affirmed the lower court's decision on a novel basis. Judge Hand disagreed with the trial court in its contention that the use of receiving sets was generally adopted by coastal tugboats operating in 1928. However, Judge Hand held that even though the use of such radios was not customary, the failure of the tugboat owner to obtain such necessary equipment still constituted negligence.

Quicknotes

JOINT LIABILITY Liability owed to an injured party by two or more parties where each party has the right to insist that the other tortfeasors be joined to the matter.

The T.J. Hooper

Owner of cargo (P) v. Tugboat (D)

60 F.2d 737 (2d Cir. 1932)

NATURE OF CASE: Appeal in action for exoneration from, or limitation of, liability.

FACT SUMMARY: Eastern Transportation Co. (Eastern) (D), the owner of two tugs, unsuccessfully appealed the refusal of the trial court to limit Eastern's (D) liability toward the owners of barges and their cargoes of coal that were lost in a storm the tugs could have avoided had they been equipped with radio receivers.

RULE OF LAW

Regardless of the custom of an industry or trade, a defendant will be held liable if his actions fall beneath the standard of the average prudent man.

FACTS: This is a petition by the Eastern Transportation Co. (Eastern) (D), as owner of the tugs *Mantrose* and *The T.J. Hooper*. The tugs were towing barges #17 and #30 belonging to the Northern Barge Co. (P). The barges carried coal owned by the New England Coal and Coke Co. and N.H. Hartwell & Son, Inc. The tugs sank in a storm, losing the barges and their cargo. The cargo owners sued the barge owners under contracts of carriage, and Northern Barge (P) sued Eastern (D) under the towing contract—both for its own loss and as bailee of the cargo. The trial court found the tugs unseaworthy because they could have secured storm warnings. The trial court held Eastern (D) and Northern Barge (D) jointly liable to the cargo owners. Eastern (D) petitioned exoneration from or limitation of liability.

ISSUE: Regardless of the custom of an industry or trade, will a defendant be held liable if his actions fall beneath the standard of the average prudent man?

HOLDING AND DECISION: (Hand, J.) Yes. Regardless of the custom of an industry or trade, a defendant will be held liable if his actions fall beneath the standard of the average prudent man. The fact that it was not a general custom for tugs to have radio receivers with which to receive weather warnings is not determinative. Reasonable prudence required the installation of such sets in the case of tugs towing heavily laden barges, strung out for half a mile and with little power to maneuver. A radio receiver would have given them necessary protection that would be available in no other way. The whole industry may have lagged in the installation of these sets, which is not to say that ordinary prudence would not regard them as necessary. Affirmed.

ANALYSIS

Professor and legal scholar William Prosser stated that, according to the majority of cases, it is the better view that not every custom is conclusive merely because it is a custom. A custom must meet the challenge of "learned reason" and be given only the evidentiary weight the situation deserves. Therefore, where common knowledge and ordinary judgment will recognize unreasonable danger, it may be that the whole trade or industry may be found negligent.

Quicknotes

CUSTOM AND USAGE A customary practice that is so widespread that it has become mandatory and has the force of law.

Lama v. Borras

Patient (P) v. Doctor (D)

16 F.3d 473 (1st Cir. 1994)

NATURE OF CASE: Appeal from jury verdict for plaintiff in medical malpractice suit.

FACT SUMMARY: Roberto Romero Lama (P) brought suit alleging medical malpractice against Dr. Pedro Borras (D) and Hospital del Maestro (D) on the basis that Dr. Borras (D) was negligent in failing to administer a conservative treatment program prior to resorting to surgery.

RULE OF LAW

In a medical malpractice case, the plaintiff must show that the physician's treatment fell below the standard of care applicable to the general practitioner, resulting in the plaintiff's injury.

FACTS: Roberto Romero Lama (Romero) (P) suffered from back pain. His physician, Alfonso, referred him to Dr. Pedro Borras (D), a neurosurgeon, who concluded that Romero had a herniated disc and scheduled him for surgery. During surgery, Dr. Borras (D) found that Romero had an "extruded" disc and attempted to remove the extruding material. Romero's symptoms remained in effect for several days after the operation and Dr. Borras (D) scheduled a second operation. Romero (P) suffered from discitis, an infection of the space between the discs. He filed suit against Dr. Borras (D) alleging negligence. The jury awarded Romero (P) $600,000, and the district court rejected Dr. Borras's (D) motion for judgment as a matter of law and for a new trial. Dr. Borras (D) appealed.

ISSUE: In a medical malpractice case, must the plaintiff show that the physician's treatment fell below the standard of care applicable to the general practitioner, resulting in the plaintiff's injury?

HOLDING AND DECISION: (Stahl, J.) Yes. In a medical malpractice case, the plaintiff must show that the physician's treatment fell below the standard of care applicable to the general practitioner, resulting in the plaintiff's injury. In order to establish a prima facie case of medical malpractice in Puerto Rico, the plaintiff must show (1) the norms of medical care and knowledge applicable to the general practitioner; (2) proof the physician failed to follow such norms in the patient's treatment; and (3) a causal relationship between the physician's act or omission and the patient's injury. The plaintiff must establish the relevant national standard of care. This is usually accomplished by expert testimony. The plaintiff must also prove by a preponderance of the evidence that the physician's negligent conduct was the factor that "most probably" caused the plaintiff's injury. Expert testimony is generally required to establish this as well. Dr. Borras (D) claimed that Romero (P) failed to establish a general medical standard governing the need for conservative treatment prior to the first operation. Here there was sufficient evidence for the jury to conclude Dr. Borras (D) failed to provide the proper conservative treatment program prior to surgery. When a physician exposes a patient to risk-prone surgery, he is liable for harm sustained that is associated with a foreseeable risk. Here discitis is a foreseeable risk of lumbar disc surgery. With respect to the issue of causation, nearly all the expert testimony stated that conservative treatment would have eliminated the need for surgery in most cases. Romero (P) introduced legally sufficient evidence to support each element of negligence by Dr. Borras (D). Affirmed.

ANALYSIS

Note that the standard of care applicable in medical malpractice cases departs from the usual standard of the "reasonable person" normally applied by juries. Courts resort to the use of custom in order to provide more consistent results. The typical standard in medical malpractice suits is that the physician use the degree of knowledge and skill possessed by physicians in good standing in the community and under similar circumstances.

Quicknotes

STANDARD OF CARE A uniform degree of behavior against which a person's conduct can be measured when determining liability in negligence cases.

Murray v. UNMC Physicians

Deceased patient's spouse (P) v. Physicians (D)

Neb. Sup. Ct., 806 N.W.2d 118 (2011)

NATURE OF CASE: Appeal from order of new trial in action for medical malpractice.

FACT SUMMARY: UNMC Physicians (D), Mrs. Murray's physicians, waited to give her an extremely expensive medicine (Flolan) until they had confirmation her insurance would cover the cost of the Flolan, because once Flolan was started, discontinuing it would have devastating consequences for the patient. Mrs. Murray died before the Flolan was administered, and her husband, Murray (P), brought suit for medical malpractice. A key issue was the appropriate standard of care and whether the standard could be tied to the need for insurance payments.

RULE OF LAW

In a medical malpractice action involving an issue of failure to provide medical treatment, the standard of care is a question for the jury where the medical treatment is extremely expensive, its abrupt discontinuance would be devastating for the patient, and physicians waited for confirmation of insurance coverage of the treatment prior to administering it.

FACTS: Mrs. Murray suffered from pulmonary arterial hypertension. Flolan, a medicine that can treat this condition, must be administered on a continuing basis for the rest of a patient's life once it is started, at a cost of around $100,000 per year. If it is discontinued, it can have devastating consequences for a patient, including death. Prior to administering Flolan to Mrs. Murray, her physicians UNMC Physicians (UNMC) (D) awaited insurance approval—because they wanted to be certain she would have a continuous, uninterrupted supply. Before insurance confirmation was received, Mrs. Murray died of cardiac arrest. Her husband, Murray (P), brought a medical malpractice action against UNMC (D). The cause of death was disputed. Murray (P) presented evidence it was arterial hypertension. UNMC (D) presented evidence it was myocarditis, an inflammation of the heart usually caused by viral or bacterial infection. Murray (P) also presented evidence earlier administration of Flolan would have prevented Mrs. Murray's death. Murray (P) moved for a directed verdict on the standard of care, arguing as a matter of law, insurance coverage cannot dictate what doctors do, but this motion was denied. Murray (P) also requested the jury be instructed if the standard of care requires prescription of a drug, it is not a defense to a claim the standard of care has been violated if the drug would not be provided until approved by an insurance carrier. That instruction was refused. The jury returned a general verdict for UNMC (D), but the trial court granted a new trial, explaining as a matter of law, a medical standard of care cannot be tied to or controlled by an insurance company or the need for payment. UNMC (D) appealed the grant of a new trial, and the state's highest court granted review.

ISSUE: In a medical malpractice action involving an issue of failure to provide medical treatment, is the standard of care a question for the jury where the medical treatment is extremely expensive, its abrupt discontinuance would be devastating for the patient, and physicians waited for confirmation of insurance coverage of the treatment prior to administering it?

HOLDING AND DECISION: (Gerrard, J.) Yes. In a medical malpractice action involving an issue of failure to provide medical treatment, the standard of care is a question for the jury where the medical treatment is extremely expensive, its abrupt discontinuance would be devastating for the patient, and physicians waited for confirmation of insurance coverage of the treatment prior to administering it. The issue in this case is a narrow one, but it appears in the context of broader policy discussions of what the appropriate standard of care should be. In this state, the standard of reasonable and ordinary care is unitary- and wealth-blind. Some argue this standard cannot be reconciled with today's healthcare marketplace, which is increasingly driven by cost and insurance concerns, and leads to physicians' declining altogether patients who cannot afford to pay or who are uninsured. On the other hand, some have argued permitting physicians to make medical decisions based on resource scarcity would compromise the fiduciary relationship between patient and physician, creating a conflict of interest because the patient's well-being would no longer be the physician's focus. Whether the legal standard of care should change to alleviate that conflict, and how it might change, has been the subject of considerable debate. It has been suggested the customary standard of care could evolve to permit the denial of marginally beneficial treatment when high costs would not be justified by minor expected benefits. Another suggestion is the standard of care should evolve to consider two separate components: (1) a skill component, addressing the skill with which diagnoses are made and treatment is rendered, that would not vary by a patient's financial circumstances and (2) a resource component, addressing deliberate decisions about how much treatment to give a patient, that would

Continued on next page.

vary so as to not demand more of physicians than is reasonable. Some have suggested physicians should be permitted to rebut the presumption of a unitary standard of care when diminution of care arises by economic necessity instead of negligence, whereas many have suggested custom should no longer be the benchmark for the standard of care, and practice standards or guidelines could be promulgated that would settle issues of resource allocation. Although these policy considerations are serious and difficult, they are not presented by this case. Contrary to the trial court's belief, this is not a case in which an insurance company overrode the medical judgment of a patient's physicians or in which those physicians allowed their medical judgment to be subordinated to a patient's ability to pay for treatment. Nor is this a case in which the parties disputed the cost-effectiveness of the treatment at issue. Rather, UNMC's (D) evidence was its decision to wait to begin Flolan treatment was not economic—it was a medical decision, based on the health consequences to the patient if the treatment is interrupted. Thus, the trial court's concerns about health care policy were misplaced in a situation in which the patient's ability to continue to pay for treatment was still a medical consideration. In other words, even when the standard of care is limited to medical considerations relevant to the welfare of the patient, and not economic considerations relevant to the welfare of the health care provider, the standard of care used in this case was still consistent with a medical standard of care. The case did not implicate other policy concerns because it did not involve a conflict of interest between the physician and patient—there was no evidence, for instance, of a financial incentive for UNMC's (D) physicians to control costs. Instead, the physicians were weighing the risk to Mrs. Murray's health of delaying treatment against the risk to her health of potentially interrupted treatment. Accordingly, it was a jury question as to whether the Flolan should have been administered immediately, and, therefore, it was error for the trial court to have ordered a new trial. Reversed.

ANALYSIS

A unitary, or wealth-blind, standard of care is defined as that which health care providers, in the same community or in similar communities and engaged in the same or similar lines of work, would ordinarily exercise and devote to the benefit of their patients under like circumstances. This standard developed in a world of fee-for-service medicine and persisted while health insurance still primarily provided first-dollar unlimited coverage. Today, however, health plans and self-insured corporations are placing increasingly stringent controls on health care resources, thereby limiting physicians' freedom to practice medicine as they see fit. As this case amply discusses, the appropriateness of this standard is increasingly being questioned in light of the realities of today's healthcare marketplace.

Quicknotes

DIRECTED VERDICT A verdict ordered by the court in a jury trial.

STANDARD OF CARE A uniform degree of behavior against which a person's conduct can be measured when determining liability in negligence cases.

Canterbury v. Spence

Patient (P) v. Surgeon (D)

464 F.2d 772 (D.C. Cir. 1972)

NATURE OF CASE: Action in negligence for damages.

FACT SUMMARY: Dr. Spence (D) performed an operation on Canterbury (P) without advising him of the risks associated with the surgery.

RULE OF LAW

A physician owes a duty to reasonably disclose to a patient all information concerning an operation that a reasonable physician in the community would disclose based on sound medical considerations.

FACTS: Canterbury (P), a minor, complained of back problems. Dr. Spence (D), after making an examination, recommended a laminectomy to correct what he thought was a ruptured disk. Dr. Spence (D) did not inform Canterbury (P) or his mother that in approximately one percent of the cases the operation resulted in paralysis. After the operation, which revealed a swollen spinal cord in poor condition rather than a ruptured disk, Canterbury (P) was placed in a post-operative unit. Canterbury (P) was allowed to vacate while unattended, contrary to Dr. Spence's (D) orders. Canterbury (P) slipped and fell off the bed which had no safety rail. No nurses were in attendance. Paralysis resulted and an emergency operation was only partially successful. Some four years later, two years after Canterbury (P) reached his majority age, suit was brought against Dr. Spence (D) for negligence in performing the operation and for failure to disclose known risks. The hospital (D) was sued for failure to have nurses in attendance and to provide a safety rail for the bed. No medical testimony was adduced with respect to normal hospital post-operative procedures. Only Dr. Spence (D) was called as an adverse witness. Dr. Spence (D) testified that the information was withheld to prevent an adverse psychological condition and because the surgery was needed. This was the prevalent practice in the medical community. Some evidence was adduced that the operation could have been negligently performed and/or could have caused the paralysis. A nonsuit was granted in favor of both Dr. Spence (D) and the hospital (D) on the ground that Canterbury (P) had failed to establish a prima facie case. The threshold question of the statute of limitations was not decided.

ISSUE: Does a physician owe a duty to reasonably disclose to a patient all information concerning an operation that a reasonable physician in the community would disclose based on sound medical considerations?

HOLDING AND DECISION: (Robinson, J.) Yes. A physician owes a duty to reasonably disclose to a patient all information concerning an operation that a reasonable physician in the community would disclose based on sound medical considerations. Exceptions are made where the patient is unconscious in an emergency situation; where the patient is unstable emotionally and the disclosure would affect his well-being; and where the risks (such as infection) are those normally associated with all operations. The mere fact that disclosure might prevent consent is immaterial. Only those facts the physician reasonably feels are relevant to an informed consent, based on his knowledge of the patient, the nature of the operation, and his experience, need be disclosed. The objective criteria against which disclosure will be measured is the reasonable medical practitioner in the community. Liability cannot be found for nondisclosure unless it was the proximate cause of the injury. If the patient would have consented anyway or the injury resulted from a preexisting or intervening condition, no liability will be found. Expert testimony is normally required to determine whether disclosure or nondisclosure was reasonable since it deals with the impact of the information on the patient. Dr. Spence's (D) testimony as to a one percent chance of paralysis and his failure to disclose are sufficient to submit the question to the jury. Reversed and remanded for new trial.

ANALYSIS

On remand the case was decided in favor of Dr. Spence (D) and the hospital (D), 509 F.2d 537 (D.C. Cir. 1975). The required disclosure should include the risk, the frequency of occurrence, alternative methods of treatment, and the medical prognosis from nontreatment. A one percent chance of loss of hearing was deemed to require disclosure in *Scott v. Wilson*, 396 S.W. 2d 532 (1965). However, a 1.5 percent chance of the loss of an eye was held not to require disclosure in *Yeates v. Harms*, 393 P.2d 982 (1964).

Quicknotes

DUTY TO DISCLOSE The duty owed by a fiduciary to reveal those facts that have a material effect on the interests of the party that must be informed.

REASONABLE CARE STANDARD The care exercised by a reasonably prudent person.

Anon.

[Parties not identified.]

K.B., 87 Eng. Rep. 791 (1703)

NATURE OF CASE: [Nature of case not stated in casebook excerpt.]

FACT SUMMARY: [Facts not stated in casebook excerpt.]

RULE OF LAW

Laws are meant to give a remedy.

FACTS: [Facts not stated in casebook excerpt.]

ISSUE: Are laws meant to give a remedy?

HOLDING AND DECISION: (Holt, C.J.) Yes. Laws are meant to give a remedy. If a law allows or prohibits something, an individual is entitled to use the law in order to obtain what is allowed by the law or to be compensated for his injuries when a violation of that law occurs.

ANALYSIS

Essentially, the court is saying that it would be counterintuitive for a law to give a right but not a remedy when one's rights are harmed.

Osborne v. McMasters

Poison victim (P) v. Drug store clerk (D)

Minn. Sup. Ct., 41 N.W. 543 (1889)

NATURE OF CASE: Action in negligence for damages.

FACT SUMMARY: Contrary to statutes, McMasters (D) sold an unlabeled poison to Osborne (P).

RULE OF LAW

The breach of a statutory duty to a member of the protected class is negligence per se.

FACTS: McMasters (D) sold an unlabeled poison to Osborne (P). Osborne (P) accidentally took it internally, evidently thinking it was something else, and died. Osborne's heirs (P) brought a wrongful death action, alleging that the violation of the criminal statute prohibiting the sale of unlabeled poisons was negligence per se. Both McMasters (D) and storeowner were sued. Counsel argued that the violation of a statutory duty was not civilly actionable unless it was based on a common-law duty of due care.

ISSUE: Is the breach of a statutory duty to a member of the protected class negligence per se?

HOLDING AND DECISION: (Mitchell, J.) Yes. The breach of a statutory duty to a member of the protected class is negligence per se. Under common law a duty must be found before alleged conduct is actionable. Where a statute imposes a duty, the breach thereof is negligence per se with respect to any member of the protected class. The statute sets the duty owed to class members. The owner of the shop is equally liable under the doctrine of respondeat superior even though he would not be liable criminally under the statute. Affirmed.

ANALYSIS

Statutes are designed to protect specific classes of individuals. Here, the public in general was being protected. If a party outside the protected class is injured, no negligence per se is involved. For example, if a plaintiff is injured by one driving without a license, it may not be negligence per se. The licensing statute has been deemed, in some courts, to be revenue-raising in nature and not enacted to protect the public in general.

Quicknotes

NEGLIGENCE Conduct falling below the standard of care that a reasonable person would demonstrate under similar conditions.

NEGLIGENCE PER SE Conduct amounting to negligence as a matter of law because it is either so contrary to ordinary prudence or it is in violation of statute.

STANDARD OF CARE A uniform degree of behavior against which a person's conduct can be measured when determining liability in negligence cases.

Martin v. Herzog

Buggy driver (P) v. Car driver (D)

N.Y. Ct. App., 126 N.E. 814 (1920)

NATURE OF CASE: Action for damages for death of plaintiff's intestate.

FACT SUMMARY: Martin's (P) decedent was killed in a collision between the buggy he was driving and Herzog's (D) automobile. Martin (P) was driving the buggy without lights, in violation of a criminal statute requiring lights.

RULE OF LAW
The unexcused omission to perform a statutory duty is negligence per se.

FACTS: Martin (P) was driving his buggy without lights when he was killed in a collision between the buggy and Herzog's (D) car. It was after dark and there was a criminal statute requiring lights. The trial judge refused Herzog's (D) request for an instruction that the absence of lights on Martin's (P) vehicle was prima facie evidence of contributory negligence and instructed instead that the jury might consider the absence of lights as some evidence of negligence, but that it was not conclusive evidence. He granted Martin's (P) request for an instruction that the fact that Martin's intestate was driving without a light is not negligence in itself. The jury returned a verdict for the plaintiff. The appellate division reversed. Martin (P) appealed to the court of appeals.

ISSUE: Is the unexcused omission of a statutory duty negligence per se?

HOLDING AND DECISION: (Cardozo, J.) Yes. The unexcused omission of the statutory duty is negligence per se. Jurors have no power to relax the duty that one traveler on the highway owes under a statute to another traveler. It is error to instruct them that they have. The omission of lights, since it was unexcused, was negligence. However, a causal connection between the negligence and the injury must also be shown. Evidence of a collision occurring after dark between a car and an unlighted buggy is evidence from which a causal connection may be inferred between the collision and the lack of signals. If nothing is shown to break the connection, there is prima facie evidence of negligence contributing to the result. Affirmed.

ANALYSIS

This case states the position, followed by a great majority of the courts, that violation of a statute is negligence per se when a statute applies to the facts and the violation is unexcused. Note, however, that the court emphasizes that one must not confuse the question of negligence with that of the causal connection between the negligence and the injury, and that conduct that is negligent is not always contributory negligence.

Quicknotes

CONTRIBUTORY NEGLIGENCE Behavior on the part of an injured plaintiff falling below the standard of ordinary care that contributes to the defendant's negligence, resulting in the plaintiff's injury.

NEGLIGENCE PER SE Conduct amounting to negligence as a matter of law because it is either so contrary to ordinary prudence or it is in violation of statute.

PRIMA FACIE Action in which the plaintiff introduces sufficient evidence to submit an issue to the judge or jury for determination.

Uhr v. East Greenbush Central School District

Parents (P) v. School district (D)

N.Y. Ct. App., 720 N.E.2d 886 (1999)

NATURE OF CASE: Appeal from summary judgment for defendant in negligence case.

FACT SUMMARY: The Uhrs (P) alleged that East Greenbush Central School District (D) was negligent when it failed to test their daughter for scoliosis as required by state statute.

RULE OF LAW

A private right of action cannot be fairly implied where it would be inconsistent with the statute's legislative scheme.

FACTS: Education Law § 905(1) required testing of all students between the ages of eight and sixteen for scoliosis at least once each school year. The Uhrs (P) claimed that the East Greenbush Central School District (the District) (D) failed to test their daughter in the 1993–1994 school year, and as a result, the ailment was allowed to progress undetected, to her detriment. The court granted the District's (D) motion for summary judgment, holding that Education Law § 905(1) did not create a private cause of action, and that the Uhrs (P) had not stated a valid claim for common-law negligence. The Uhrs (P) appealed, claiming a private cause of action may be fairly implied when the statute is silent.

ISSUE: Can a private right of action be fairly implied where it would be inconsistent with the statute's legislative scheme?

HOLDING AND DECISION: (Rosenblatt, J.) No. A private right of action cannot be fairly implied where it would be inconsistent with the statute's legislative scheme. Here, the legislature has vested the Commissioner of Education with the duty to implement Education Law and to adopt rules and regulations for that purpose. Education Law § 905(1) provides that school authorities shall not suffer any liability that would not have existed in the absence of that section. When creating the statutory duty for school districts to test students for scoliosis, the legislature clearly precluded any private cause of action based on that statutory duty. Affirmed.

ANALYSIS

The court found that the school district did have a statutory duty to test the students. It also found that the legislature had clearly contemplated administrative enforcement of the statute. The language of the statute clearly sought to immunize the school districts from any liability that might arise out of the scoliosis-screening program.

Quicknotes

BREACH The violation of an obligation imposed pursuant to contract or law, by acting or failing to act.

DUTY An obligation owed by one individual to another.

IMMUNITY Exemption from a legal obligation.

NEGLIGENCE Conduct falling below the standard of care that a reasonable person would demonstrate under similar conditions.

Baltimore and Ohio R.R. v. Goodman

Railroad company (D) v. Accident victim (P)

275 U.S. 66 (1927)

NATURE OF CASE: Action in damages for wrongful death.

FACT SUMMARY: Goodman (P) was killed when struck by a train at a blind railroad crossing.

> **RULE OF LAW**
> When a plaintiff perceives a risk and fails to adequately take precautions to guard against it, no recovery will be allowed, and the judge must direct a verdict in favor of the defendant.

FACTS: Goodman (P) was driving his truck when he approached a blind railroad crossing without signals or guardrails. Goodman (P) slowed to approximately 10 mph. However, as Goodman (P) approached the track he finally saw the train and could not stop in time. Goodman (P) was killed, and his heirs (P) filed a wrongful death action. Baltimore and Ohio Railroad (D) alleged that Goodman's (P) death resulted from his own negligence. The court refused to direct a verdict on the above evidence, and the jury found for the heirs (P).

ISSUE: When a plaintiff perceives a risk and fails to adequately take precautions to guard against it, will no recovery be allowed, and must the judge direct a verdict in favor of the defendant?

HOLDING AND DECISION: (Holmes, J.) Yes. When a plaintiff perceives a risk and fails to adequately take precautions to guard against it, no recovery will be allowed, and the judge must direct a verdict in favor of the defendant. Here, the risk was known. Goodman (P) was required to approach the tracks in a safe manner. If necessary he should have come to a complete stop, gotten out, and looked to see if a train was approaching. Goodman (P) knew that he, not the train, would have to stop. Driving at even 10 mph in a situation such as this is unsafe and negligent. Goodman's (P) negligence was the proximate cause of his death. In a clear-cut situation such as this one, the judge should have directed a verdict in favor of the Baltimore and Ohio Railroad (D). Reversed.

ANALYSIS

In *Torgeson v. Missouri K.T.R.R.*, 124 Kan. 798 (1928), someone took the advice offered above and got out and looked both ways. However, by the time he started his car again a train came by and struck it. Where the railroad crossing has warning devices, a plaintiff has the right to rely on them. *Toschi v. Christian*, 149 P.2d 848 (1944). Once the railroad has undertaken a duty to warn drivers of oncoming trains, the rule applied above is not utilized.

Quicknotes

DIRECTED VERDICT A verdict ordered by the court in a jury trial.

PROXIMATE CAUSE The natural sequence of events without which an injury would not have been sustained.

Pokora v. Wabash Ry.

Car driver (P) v. Railroad company (D)

292 U.S. 98 (1934)

NATURE OF CASE: Action for damages in negligence.

FACT SUMMARY: Pokora (P) was injured when his vehicle was struck by an oncoming train obscured by railroad cars that had been left at the crossing.

RULE OF LAW

A plaintiff is not required to get out of his vehicle to see if a train is approaching to avoid contributory negligence.

FACTS: Wabash Ry. (D) had a siding near a railroad crossing. Wabash left railroad cars at the siding. The cars obscured the view of oncoming trains. Pokora (P) approached the crossing, stopped, and heard nothing. Pokora (P) then crossed and was struck by a train. Based on *Baltimore and Ohio R.R. v. Goodman*, 275 U.S. 66 (1927), the court directed a verdict in favor of Wabash Ry. (D). It held that Pokora's (P) failure to get out of his car and look was contributory negligence.

ISSUE: Is a plaintiff required to get out of his vehicle to see if a train is approaching to avoid contributory negligence?

HOLDING AND DECISION: (Cardozo, J.) No. A plaintiff is not required to get out of his vehicle to see if a train is approaching to avoid contributory negligence. That is an extremely unusual standard of behavior. Moreover, it is of doubtful benefit. By the time a party gets back to his car and attempts to cross, a train that could not have been seen at the time he looked could be upon him. Judges should refrain from framing standards of conduct that amount to rules of law. Extraordinary situations may not wisely or fairly be subjected to tests or regulations that are only fitting for the commonplace. Pokora (P) is not guilty of contributory negligence solely for failing to get out of his vehicle. Reversed and remanded.

ANALYSIS

A judge should not set an abnormal standard of care. Again, the reasonable man standard should be applied in determining whether a plaintiff is contributorily negligent. Extraordinary situations must be decided on facts peculiar to the case since we have no experience with which to decide what a reasonable man might do under such circumstances. Such decisions are better left to the trier of fact, who may decide on the basis of all of the evidence.

Quicknotes

CONTRIBUTORY NEGLIGENCE Behavior on the part of an injured plaintiff falling below the standard of ordinary care that contributes to the defendant's negligence, resulting in the plaintiff's injury.

Byrne v. Boadle

Pedestrian (P) v. Shop owner (D)

Ex., 159 Eng. Rep. 299 (1863)

NATURE OF CASE: Action to recover damages for negligence.

FACT SUMMARY: While Byrne (P) was walking along the street, passing Boadle's (D) shop, a barrel fell from the shop window and struck Byrne (P), injuring him.

RULE OF LAW
When it is highly probable that an injury is due to the negligence of the defendant, and the defendant has better access to the evidence concerning the injury, the doctrine of res ipsa loquitur creates an inference that the defendant was negligent and puts the burden on defendant to introduce contrary evidence.

FACTS: Byrne (P) was walking in a public street past Boadle's (D) flour shop, when a barrel of flour rolled out of the window above Byrne (P), striking and injuring him. The trial court nonsuited Byrne (P), ruling that there was no evidence of any negligence.

ISSUE: When it is highly probable that an injury is due to the negligence of the defendant, and the defendant has better access to the evidence concerning the injury, does the doctrine of res ipsa loquitur create an inference that the defendant was negligent and put the burden on defendant to introduce contrary evidence?

HOLDING AND DECISION: (Baron Pollock, J.) Yes. When it is highly probable that an injury is due to the negligence of the defendant, and the defendant has better access to the evidence concerning the injury, the doctrine of res ipsa loquitur creates an inference that the defendant was negligent and puts the burden on defendant to introduce contrary evidence. According to the ancient doctrine of res ipsa loquitur, "the thing speaks for itself." The mere fact that a barrel of flour fell on a passerby outside of Boadle's (D) flour shop is prima facie evidence of the latter's negligence, and Byrne (P) cannot be expected to prove that it could not have happened without some negligence. If there are any facts inconsistent with a finding of negligence, it is for Boadle (D) to prove them. Reversed.

ANALYSIS

This is one of the earliest cases applying the doctrine of res ipsa loquitur. In a later English case, the rule was stated as follows: "There must be reasonable evidence of negligence; but where the thing is shown to be under the management of the defendant or his servants, and the accident is such as in the ordinary course of things does not happen if those who have the management use proper care, it affords reasonable evidence, in the absence of explanation by the defendants, that the accident arose from want of care." To invoke the doctrine, the plaintiff need not explain away all possibilities as long as he shows that such accidents do not occur without negligence; the burden of proof is then shifted to the defendant.

Quicknotes

PRIMA FACIE Action in which the plaintiff introduces sufficient evidence to submit an issue to the judge or jury for determination.

RES IPSA LOQUITUR A rule of law giving rise to an inference of negligence where the instrument inflicting the injury is in the exclusive control of the defendant and where such harm could not ordinarily result in the absence of negligence.

Colmenares Vivas v. Sun Alliance Insurance Co.

Tourists riding escalators (P) v. Insurance company (D)

807 F.2d 1102 (1st Cir. 1986)

NATURE OF CASE: Appeal from directed verdict denying damages for negligence.

FACT SUMMARY: Colmenares (P) suffered injuries while riding an escalator insured by Sun Alliance Insurance Co. (D).

RULE OF LAW

The control requirement of the doctrine of res ipsa loquitur is satisfied where the defendant is ultimately responsible for the agent or instrument causing the injury.

FACTS: Mr. and Mrs. Colmenares (P) were injured while riding an airport escalator in Puerto Rico. The Colmenares (P) sued Sun Alliance Insurance Co. (Sun) (D), the insurance carrier for the Port Authority, the airport owner, and the operator for negligence. Sun (D) brought a third-party action against Westinghouse Electric Corp. (Westinghouse) (D) based on a maintenance contract between the parties that required Westinghouse (D) to inspect, maintain, adjust, and repair the escalator and handrail as needed, and to keep the escalator in a safe operating condition. The court ruled that there was no evidence that the Port Authority was negligent. The court also held that the case could not go to the jury based on the theory of res ipsa loquitur because the instrument causing the injury, the escalator, was not in the exclusive control of the Authority. The court then granted Sun's (D) motion for a directed verdict. The Colmenares (P) appealed.

ISSUE: Is the control requirement of the doctrine of res ipsa loquitur satisfied where the defendant is ultimately responsible for the agent or instrument causing the injury?

HOLDING AND DECISION: (Bownes, J.) Yes. The control requirement of the doctrine of res ipsa loquitur is satisfied where the defendant is ultimately responsible for the agent or instrument causing the injury. The injury-causing escalator was the property and under the exclusive control of the Port Authority. Even though such control was shared by Westinghouse (D), the Port Authority had a nondelegable duty of care to maintain the escalator in a safe condition. Therefore, the Port Authority effectively had exclusive control over the escalator for purposes of applying the res ipsa loquitur doctrine. The public is entitled to rely on the Port Authority, not its agents or contractors, for the safe condition of the escalator. Reversed and remanded.

DISSENT: (Torruella, J.) The malfunction of the escalator does not by itself raise an inference of negligence without additional proof of the cause of the malfunction. The court has no basis of common knowledge to infer that the escalator's malfunction was the result of its operator's negligence.

ANALYSIS

The exclusive control issue is often tricky in the case of multiple defendants. For example, in one case the court refused to apply the res ipsa loquitur doctrine to infer negligence in an airplane crash against a large number of the plane's manufacturers and repairs because the plaintiff failed to sue the company that had performed the most recent repairs. *Winns v. Rockwell International Corp.*, 705 F.2d 1449, 1454 (5th Cir. 1983).

Quicknotes

DUTY OF CARE A principle of negligence requiring an individual to act in such a manner as to avoid injury to a person to whom he or she owes an obligatory duty.

RES IPSA LOQUITUR A rule of law giving rise to an inference of negligence where the instrument inflicting the injury is in the exclusive control of the defendant and where such harm could not ordinarily result in the absence of negligence.

Ybarra v. Spangard

Surgery patient (P) v. Surgeon (D)

Cal. Sup. Ct., 154 P.2d 687 (1944)

NATURE OF CASE: Action to recover damages for personal injuries due to negligent malpractice.

FACT SUMMARY: Ybarra (P) suffered an injury to his right arm and shoulder while he was unconscious having his appendix removed under the care of six doctors and medical employees (D).

RULE OF LAW

Where an unexplained injury occurs during a medical procedure to a part of the body not under treatment, res ipsa loquitur applies to permit negligence to be inferred against all the doctors and medical employees who took part in caring for the injured patient.

FACTS: Ybarra (P) consulted Dr. Tilley (D), who diagnosed appendicitis. Dr. Tilley (D) arranged for an appendectomy to be performed by Dr. Spangard (D) at a hospital under the ownership and management of Dr. Swift (D). Ybarra (P) was wheeled into the operating room by nurse Gisler (D) and anesthetized by Dr. Reser (D). Dr. Reser (D) laid him back against two hard objects at the top of his shoulders. Ybarra (P) awoke the next morning in his hospital room attended by Thompson (D) and another nurse. When Ybarra (P) awakened he felt a sharp pain between his neck and his right shoulder. The pain spread down his arm, and after his release from the hospital he developed paralysis and atrophy of the muscles around the shoulder. Dr. Reser (D) and the nurses were employees of Dr. Swift (D); the other doctors (D) were independent contractors. The medical personnel (D) claimed that res ipsa loquitur should not apply against them because Ybarra (P) did not show an injury caused by an instrumentality under a defendant's control in that he did not show which of the several instrumentalities that he came in contact with in the hospital caused his injury, and did not show that any one particular defendant had exclusive control over any particular instrumentality. The court held for the defendants.

ISSUE: Where an unexplained injury occurs during a medical procedure to a part of the body not under treatment, does res ipsa loquitur apply to permit negligence to be inferred against all the doctors and medical employees who took part in caring for the injured patient?

HOLDING AND DECISION: (Gibson, C.J.) Yes. Where an unexplained injury occurs during a medical procedure to a part of the body not under treatment, res ipsa loquitur applies to permit negligence to be inferred against all the doctors and medical employees who took part in caring for the injured patient. Every defendant in whose custody Ybarra (P) was placed for any period was under a duty to exercise ordinary care for his safety. The control at one time or another of one or more of the various agencies or instrumentalities that might have harmed Ybarra (P) was in the hands of every defendant or of his employees or temporary servants. Ybarra (P) was unconscious; it is unreasonable to require him to identify any one person as the one who did the negligent act in order to get his case before the jury. Reversed.

ANALYSIS

This case is a prime example of the "smoking out the evidence" policy sometimes relied on by courts in invoking res ipsa loquitur. Obviously, the medical personnel would keep silent to avoid implicating one of their number.

Quicknotes

ORDINARY CARE The degree of care exercised by a reasonable person when conducting everyday activities or under similar circumstances; synonymous with due care.

RES IPSA LOQUITUR A rule of law giving rise to an inference of negligence where the instrument inflicting the injury is in the exclusive control of the defendant and where such harm could not ordinarily result in the absence of negligence.

CHAPTER 4

Plaintiff's Conduct

Quick Reference Rules of Law

Butterfield v. Forrester

Horseback rider (P) v. Landowner (D)

K.B., 103 Eng. Rep. 926 (1809)

NATURE OF CASE: Appeal of personal injury judgment in favor of defendant (D).

FACT SUMMARY: While riding very fast, Butterfield (P) ran into an obstruction that Forrester (D) had put in the road and was injured.

RULE OF LAW

A plaintiff will not be able to recover where his lack of due care contributed to the occurrence of the accident.

FACTS: Forrester (D) was making some repairs on his house and put up a pole across the road. However, passage was still possible. Butterfield (P) was riding very fast on the road, did not see the pole, and ran into it. He fell with his horse and was injured. There was no evidence of his being intoxicated. There was evidence that it was possible to see the obstruction from 100 yards away at the time of the accident and that, had Butterfield (P) not been riding so fast, he might have seen and avoided the pole. The jury found in favor of Forrester (D) and Butterfield (P) appealed.

ISSUE: Will a plaintiff be able to recover where his lack of due care contributed to the occurrence of the accident?

HOLDING AND DECISION: (Per curiam) No. A plaintiff will not be able to recover where his lack of due care contributed to the occurrence of the accident. In order for Forrester (D) to have been liable not only would the pole have had to have been in the road, but Butterfield (P) would have had to have used ordinary care in navigating by it, which Butterfield (P) did not. Rule refused.

ANALYSIS

This case states the defense of contributory negligence. The following theories have been used to support the theory: plaintiff is denied recovery to punish him for his own misconduct; plaintiff must come into court with "clean hands"; the defense is a deterrent to plaintiff's negligence; plaintiff's negligence is a superseding cause which makes the defendant's negligence no longer the proximate cause. The same standard is used as to determine negligence: the average reasonable person.

Quicknotes

CONTRIBUTORY NEGLIGENCE Behavior on the part of an injured plaintiff falling below the standard of ordinary care that contributes to the defendant's negligence, resulting in the plaintiff's injury.

PROXIMATE CAUSE The natural sequence of events without which an injury would not have been sustained.

Beems v. Chicago, Rock Island & Peoria R.R.

Railroad brakeman (P) v. Railroad company (D)

Iowa Sup. Ct., 12 N.W. 222 (1882)

NATURE OF CASE: Appeal from award granting damages for negligence.

FACT SUMMARY: The Chicago, Rock Island & Peoria Railroad (D) contended that the fact Beems (P) attempted to uncouple the railroad cars while the train was moving at an unusual rate of speed constituted contributory negligence that barred his recovery for the injuries resulting therefrom.

RULE OF LAW
The lack of contributory negligence on the part of the plaintiff renders the negligent defendant completely liable.

FACTS: Beems (P), a brakeman for the Chicago, Rock Island & Peoria Railroad (D), attempted to uncouple two railroad cars while the train was moving. Before Beems (P) attempted to do uncouple the cars, he signaled to other Railroad (D) employees to slow the speed of the train, but his signals were disregarded. His foot became caught between the rails, and he was killed by the train. His estate sued, contending the Railroad (D) employees were negligent in failing to slow the train on his order. The Railroad (D) defended, contending he was contributorily negligent in climbing between the cars while the train was proceeding at an unusual rate of speed, and therefore, even if the employees were negligent Beems (P) could not recover. The trial court instructed the jury that Beems (P) could not recover unless the employees were negligent. The jury found for Beems (P), and the Railroad (D) moved for a judgment notwithstanding the verdict, which was denied.

ISSUE: Does the lack of contributory negligence on the part of the plaintiff render the negligent defendant completely liable?

HOLDING AND DECISION: (Beck, J.) Yes. The lack of contributory negligence on the part of the plaintiff renders the negligent defendant completely liable. In this case it was proper for the jury to conclude from the evidence that Beems (P) acted reasonably in relying on the employees to comply with his signals to slow the train down. Therefore, he was not negligent in boarding the train and attempting to uncouple the cars while the train was in motion. Lacking a finding of contributory negligence, the Railroad (D) was completely liable for the negligence of its employees. Affirmed.

ANALYSIS

Contributory negligence is a complete defense to liability for a defendant's negligence. It is believed a plaintiff should not recover if his own negligent actions contribute to the injury. Contributory negligence is not a defense to an intentional tort or where the defendant's conduct was shown to be wanton and reckless. Further, contributory negligence is not a defense where the defendant had the last clear chance to avoid the accident.

Quicknotes

CONTRIBUTORY NEGLIGENCE Behavior on the part of an injured plaintiff falling below the standard of ordinary care that contributes to the defendant's negligence, resulting in the plaintiff's injury.

WANTON AND RECKLESS Unlawful intentional or reckless conduct without regard to the consequences.

Gyerman v. United States Lines Co.

Longshoreman (P) v. Shipping company (D)

Cal. Sup. Ct., 498 P.2d 1043 (1972)

NATURE OF CASE: Appeal from a finding that plaintiff's contributory negligence barred his cause of action.

FACT SUMMARY: Gyerman (P), a longshoreman, was injured while unloading fishmeal sacks for United States Lines Co. (D), but the trial court held that Gyerman's (P) conduct was also negligent and barred his cause of action.

RULE OF LAW

The burden of proving all aspects of the affirmative defense of contributory negligence, including causation, rests on the defendant, unless the elements of the defense may be inferred from the plaintiff's evidence.

FACTS: Gyerman (P), a longshoreman, was injured while unloading fishmeal sacks in the warehouse of United States Lines Co. (D). Before he began work, Gyerman (P) noted that the packs were dangerously stacked. He complained to his supervisor that it was dangerous to proceed with the work and was told that nothing could be done about the situation. Gyerman (P) proceeded with the work and was injured. The trial judge found United States Lines (D) was negligent in its failure to stack the sacks properly, but further found that Gyerman's (P) negligence in failing to stop work in the face of a known danger barred his cause of action. Gyerman (P) appealed.

ISSUE: Does the burden of proving all aspects of the affirmative defense of contributory negligence, including causation, rest on the defendant, unless the elements of the defense may be inferred from the plaintiff's evidence?

HOLDING AND DECISION: (Sullivan, J.) Yes. The burden of proving all aspects of the affirmative defense of contributory negligence, including causation, rests on the defendant, unless the elements of the defense may be inferred from the plaintiff's evidence. Contributory negligence is conduct on the part of the plaintiff that falls below the standard to which he should conform for his own protection, and that is a legally contributing causal connection with the negligence of the defendant in bringing about the plaintiff's harm. Merely because plaintiff asserts that his own negligence, if any, could not have caused his injury, does not shift to him the burden of proof on the issue. The fundamental question is whether the plaintiff, as "the negligent actor has so produced the harm to himself. . .for which he is sought to be held responsible. . .as to make the law regard his conduct as the cause of the harm." It is obvious here that Gyerman (P) did not create or maintain the dangerous conditions. The trial court found that United States Lines (D) had control of the cargo and directed its disposition and high stacking throughout the warehouse. United States Lines (D) alone created the risk of harm that materialized in the toppling of the stacks. Reversed and remanded.

ANALYSIS

Courts have long held that contributory negligence is invalid as a defense for negligence where the defendant bases the claim on plaintiff's breach of a safety regulation. See *Koenig v. Patrick Construction Corp.*, 298 N.Y. 313, 83 N.E. 2d 133 (1948). In *Osborne v. Salvation Army*, 107 F.2d 929 (2d Cir. 1939), the court stated: "It is the general rule that a plaintiff may not waive a statute enacted for his protection and that he cannot do so because of assumption of risk is clear. To bar recovery in an action brought under the (workman's safety) statute because the plaintiff's acts contributed to his injuries would seem to render its enforcement entirely ineffective."

Quicknotes

AFFIRMATIVE DEFENSE An assertion raised by the defendant in the answer, permitting the introduction of additional evidence to address or refute a plaintiff's allegations; an affirmative defense shift the burden of proof to the defendant to establish all the elements of the defense.

CAUSATION The aggregate effect of preceding events that bring about a tortious result; the causal connection between the actions of a tortfeasor and the injury that follows.

CONTRIBUTORY NEGLIGENCE Behavior on the part of an injured plaintiff falling below the standard of ordinary care that contributes to the defendant's negligence, resulting in the plaintiff's injury.

PROXIMATE CAUSE The natural sequence of events without which an injury would not have been sustained.

LeRoy Fibre Co. v. Chicago, Milwaukee and St. Paul Ry.

Fiber company (P) v. Railroad (D)

232 U.S. 340 (1914)

NATURE OF CASE: Appeal from a finding of contributory negligence barring plaintiff's recovery.

FACT SUMMARY: LeRoy Fibre Co. (P) was found to be contributorily negligent in stacking straw on its property so near Chicago, Milwaukee and St. Paul Ry.'s (Chicago) (D) right of way as to allow sparks from Chicago's (D) railroad engine to ignite and destroy the straw.

RULE OF LAW

The rights of one man in the use of his property cannot be limited by the wrongs of another.

FACTS: LeRoy Fibre Co. (LeRoy) (P), makers of flax, brought suit against Chicago, Milwaukee and St. Paul Ry. (Chicago) (D) when straw on LeRoy's (P) property was ignited by Chicago's (D) railroad engine. The engine was on Chicago's (D) right of way, which passed near where the 700 tons of straw were stacked on LeRoy's (P) property. The jury, consistent with its instructions, found LeRoy (P) contributorily negligent by placing the straw within 100 feet of the right of way. LeRoy (P) appealed.

ISSUE: Can the rights of one man in the use of his property be limited by the wrongs of another?

HOLDING AND DECISION: (McKenna, J.) No. The rights of one man in the use of his property cannot be limited by the wrongs of another. We concur with the simple requirement of the law, that everyone must use his property so as not to injure others. There is no exception to this rule merely because the defendant happens to be a railroad. Such operation is a legitimate use of property; other property in its vicinity may suffer inconveniences and be subject to risks by it, but a risk from wrongful operation is not one of them. Reversed.

CONCURRENCE: (Holmes, J.) If a man stacked his flax so near to a railroad that it obviously was likely to be set fire to by a well-managed train, I should say that he could not throw the loss upon the railroad by the oscillating result of an inquiry by the jury whether the railroad used due care. I should say that although of course he had a right to put his flax where he liked upon his own land, the liability of the railroad for a fire was absolutely conditioned upon the stacks being at a reasonably safe distance from the train.

ANALYSIS

Justice Holmes suggests a somewhat radical complication here in the theory of negligence, *i.e.*, a possibility that judgment of the negligence of the actor may depend on a judgment of the negligence of the victim, and vice versa. Compare this reasoning to the next case, *Derheim v. N. Fiorito*, 80 Wash. 2d 161, 492 P.2d 1030 (1972), a more recent case which espouses the modern view that "a defendant whose negligence proximately causes an injury to the plaintiff 'takes the plaintiff as he finds him.'"

Quicknotes

CONTRIBUTORY NEGLIGENCE Behavior on the part of an injured plaintiff falling below the standard of ordinary care that contributes to the defendant's negligence, resulting in the plaintiff's injury.

Derheim v. N. Fiorito Co.

Car accident victim (P) v. Truck driver (D)

Wash. Sup. Ct., 492 P.2d 1030 (1972)

NATURE OF CASE: Appeal from a verdict and judgment for plaintiff in a personal injury action.

FACT SUMMARY: N. Fiorito Co. (D), charged with negligence for injuries sustained by Derheim (P) in an auto accident between a Derheim (P) and an N. Fiorito Co. truck, claimed Derheim (P) was contributorily negligent for not using his car seatbelt.

RULE OF LAW

A defendant may not claim contributory negligence by the plaintiff, where the plaintiff's injuries are increased by his failure to use a seatbelt.

FACTS: Derheim (P) brought a personal injury action against N. Fiorito Co., (D) arising from the collision of Derheim's (P) car with a truck owned by N. Fiorito Co. (D) when the driver of the truck (D) made an illegal turn. When N. Fiorito Co. (D) was prevented from claiming contributory negligence by Derheim (P) because of Derheim's (D) failure to use his car seatbelt at the time of the accident, N. Fiorito Co. (D) appealed.

ISSUE: May a defendant claim contributory negligence by the plaintiff, where the plaintiff's injuries are increased by his failure to use his seatbelt?

HOLDING AND DECISION: (Hunter, J.) No. A defendant may not claim contributory negligence by the plaintiff, where the plaintiff's injuries are increased by his failure to use his seatbelt. Courts have traditionally said a defendant whose negligence proximately causes an injury to a plaintiff "takes plaintiff as he finds him." We believe failure to use a seatbelt is conduct which occurs before defendant's negligence, as opposed to contributory negligence which customarily is thought of in terms of conduct contributing to the accident itself. It seems extremely unfair to mitigate the damages of one who sustains those damages in an accident for which he was in no way responsible, particularly where, as is the case here, there is no statutory duty to wear seatbelts. Affirmed.

ANALYSIS

Contrast the opinion of the Washington court here with a later New York Court of Appeals decision in *Spier v. Barker*, 35 N.Y. 2d. 444, 323 N.E. 2d 164, 363 N.Y.S. 2d 916 (1974). In *Spier*, the court decided, "We today hold that nonuse of an available seatbelt, and expert testimony thereto, is a factor which the jury may consider, in light of all the other facts received in evidence, in arriving at its determination as to whether the plaintiff has exercised due care, not only to avoid injury to himself, but to mitigate any injury he would likely sustain." See Kircher, "Seat Belt Defense-State of the Law," 53 *Marq. L. Rev.* 172, 186.

Quicknotes

ASSUMPTION OF RISK DOCTRINE An affirmative defense to a negligence suit by the defendant contending that the plaintiff knowingly and voluntarily subjected himself to the hazardous condition and wholly absolving the defendant of liability for injuries incurred.

COMPARATIVE NEGLIGENCE Doctrine whereby the court in assessing the appropriate measure of damages compares the relative fault of the parties and reduces the amount of damages to be collected by the plaintiff in proportion to his degree of fault.

CONTRIBUTORY NEGLIGENCE Behavior on the part of an injured plaintiff falling below the standard of ordinary care that contributes to the defendant's negligence, resulting in the plaintiff's injury.

MITIGATION OF DAMAGES A plaintiff's implied obligation to reduce the damages incurred by taking reasonable steps to prevent additional injury.

Fuller v. Illinois Central R.R.

Wagon rider (P) v. Railroad (D)

Miss. Sup. Ct., 56 So. 783 (1911)

NATURE OF CASE: Appeal from judgment for the defendant in a negligence action.

FACT SUMMARY: After Fuller (P), who was riding in a one-horse wagon crossing a railroad track, was hit by an Illinois Central Railroad (D) train and killed, Fuller's (P) representative argued that the train's engineer had the last clear chance to avoid the accident.

RULE OF LAW

The contributory negligence of a party injured will not defeat the action if it is shown that the defendant might, by the exercise of reasonable care and prudence, have avoided the consequence of the injured party's negligence.

FACTS: Fuller (P), a man over seventy years old, was riding his one-horse wagon on a dirt road that crossed a stretch of the Illinois Central Railroad's (the Railroad) (D) track that ran perpendicular to it. Fuller (P) had his head down and did not observe the Railroad's (D) oncoming train. The train came down the tracks an hour late, faster than the usual 40 mph. The engineer could have stopped the train within 200 feet, but he did not slow the train at all. The only signal he gave was a routine whistle blast twenty seconds before the train hit the wagon and killed Fuller (P). Fuller's (P) representative sued the Railroad (D), and the Railroad (D) offered a defense of contributory negligence. Fuller's (P) representative argued that the Railroad's (D) engineer had the last clear chance to avoid injury either by braking or promptly sounding a warning-whistle. At trial, judgment was given for the Railroad (D), and Fuller's (P) representative appealed.

ISSUE: Will the contributory negligence of a party injured defeat the action if it is shown that the defendant might, by the exercise of reasonable care and prudence, have avoided the consequence of the injured party's negligence?

HOLDING AND DECISION: (McLain, J.) No. The contributory negligence of a party injured will not defeat the action if it is shown that the defendant might, by the exercise of reasonable care and prudence, have avoided the consequence of the injured party's negligence. This principle is known as the doctrine of "last clear chance" and has met with practically universal favor. The facts here show that for a distance of 660 feet west of the crossing where Fuller (P) was killed, the track was straight, and there were no obstructions; there was nothing to prevent those in charge of the Railroad's (D) train from seeing Fuller's (P) perilous position. No alarm was given. Nothing was done to warn Fuller (P) of the approaching train, and he was unconscious of its approach. The only warning was too late to be of any benefit whatever. Fuller (P) was in a wagon, and the engineer could have seen that he was going to cross the track and could only with difficulty extricate himself from his perilous position. Reversed and remanded.

ANALYSIS

In the early cases, the contributory negligence defense worked to absolutely bar recovery by a negligent plaintiff. The last clear chance principle, as set forth in *Fuller*, allowed a plaintiff who was contributorily negligent to recover if he could prove that the defendant was also negligent by failing to use reasonable care to avoid the incident and he had the existing opportunity to avoid the harm. Thus, the last clear chance doctrine is really a method whereby responsibility is placed where it best reduces the likelihood of an accident.

Quicknotes

CONTRIBUTORY NEGLIGENCE Behavior on the part of an injured plaintiff falling below the standard of ordinary care that contributes to the defendant's negligence, resulting in the plaintiff's injury.

LAST CLEAR CHANCE DOCTRINE An attempt by the courts to reduce the inherent unfairness of absolving the defendant of liability completely where the plaintiff has committed contributory negligence; the plaintiff is permitted to recover despite a finding of contributory negligence where the defendant was the last party capable of preventing the injury.

Lamson v. American Axe & Tool Co.

Axe company employee (P) v. Axe company (D)

Mass. Sup. Jud. Ct., 58 N.E. 585 (1900)

NATURE OF CASE: Appeal from a directed verdict denying damages for negligence.

FACT SUMMARY: Lamson (P) was injured when a hatchet fell from an inadequate rack located above his workbench.

RULE OF LAW

A person cannot recover for negligently inflicted injuries when he has acted to assume the risk of such injuries.

FACTS: Lamson (P) was employed by American Axe Co. (D) to paint hatchets. He worked at a bench above which was a rack where he placed the hatchets to dry. The racks, which safely held the hatchets, were replaced by American Axe (D) with a rack that could not hold the hatchets when jarred sharply by nearby machinery. The jarring was a common occurrence. Lamson (P) complained to his supervisor about the danger and was told to use the racks or leave. Lamson (P) continued to work at the bench and was injured when a hatchet fell from the racks. Lamson (P) sued America Axe (D) for negligence. The trial court entered a directed verdict for American Axe (D) on the basis Lamson (P) assumed the risk of the injury. Lamson (P) appealed.

ISSUE: Can a person recover for negligently inflicted injuries when he has acted to assume the risk of such injuries?

HOLDING AND DECISION: (Holmes, C.J.) No. A person cannot recover for negligently inflicted injuries when he has acted so to assume the risk of such injuries. Lamson (P) was well aware of the risk of injury presented by the rack and when given the choice of leaving or staying and working under those conditions, he chose to stay. As a result, he assumed the risk of such injury and cannot recover. Exceptions overruled.

ANALYSIS

In order to assume a risk a person must be shown to have recognized and actually understood the risk of injury, and that he voluntarily chose to undertake it. The unreasonable assumption of a risk may also give rise to contributory negligence as an additional defense to liability. If a defendant is under a duty to make a condition safe, a plaintiff's reasonable assumption of risk will not bar recovery.

Quicknotes

ASSUMPTION OF RISK DOCTRINE An affirmative defense to a negligence suit by the defendant contending that the plaintiff knowingly and voluntarily subjected himself to the hazardous condition and wholly absolving the defendant of liability for injuries incurred.

Ives v. S. Buffalo Ry.

Employee (P) v. Employer (D)

94 N.E. 431 (N.Y. 1911)

NATURE OF CASE: [Appeal in action challenging the constitutionality of the nation's first workers' compensation statute.]

FACT SUMMARY: [New York passed the nation's first worker's compensation statute. When an employee (P) sought compensation under the statute, the employer (D) challenged the statute as unconstitutional.]

RULE OF LAW

A statute that imposes on employers in certain designated occupations an absolute liability for injuries sustained by employees, except in certain limited cases, without any fault of the employer, is unconstitutional.

FACTS: [New York passed the nation's first worker's compensation statute. The statute provided, in part, that employers in specified industries would be liable for any injury to a worker arising out of and in the course of the employment by "a necessary risk or danger of the employment or one inherent in the nature thereof; . . . provided that the employer shall not be liable in respect of any injury to the workman which is caused in whole or in part by the serious and willful misconduct of the workman." When an employee (P) sought compensation under the statute, the employer (D) challenged the statute as unconstitutional. New York's highest court, the Court of Appeals, granted review in the case.]

ISSUE: Is a statute that imposes on employers in certain designated occupations an absolute liability for injuries sustained by employees, except in certain limited cases, without any fault of the employer, unconstitutional?

HOLDING AND DECISION: (Werner, J.) Yes. A statute that imposes on employers in certain designated occupations an absolute liability for injuries sustained by employees, except in certain limited cases, without any fault of the employer, is unconstitutional. The statute, judged by common-law standards is revolutionary. The statute's rule of liability is that the employer is responsible to the employee for every accident in the course of the employment, whether the employer is at fault or not, and whether the employee is at fault or not, except when the employee's fault is so serious that it constitutes serious and willful misconduct. The radical character of this legislation is at once revealed by contrasting it with the rule of the common law, under which the employer is liable for injuries to employees only when the employer is guilty of some act or acts of negligence that caused the occurrence out of which the injuries arise, and then only when the employee is shown to be free from any negligence that contributes to the occurrence. The principle of law embodied in the statute, if left unchecked, could be extended to situations beyond the employment context that strike at the core of society. For example, poverty and misfortune from every cause are detrimental to the state. Therefore, it likely would be beneficial to the welfare of all concerned if there could be a more equal distribution of wealth in society. Many persons have much more property than they can use to their advantage, and many more find it impossible to get the means for a comfortable existence. If the Legislature can say to an employer, "You must compensate your employee for an injury not caused by you or by your fault," what would stop it from going further and forcing those who are more affluent to share their wealth with those less fortunate who can barely subsist, so they do not become a charge upon the state? [The court held that the statute was unconstitutional, as it was not a legitimate exercise of the police power and took the employer's property without due process.]

CONCURRENCE: (Cullen, C.J.) There is no principle of law pursuant to which a person can be compelled to indemnify another for loss, unless it is based on contract or fault. Otherwise, it could be argued that it is a mere modification of the common law that would permit the Legislature to force a person to pay their neighbor's debts.

ANALYSIS

Applying a suggestion made by the court in *Ives* as to what might render the workers' compensation act constitutional, the New York legislature amended the New York Constitution to permit such a statute, and, six years after *Ives* was handed down, a unanimous U.S. Supreme Court upheld the statute as constitutional in *New York Central Railroad v. White,* 243 U.S. 188 (1917), concluding that "the prescribed scheme of compulsory compensation is not repugnant to the provisions of the Fourteenth Amendment."

Quicknotes

DUE PROCESS The constitutional mandate requiring the courts to protect and enforce individuals' rights and

Continued on next page.

liberties consistent with prevailing principles of fairness and justice and prohibiting the federal and state governments from such activities that deprive its citizens of life, liberty, or property interest.

POLICE POWERS The power of a government to impose restrictions on the rights of private persons, so long as those restrictions are reasonably related to the promotion and protection of public health, safety, morals, and the general welfare.

WORKER'S COMPENSATION ACT The statutory right of an employee to claim fixed benefits (primarily loss of earnings and medical expenses) from the employer for injury or disease arising out of and in the course of employment. The compensation scheduled under the Act is an exclusive remedy, barring any common-law remedy which the employee may have had.

Murphy v. Steeplechase Amusement Co.

Injured rider (P) v. Amusement park (D)

N.Y. Ct. App., 166 N.E. 173 (1929)

NATURE OF CASE: Action to recover damages for personal injuries.

FACT SUMMARY: Murphy (P) was injured when he fell while riding an amusement ride—"The Flopper"—which was a moving belt that ran up an inclined plane and caused people to fall on padded walls and flooring.

RULE OF LAW

One who takes part in a sport accepts the dangers that inhere in it insofar as they are obvious and necessary and they are not so serious as to justify the belief that precautions of some kind must have been taken to avert them.

FACTS: While visiting the amusement park at Coney Island, New York, run by Steeplechase Amusement Co. (Steeplechase) (D), Murphy (P), his wife, and their friends decided to ride "The Flopper" after watching others do so. "The Flopper" consists of a moving belt, running up an inclined plane, on which passengers sit or stand. There are four-foot high padded walls on either side of the groove in which the belt runs and padded flooring beyond those walls at the same angle as the belt (which is driven by a motor that runs on electrical current). The whole purpose of the ride was the laughter and merriment occasioned by the numerous spills the passengers took. In fact, Mrs. Murphy, who preceded her husband in boarding the ride, testified that she took a chance when she was asked if she thought a fall might be expected. When Murphy (P) fell on the ride, however, he blamed the fractured kneecap he suffered on a sudden start and stop of the belt. In a suit to recover for his injuries, Murphy (P) specifically charged that (1) the belt was dangerous to life and limb, (2) it was not properly equipped to prevent injuries to persons using it, (3) it was operated at a fast and dangerous rate of speed, and (4) there was no proper railing, guard, or other device to prevent a fall. At trial, Murphy (P) gave uncorroborated testimony (which was also contradicted by photographs and witnesses for Steeplechase [D]) that he fell on wood and not canvas padding. At the same trial, the president of Steeplechase (D) said such an accident had never occurred before, but a nurse in the emergency hospital serving the amusement park said there had been other injuries (she did not know how many), none of which involved broken bones or serious injuries. On this evidence, a verdict in favor of Murphy (P) was entered. Following an affirmation of that verdict on appeal, Steeplechase (D) brought the matter before this court on appeal.

ISSUE: Does one who takes part in a sport accept the dangers that inhere in it insofar as they are obvious and necessary and they are not so serious as to justify the belief that precautions of some kind must have been taken to avert them?

HOLDING AND DECISION: (Cardozo, C.J.) Yes. One who takes part in a sport accepts the dangers that inhere in it insofar as they are obvious and necessary and they are not so serious as to justify the belief that precautions of some kind must have been taken to avert them. The purpose of the ride in question was to illicit amusement and merriment from the spills taken by the riders. This was observed by Murphy (P) before he got on the ride. His injuries are no more than what common experience tells us could well happen at any time as the consequence of a sudden fall. As to the allegation that an abnormal and extraordinary spasm in the machine's operation caused the fall, such a bare allegation is insufficient to provide the basis for a verdict absent some evidence firmer than a mere descriptive epithet (Murphy's [P] saying that he felt a jerk). All in all, the best advice is for the timorous to stay at home. Otherwise, they must accept the risks inherent in the actions and adventures they undertake. Thus, the judgment is reversed, and a new trial granted.

ANALYSIS

The legal maxim "volenti non fit injuria" (no wrong is done to one who is willing)—cited by the court—is the basis for the assumption of risk doctrine. Precisely what one has "willingly" chosen to risk is usually determined subjectively. However, there are certain risks all adults are held to appreciate.

Quicknotes

ASSUMPTION OF RISK DOCTRINE An affirmative defense to a negligence suit by the defendant contending that the plaintiff knowingly and voluntarily subjected himself to the hazardous condition and wholly absolving the defendant of liability for injuries incurred.

Dalury v. S-K-I, Ltd.

Skier (P) v. Ski resort (D)

Vt. Sup. Ct., 670 A.2d 795 (1995)

NATURE OF CASE: Appeal from summary judgment for defendant in negligence action.

FACT SUMMARY: Dalury (P), who had signed a liability release form, was injured at S-K-I, Ltd. (D), a ski resort, after colliding with a metal pole that formed part of a control maze for a ski lift line.

RULE OF LAW

A standard signed liability waiver form may be held unenforceable if it violates public policy.

FACTS: Dalury (P) purchased a season pass at S-K-I, Ltd. (D) and signed a standard release-from-liability form and a photo identification card, which also contained the waiver language. The waiver stated that Dalury (P) acknowledged the risks inherent in skiing and that S-K-I (D) accepted no responsibility for "personal injury or property damage resulting from negligence, conditions of the premises, operations of the ski area, or actions or omissions of employees." Dalury (P) was badly injured when he collided with a metal pole used for directing the ski lift lines. Dalury (P) brought suit, and the trial judge granted summary judgment for S-K-I (D) on the basis of the waiver form. On appeal, Dalury (P) contended that the release was unenforceable as a matter of law because it violated public policy.

ISSUE: May a standard signed liability waiver form be held unenforceable if it violates public policy?

HOLDING AND DECISION: (Johnson, J.) Yes. A standard signed liability waiver form may be held unenforceable if it violates public policy. Even a well-drafted liability release form may be void if enforcement would be contrary to public policy. In determining whether an exculpatory agreement violates public policy, the standard to be used is that found in *Wolf v. Ford*, 644 A.2d 522 (Md. 1994), which balanced the "totality of the circumstances of a given case against the backdrop of current societal expectations." Thousands of people buy lift tickets at S-K-I (D) every season; therefore a legitimate public interest is implicated. Under Vermont premises liability law, a business invitee has the right to assume that the premises are reasonably safe for the purposes for which they are being used. This standard applies to ski resorts too. S-K-I (D) is in the best position to insure against risks by properly maintaining their premises and training their employees. It would be illogical to put risks on skiers that S-K-I (D) is far better able to control and prevent. Dalury's (P) acknowledgment of the inherent risks of skiing, as expressed in the waiver form, should not allow S-K-I (D) to escape liability if they have been negligent. Reversed and remanded.

ANALYSIS

This was a case of first impression in Vermont and the holding reflects the majority approach for deciding whether public policy interests are implicated. However, the court declined to adopt a formulaic inquiry. A typical example of such an inquiry is the one developed in Colorado which balances (1) the existence of a duty to the public, (2) the nature of the service performed, (3) whether the contract was fairly entered into, and (4) whether the intention of the parties is expressed in clear and unambiguous language. *Jones v. Dressel*, 623 P.2d 370 (Colo. 1981).

Quicknotes

ASSUMPTION OF RISK DOCTRINE An affirmative defense to a negligence suit by the defendant contending that the plaintiff knowingly and voluntarily subjected himself to the hazardous condition and wholly absolving the defendant of liability for injuries incurred.

WAIVER The intentional or voluntary forfeiture of a recognized right.

Li v. Yellow Cab Co. of California

Auto accident victim (P) v. Cab company (D)

Cal. Sup. Ct., 532 P.2d 1226 (1975)

NATURE OF CASE: Appeal from denial of damages for negligence.

FACT SUMMARY: Nga Li (P) was injured in an automobile accident with a driver from the Yellow Cab Co. of California (D), but she was denied any compensation for her injuries because of her own contributory negligence.

RULE OF LAW

In California, contributory negligence is hereafter replaced with a system of "pure comparative negligence"; and, under this system, liability for negligently caused damage is assigned in direct proportion to the amount of negligence of the involved parties.

FACTS: Nga Li (P) made a left-hand turn into an intersection when a cab of the Yellow Cab Co. of California (D) was approaching from the opposite direction. This cab entered the intersection at an unsafe speed after the traffic signal had turned yellow. As a result, the cab struck Nga Li's (P) car, and she was injured. Thereafter, Nga Li (P) brought an action for damages against the Yellow Cab Co. of California (D) based upon the negligence of the cab driver. The trial court, though, held that Nga Li (P) was barred from any recovery because she was contributorily negligent. Thereupon, Nga Li (P) appealed on the ground that her contributory negligence should not have totally barred her recovery.

ISSUE: Must the doctrine of contributory negligence be followed in California today?

HOLDING AND DECISION: (Sullivan, J.) Yes. In California, contributory negligence is hereafter replaced with a system of "pure comparative negligence"; and, under this system, liability for negligently caused damage is assigned in direct proportion to the amount of negligence of the involved parties. This replacement is necessary in order to promote basic fairness, which demands that responsibility for damage be proportioned according to fault (i.e., that no one be allowed to escape liability for his or her negligence). As such, Nga Li (P) can recover from the Yellow Cab Co. of California (D) those damages that are proportionate to the cab company's amount of negligence. Reversed.

ANALYSIS

This case illustrates a recent trend that attempts to avoid the harshness of the contributory negligence system (i.e., where any negligence by the injured party bars his recovery from the tortfeasor). Note that there are three forms of comparative negligence systems. First, there is the "pure" system discussed in this case. Second, there is the system in which the injured party can only recover if his negligence is "less than" the tortfeasor's. Third, there is the system in which the injured party can only recover if his negligence is "not greater than" the tortfeasor's.

Quicknotes

COMPARATIVE NEGLIGENCE Doctrine whereby the court in assessing the appropriate measure of damages compares the relative fault of the parties and reduces the amount of damages to be collected by the plaintiff in proportion to his degree of fault.

CONTRIBUTORY NEGLIGENCE Behavior on the part of an injured plaintiff falling below the standard of ordinary care that contributes to the defendant's negligence, resulting in the plaintiff's injury.

Pinnick v. Cleary

Motorist (P) v. Motorist (D)

Mass. Sup. Ct., 271 N.E.2d 592 (1971)

NATURE OF CASE: Petition for declaratory relief challenging as unconstitutional a newly enacted statute providing for a "no fault" personal injury protection scheme for automobile accidents.

FACT SUMMARY: [Pinnick (P), a motorist who was injured by the negligence of another motorist, Cleary (D), challenged as unconstitutional a just-enacted statute, c. 670, that departed from the common law by providing for a "no fault" personal injury protection scheme for automobile accidents.]

RULE OF LAW

A statutory "no fault" personal injury protection scheme for automobile accidents, which abrogates the common law, does not unconstitutionally deprive an injured motorist of a vested property interest without due process.

FACTS: The Massachusetts legislature enacted a statute, c. 670, that departed from the common law by providing for a "no fault" personal injury protection scheme for automobile accidents. Specifically, if an injury occurred on the road, motorists were assured of the probability of quick and efficient payment of up to a set amount of defined losses incurred. In cases of accidents in which the motorist was not negligent, the motorist thus would avoid the uncertainty, delay, and cost of a tort proceeding, but still retained the option of recovering more through litigation if the facts warranted the bringing of a tort action. [A few days after c. 670 became effective, Pinnick (P) was injured in an automobile accident caused by Cleary's (D) negligence. When Pinnick (P) attempted to recover damages from Cleary (D) in a tort action, Cleary (D) raised c. 670 as a defense. Pinnick (P) then petitioned the Massachusetts Supreme Judicial Court for declaratory relief, asserting that c. 670 was unconstitutional.] Pinnick (P) argued, inter alia, that the tort action Pinnick (P) would have been able to bring in the absence of c. 670 constituted a "vested property right," which c. 670 unconstitutionally deprived without due process. The Court granted Pinnick's (P) petition.

ISSUE: Does a statutory "no fault" personal injury protection scheme for automobile accidents, which abrogates the common law, unconstitutionally deprive an injured motorist of a vested property interest without due process?

HOLDING AND DECISION: (Reardon, J.) No. A statutory "no fault" personal injury protection scheme for automobile accidents, which abrogates the common law, does not unconstitutionally deprive an injured motorist of a vested property interest without due process. In arguing that the cause of action abrogated by c. 670 constitutes a vested property right, Pinnick (P) ignores the distinction between a cause of action that has accrued and the expectation that every citizen has that, upon the occurrence of a legal wrong, redress will be available according to the rules of statutory and common law applicable at that time. Although a legislature is restricted in the extent to which it can retroactively affect common-law rights of redress that have already accrued, there is ample authority for the legal principle that no person has a vested interest in any rule of law entitling them to insist that such rule will remain unchanged for the person's benefit. Here, however, c. 670 has not attempted to abolish the right of tort recovery and leave the automobile accident victim without redress. To the contrary, it has affected the automobile accident victim's substantive rights of recovery only in one respect and has simply altered the method of enforcing them in all others. Therefore, c. 670 may be judged by the test applied in workmen's compensation cases: whether the statute provides an adequate and reasonable substitute for preexisting rights. However, in applying that test in the automobile context, the effect of an automobile "no fault" statute cannot be viewed, as in the workers' compensation context, from the respective perspectives of plaintiffs and defendants, because these are not preexisting categories in the automobile context, as are the employers and employees affected by a workmen's compensation act; every driver is a potential plaintiff and, equally, a potential defendant. Notwithstanding that c. 670 may have the effect of depriving the automobile accident victim of damages for pain and suffering, the exchange of rights involved with respect to the driver in an accident in which the driver was not negligent bears considerable resemblance to that effected by workers' compensation statutes with respect to employees that has been upheld by the United States Supreme Court in *New York Central Railroad v. White*, 243 U.S. 188 (1917).

ANALYSIS

One of the stated desired effects of c. 670 on all motorists alike was to make available to them compulsory insurance at lower rates resulting from the savings to insurance companies in administrative expenses

Continued on next page.

and total payments that were expected to follow from c. 670. In a concurrence in the result, Chief Justice Tauro opined that the Court's reliance on *New York Central Railroad v. White,* 243 U.S. 188 (1917), was misplaced, not only because *White* arose under New York's laws and constitution, but because Massachusetts' workers' compensation law, which was drafted for the benefit of the employee, and not to reduce insurance rates, permitted an employee to retain the employee's common-law rights as an alternative to coverage by the workers' compensation statute, and, more significantly, because workers' compensation creates no classifications for employees and treats equally all persons coming within its coverage.

Quicknotes

DUE PROCESS The constitutional mandate requiring the courts to protect and enforce individuals' rights and liberties consistent with prevailing principles of fairness and justice and prohibiting the federal and state governments from such activities that deprive its citizens of life, liberty, or property interest.

NO FAULT INSURANCE An insurance contract under which the insured party is indemnified by the party's insurance company for losses, regardless of the source of the cause of loss. When applied to automobile insurance, a statutory scheme whereby a policyholder and the policyholder's passengers are reimbursed by the policyholder's insurer without proof of fault, in exchange for being restricted in the right to seek recovery through the court system for losses caused by other parties.

WORKER'S COMPENSATION ACT The statutory right of an employee to claim fixed benefits (primarily loss of earnings and medical expenses) from the employer for injury or disease arising out of and in the course of employment. The compensation scheduled under the Act is an exclusive remedy, barring any common-law remedy which the employee may have had.

CHAPTER 5

Causation

Quick Reference Rules of Law

CHAPTER 5

New York Central R.R v. Grimstad

Railroad (D) v. Barge captain (P)

264 F. 334 (2d Cir. 1920)

NATURE OF CASE: Suit to recover damages for wrongful death.

FACT SUMMARY: Grimstad's (P) husband, captain of a barge owned by New York Central R.R. (D), fell into the water and drowned. The boat was not equipped with life preservers, and the victim did not know how to swim.

RULE OF LAW
A negligent party is liable only for those damages that were actually caused by his negligence.

FACTS: Grimstad's (P) husband, who did not know how to swim, was captain of the *Grayton*, a barge owned by New York Central R.R. (the Railroad) (D). While docked in Brooklyn, the *Grayton* was struck by a tugboat. Mrs. Grimstad (P) came out of the *Grayton's* cabin and found her husband in the water, arms outstretched. She ran back into the cabin and returned with a small line, but by then her husband had disappeared. Mrs. Grimstad (P) later brought suit under the Federal Employers' Liability Act, seeking damages for the death of her husband. Mrs. Grimstad (P) alleged that his drowning had been the result of the Railroad's (D) negligence in failing to equip the *Grayton* with life-preservers and other safety appliances, including life buoys. From a jury verdict in favor of Mrs. Grimstad (P), the Railroad (D) appealed, arguing that any negligence on its part had been inconsequential because Grimstad would have drowned anyway.

ISSUE: Is a negligent party liable only for those damages that were actually caused by his negligence?

HOLDING AND DECISION: (Ward, C.J.) Yes. A negligent party is liable only for those damages that were actually caused by his negligence. The jury found that the Railroad (D) was negligent in not equipping the Grayton with life preservers, but a life preserver is intended to be put on before a person gets into the water. A life buoy, on the other hand, is to be thrown to a person who has already fallen into the water, but there has been no showing that the absence of life buoys contributed to Grimstad's death. It is likely that Mrs. Grimstad (P) would have found a buoy too late to save her husband. Or, she might not have thrown it accurately enough for him to seize it. In fact, even if Grimstad had been able to grasp a life buoy, he might not have been saved from drowning. Thus, there was no showing that the Railroad's (D) negligence, if any, caused Grimstad's death. Therefore, the Railroad's (D) motion to dismiss the complaint should have been granted. Reversed.

ANALYSIS

Causation is a necessary element of any cause of action that sounds in tort. Thus, a party is not liable unless his conduct can be shown to have been the cause in fact of the damages suffered by someone else. It is sometimes said that the defendant's conduct is actionable only if the plaintiff would have incurred no damages "but for" the defendant's acts. The "but for" test does not enjoy widespread acceptance, however, since it does not adequately dispose of the causation issue in every case. Courts generally prefer to ignore any prescribed causation test, most electing instead to resolve the causation issue according to the facts of each particular case.

Quicknotes

CAUSE IN FACT The event without which an injury would not have been incurred.

Zuchowicz v. United States

Decedent's estate (P) v. Federal government (D)

140 F.3d 381 (2d Cir. 1998)

NATURE OF CASE: Appeal from damage award for plaintiff in negligence action.

FACT SUMMARY: Mrs. Zuchowicz (P) brought suit against the Government (D), alleging the Government's (D) negligence in prescribing an overdose of Danocrine, thereby causing her to develop primary pulmonary hypertension.

RULE OF LAW

Where a negligent act increases the chances that a particular type of accident would occur, and such an accident does in fact occur, a court may conclude that the negligent conduct was the cause of the injury.

FACTS: Mrs. Zuchowicz (P) filed a prescription for Danocrine at the Naval Hospital. The prescription incorrectly instructed her to take 1600 milligrams of Danocrine per day. Defendants stipulated its doctors and/or pharmacists were negligent and violated the prevailing standard of care by prescribing this dosage. Mrs. Zuchowicz (P) took 1600 milligrams per day for one month, and 800 milligrams per day thereafter. She experienced abnormal weight gain, bloating, edema, hot flashes, night sweats, a racing heart, chest pains, dizziness, headaches, acne, and fatigue. She was examined by an obstetrician/gynecologist who told her to stop taking the drug. Shortly thereafter, she was diagnosed with primary pulmonary hypertension (PPH). She was on the waiting list for a lung transplant when she became pregnant. She gave birth to a son and died one month later. Mrs. Zuchowicz's (P) expert witness testified that he was confident that the prescribed overdose caused her illness. The district court awarded plaintiff's husband, as representative of Mrs. Zuchowicz's (P) estate, $1,034,236.02 in damages. The Government (D) appealed.

ISSUE: Where a negligent act increases the chances that a particular type of accident would occur, and such an accident does in fact occur, may a court conclude that the negligent conduct was the cause of the injury?

HOLDING AND DECISION: (Calabresi, J.) Yes. Where a negligent act increases the chances that a particular type of accident would occur, and such an accident does in fact occur, a court may conclude that the negligent conduct was the cause of the injury. On the basis of the expert testimony alone the court could have held that the prescribed overdose more likely than not caused Mrs. Zuchowicz's (P) illness. In order for the causation element to be satisfied, the trier of fact must be able to determine, by a preponderance of the evidence, that the defendant's negligence was responsible for the injury. Here the trier of fact must be able to conclude that the overdose was, more likely than not, the cause of Mrs. Zuchowicz's (P) illness and ultimate death. Courts have held that where a negligent act was deemed wrongful because the act increased the chances that a particular type of accident would occur, and such an accident did in fact happen, this was sufficient to support a finding by the trier of fact that the negligent conduct caused the injury. Then the burden shifts to the negligent party to show evidence rebutting such but for cause and showing that the wrongful conduct was not a substantial factor. Here Mrs. Zuchowicz (P) met her burden of demonstrating that the excessive dosage was a substantial factor in causing her illness. Affirmed.

ANALYSIS

Cause-in-fact is also an issue in slip-and-fall cases. In such cases courts have noted that the mere fact that such injury could have occurred in the absence of negligence is insufficient to break the chain of causation, where the defendant's conduct greatly increases the chances of injury and is of the type that would normally lead to the happening of such an injury, *Reynolds v. Texas & Pacific Ry.*, 37 La. Ann. 694, 698 (1885).

Quicknotes

CAUSATION The aggregate effect of preceding events that bring about a tortious result; the causal connection between the actions of a tortfeasor and the injury that follows.

CAUSE IN FACT The event without which an injury would not have been incurred.

Union Stock Yards Co. of Omaha v. Chicago, Burlington, & Quincy R.R.

Terminal company (P) v. Railroad company (D)

196 U.S. 217 (1905)

NATURE OF CASE: Suit for recovery of damages.

FACT SUMMARY: Union Stock Yards Co. of Omaha (P) brought suit against the Chicago, Burlington, & Quincy Railroad (D) for recovery of damages it paid to one of its employees who was injured as the result of a defective nut in one of the switching cars, which was undetected since both parties failed to conduct a reasonable inspection.

RULE OF LAW

When two parties commit a joint offense, neither can seek indemnity or contribution from the other, unless the action of one party was primarily responsible for the resulting injury.

FACTS: Union Stock Yards Co. of Omaha (Union) (P) was responsible for moving the switching cars for the Chicago, Burlington, & Quincy Railroad (the Railroad) (D) in its stockyard. One of the cars had a defective nut, which either party could have discovered through reasonable inspection; neither party carried out such an inspection and Union's (P) employee suffered injuries. Union (P) paid damages to the employee and sued the Railroad (D) for recovery.

ISSUE: When two parties commit a joint offense, can either seek indemnity or contribution from the other, unless the action of one party was primarily responsible for the resulting injury?

HOLDING AND DECISION: (Day, J.) No. When two parties commit a joint offense, neither can seek indemnity or contribution from the other, unless the action of one party was primarily responsible for the resulting injury. The general rule is that one of several tortfeasors may not recover against another, even if he was compelled to pay all the damages for any injuries sustained. An exception to the rule has been found so that the principal wrongdoer be made to bear the ultimate loss, and thus less culpable parties have been able to avoid liability. In *Gray v. Boston Gas Light Co.*, 114 Mass. 149 (1873), the court stated the rule that if two parties, acting together, commit an illegal or wrongful act, then the party who is held responsible cannot have indemnity or contribution from the other because each is equally culpable for the damage. The rule does not apply, however, when one party commits the action and the other is exposed to liability and suffers damage therefrom. In that case, the party may recover against the party whose wrongful act exposed him to liability. Here both parties were negligent in failing to inspect the car before putting it into use by persons who may be injured. This case does not fall into the exception to the general rule barring recovery of indemnity or contribution. [Affirmed.]

ANALYSIS

At common law where joint tortfeasors have acted in concert, the release by the plaintiff of one affected a release as to all other defendants, in the absence of an agreement otherwise. The tortfeasors were considered a single person with an undividable duty of care to the plaintiff. Modern courts, however, have rejected this rationale.

Quicknotes

CONTRIBUTION The right of a person or party who has compensated a victim for his injury to seek reimbursement from others who are equally responsible for the injury in proportional amounts.

INDEMNITY The duty of a party to compensate another for damages sustained.

TORTFEASOR Party that commits a tort or wrongful act.

American Motorcycle Association v. Superior Court

Association (D) v. Motorcycle racer (P)

Cal. Sup. Ct., 578 P.2d 899 (1978)

NATURE OF CASE: Appeal from denial of claim for partial indemnity.

FACT SUMMARY: Glen Gregos (P) was injured in a cycle meet negligently organized by American Motorcycle Association (AMA) (D). AMA (D) cross-complained for contribution from Gregos's parents for the negligence allocable to the improper supervision of Glen (P).

RULE OF LAW

Under a comparative negligence formula of recovery, the equitable indemnity doctrine should be modified so as to permit a partial indemnity among concurrent tortfeasors on a proportional basis.

FACTS: Glen Gregos (P) was injured during a cycle meet and brought an action against American Motorcycle Association (AMA) (D) for damages. Liability was found on AMA's (D) part and damages awarded. AMA (D) then cross-complained for partial indemnity for the negligence of Gregos's parents for their negligent supervision of Gregos (P). The cross-complaint was dismissed, and AMA (D) appealed.

ISSUE: Under a comparative negligence formula of recovery, should the equitable indemnity doctrine be modified so as to permit a partial indemnity among concurrent tortfeasors on a proportional basis?

HOLDING AND DECISION: (Tobriner, J.) Yes. Under a comparative negligence formula of recovery, the equitable indemnity doctrine should be modified so as to permit a partial indemnity among concurrent tortfeasors on a proportional basis. While the comparative negligence theory requires the assessment of fault attributable to each defendant, joint and severable liability is not completely wiped away by the development. A plaintiff should still be able to obtain full recovery from any one defendant who was responsible; however, in most cases the percentage of liability will also operate as the percentage of the entire judgment that a particular defendant will pay. Furthermore, partial indemnity should be permitted as among concurrent tortfeasors on a proportional basis. Reversed.

DISSENT: (Clark, J.) The principle of joint and several liability is inconsistent with a comparative negligence formula. In this respect the majority opinion is undermining the formula. Furthermore, the incentive to settle a case for a proportional amount is lost where the possibility exists for recovery of all the judgment from one party.

ANALYSIS

The majority opinion is somewhat vague on when joint and several liability is available after a determination of the percentages of fault. Clearly, the court did not want to deprive the plaintiffs the opportunity to collect a judgment from one tortfeasor if all others are insolvent.

Quicknotes

COMPARATIVE NEGLIGENCE Doctrine whereby the court, in assessing the appropriate measure of damages, compares the relative fault of the parties and reduces the amount of damages to be collected by the plaintiff in proportion to his degree of fault.

INDEMNITY The duty of a party to compensate another for damages sustained.

JOINT AND SEVERAL LIABILITY Liability amongst tortfeasors allowing the injured party to bring suit against any of the defendants, individually or collectively, and to recover from each up to the total amount of damages awarded.

Kingston v. Chicago & N.W. Ry.

Fire victim (P) v. Railroad company (D)

Wis. Sup. Ct., 211 N.W. 913 (1927)

NATURE OF CASE: Action for damages in negligence.

FACT SUMMARY: Sparks from a train united with a fire of unknown origin to destroy Kingston's (P) property.

RULE OF LAW

A party causing a fire that unites with another man-made fire is liable for all damages caused by the united fires.

FACTS: Sparks from a train owned by Chicago and N.W. Ry. (Chicago) (D) caused a fire. The fire spread and united with another fire of a relatively minor nature, which was apparently set by an unknown third party. The united fires destroyed Kingston's (P) property. Chicago (D) attempted to argue that the uniting of the two fires, either of which would have destroyed Kingston's (P) property, absolved it of liability since the other fire was an intervening cause and would have destroyed Kingston's (P) property anyway.

ISSUE: Is a party causing a fire that unites with another man-made fire liable for all damages caused by the united fires?

HOLDING AND DECISION: (Owen, J.) Yes. A party causing a fire that unites with another man-made fire is liable for all damages caused by the united fires. If both parties starting the separate blazes were known, they would be jointly liable for the destruction of Kingston's (P) property. The fact that one of the parties is unknown will not excuse Chicago (D) from its joint and several liability. Here, either fire would have destroyed the property. In such a case, the mere fact that one of the parties is unknown is immaterial. This is not a case where a lesser fire is swallowed up by a much greater fire, thereby losing its identity. The fires were approximately equal in size and magnitude. Kingston (P) need not prove the origin of the other fire. If it had a natural origin and would have burned Kingston's (P) property anyway, Chicago (D) might not be liable. Here, since both fires were caused by human negligence or design, Chicago (D) is jointly and severally liable. Affirmed.

ANALYSIS

Where two defendants are negligent and their conduct unites to cause a single injury, the courts may apportion the negligence between them awarding damages based on the proportion. In *Smith v. J.C. Penney Co.*, 525 P.2d 1299 (1974), the court found that the manufacturer of a coat containing flammable material was a joint tortfeasor with the party who negligently set the coat on fire. The same rationale applies where two parties collide with plaintiff's vehicle. *Madduk v. Donaldson*, 108 N.W. 2d 33 (1961).

Quicknotes

JOINT AND SEVERAL LIABILITY The liability of multiple tortfeasors whose causal connection to the injury cannot be separated and who are therefore found equally liable; all tortfeasors are responsible for the entire amount of the injury.

Summers v. Tice

Shooting victim (P) v. Gunman (D)

Cal. Sup. Ct., 199 P.2d 1 (1948)

NATURE OF CASE: Damages for personal injury.

FACT SUMMARY: Summers (P) sued two defendants for personal injury caused when both defendants shot in his direction.

RULE OF LAW

When two or more persons by their acts are possibly the sole cause of harm, and the plaintiff has introduced evidence that one of the two persons is culpable (responsible), then the defendant has the burden of proving that the other person was the sole cause of the harm.

FACTS: Summers (P) and the two defendants were members of the same hunting party. Both defendants fired at the same time at a quail in the direction of Summers (P). Summers (P) was struck in the eye by a shot from one of the two guns. There was no evidence from which to determine which gun had caused the injury. The trial court held both defendants liable. They appealed on grounds they were not joint tortfeasors, they were not acting in concert, and there was insufficient evidence to show which defendant was guilty of the negligence which caused the injuries.

ISSUE: When two or more persons by their acts are possibly the sole cause of harm, and the plaintiff has introduced evidence that one of the two persons is culpable, does the defendant have the burden of proving that the other person was the sole cause of the harm?

HOLDING AND DECISION: (Carter, J.) Yes. When two or more persons by their acts are possibly the sole cause of harm, and the plaintiff has introduced evidence that one of the two persons is culpable, then the defendant has the burden of proving that the other person was the sole cause of the harm. The reason behind the rule that each joint tortfeasor is responsible for the whole damage is the practical unfairness of denying the injured person redress simply because he cannot prove how much damage each did, when it is certain that between the defendants they did all the damage. The rule applies whenever the harm has plural causes, and not merely when the causes acted in conscious concert. Here it is clear the two defendants were the sole cause of plaintiff's injuries. Plaintiff has introduced evidence that one of the two defendants is culpable. The defendants now have the burden of proving which of them is the sole cause of the harm. Judgment for plaintiff is affirmed.

ANALYSIS

At common law, two situations in which two or more defendants acted tortiously toward the plaintiff gave rise to what is now referred to as joint and several liability: where the defendants acted in concert to cause the harm, and where the defendants acted independently but caused indivisible harm. Liability in the case of concerted action is a form of vicarious liability, in which all the defendants will be responsible for the harm actually caused by only one of the defendants.

Quicknotes

JOINT AND SEVERAL LIABILITY Liability amongst tortfeasors allowing the injured party to bring suit against any of the defendants, individually or collectively, and to recover from each up to the total amount of damages awarded.

TORTFEASOR Party that commits a tort or wrongful act.

Sindell v. Abbott Laboratories

Daughter of drug recipient (P) v. Drug manufacturer (D)

Cal. Sup. Ct., 607 P.2d 924 (1980)

NATURE OF CASE: Appeal from dismissal of putative class actions for personal injuries allegedly resulting from prenatal exposure to diethylstilbestrol (DES).

FACT SUMMARY: Sindell (P) brought class actions alleging that she and other women similarly situated to her had suffered various personal injuries from prenatal exposure to diethylstilbestrol (DES), which numerous drug manufacturers (D) had produced, marketed, and distributed over a 30-year period, but she could not identify which named drug manufacturer (D) had produced the DES given to her mother.

RULE OF LAW

Where an innocent tort plaintiff brings an action against multiple manufacturers of a product that has allegedly injured the plaintiff, but the plaintiff cannot identify which manufacturer's product in fact caused the plaintiff's injuries, the plaintiff's action nevertheless may proceed where it is possible to measure each manufacturer's market share of the product; where the manufacturers of a substantial share of the product are joined in the action; and where, if the named manufacturers cannot show they did not manufacture the injury-causing product, they may cross-complain against other manufacturers, not joined in the action, which they can allege might have supplied the injury-causing product.

FACTS: Sindell (P) brought class actions alleging that she and other women similarly situated to her had suffered various personal injuries from prenatal exposure to diethylstilbestrol (DES), a synthetic compound of the female hormone estrogen that was administered to women during pregnancy for the purpose of preventing miscarriage. Daughters of women to whom DES was administered were at risk of suffering from cancerous vaginal and cervical growths and possibly requiring expensive and repeated testing, monitoring, surgeries, and treatment. DES was manufactured, marketed, and distributed between 1941 and 1971 by over 200 producers from an identical drug formula. In 1947, the Food and Drug Administration (FDA) authorized the marketing of DES as a miscarriage preventative, but only on an experimental basis, with a requirement that the drug contain a warning label to that effect. In one action, Sindell (P) alleged that various drug manufacturers (D) were jointly and individually negligent in that they manufactured marketed and promoted DES as a safe and efficacious drug to prevent miscarriage, without adequate testing or warning, and without monitoring or reporting its effect, and that they knew or should have known that, in fact, DES was a carcinogenic substance that was dangerous to the daughters of the mothers to whom it was administered. In a second action, Sindell (P) alleged that the drug manufacturers (D) were jointly liable regardless of which particular brand of DES was ingested by Sindell's (P) mother because the drug manufacturers (D) collaborated in marketing, promoting, and testing the drug, relied upon one another's tests, and adhered to an industrywide safety standard. She also alleged that the drug was produced from a common and mutually agreed upon formula as a fungible drug interchangeable with other brands of the same product. Finally, she alleged that the drug manufacturers (D) were jointly liable since they acted in concert, on basis of express and implied agreements, and in reliance upon and ratification and exploitation of one another's testing and marketing methods. The trial court dismissed Sindell's (P) actions on the grounds that she could not prove which of the named drug manufacturers (D) had produced the DES given to her mother. The state's highest court granted review.

ISSUE: Where an innocent tort plaintiff brings an action against multiple manufacturers of a product that has allegedly injured the plaintiff, but the plaintiff cannot identify which manufacturer's product in fact caused the plaintiff's injuries, may the plaintiff's action nevertheless proceed where it is possible to measure each manufacturer's market share of the product; where the manufacturers of a substantial share of the product are joined in the action; and where, if the named manufacturers cannot show they did not manufacture the injury-causing product, they may cross-complain against other manufacturers, not joined in the action, which they can allege might have supplied the injury-causing product?

HOLDING AND DECISION: (Mosk, J.) Yes. Where an innocent tort plaintiff brings an action against multiple manufacturers of a product that has allegedly injured the plaintiff, but the plaintiff cannot identify which manufacturer's product in fact caused the plaintiff's injuries, the plaintiff's action nevertheless may proceed where it is possible to measure each manufacturer's market share of the product; where the manufacturers of a substantial share of the product are joined in the action; and where, if the named manufacturers cannot show they did not manufacture the injury-causing product, they may cross-complain against other manufacturers, not joined in the action, which they can allege might have supplied the injury-causing product. Although the general rule is that a plaintiff's injuries must be caused directly by the defendant, or by an instrumentality directly controlled by the defendant, there are three existing exceptions to this rule. The first exception, also known as the "alternative liability" theory, is that under certain circumstances, where a plaintiff cannot identify which of two or more defendants caused an injury, the burden of proof may shift to the defendants to show that they were not responsible for the harm. Here, the drug manufacturers (D) argue that the alternative liability theory is inapplicable because they are in no better position than Sindell (P) to identify which among them actually manufactured the DES given to Sindell's (P) mother. However, even if that were so, that would not per se prevent the application of the theory, since the manufacturers (D) might be able to show they did not manufacture the injury-causing substance—as where they did not start manufacturing DES until after Sindell (P) was born. Nevertheless, the alternative liability theory is inapplicable here because not all DES manufacturers have been joined in Sindell's (P) actions, so that it would be impossible to properly apportion liability among them under the alternative liability theory. Here, since any one of 200 companies that manufactured DES might have made the product that harmed Sindell (P), there is no rational basis upon which to infer that any defendant in this action caused her injuries, nor even a reasonable possibility that they were responsible. The second exception to the general rule arises when there has been "concert of action" among multiple potential tortfeasors. However, here, the record does not demonstrate the requisite common plan or tacit understanding among the defendants necessary to sustain the exception. The third exception to the general rule, known as the "enterprise theory" of liability, also is inapplicable here. Thus, none of the existing exceptions apply, and, seemingly, the dismissal of the actions should be upheld. However, the court decides to craft a fourth exception that will enable Sindell's (P) actions to go forward, as there are forceful arguments in favor of holding that she has a cause of action, the most persuasive of which is that as between an innocent plaintiff and negligent defendants, the latter should bear the cost of the injury. Sindell (P) is not at fault in failing to provide evidence of causation, and although the absence of such evidence is not attributable to the DES manufacturers (D) either, their conduct in marketing a drug the effects of which are delayed for many years played a significant role in creating the unavailability of proof. Also, from a broader policy standpoint, the DES manufacturers (D) are better able to bear the cost of injury resulting from the manufacture of a defective product. Accordingly, as here, where all defendants produced a drug from an identical formula and the manufacturer of the DES that caused the plaintiff's injuries cannot be identified, through no fault of the plaintiff, an expanded, modified alternative liability theory is applicable. Under this new theory, it is reasonable to measure the likelihood that any of the defendants supplied the product which allegedly injured plaintiff by the percentage which the DES sold by each of them bears to the entire production of the product sold by all the manufacturers. To make this exception fair to the manufacturers (D), those manufacturers (D) representing a substantial share of the market for the product (here, DES) must be joined—so that the injustice of shifting the burden of proof to defendants to demonstrate that they could not have made the substance which injured the plaintiff is significantly diminished. The presence in the action of a substantial share of the appropriate market also provides a ready means to apportion damages among the defendants, and each defendant will be held liable for the proportion of the judgment represented by its share of that market unless it demonstrates that it could not have made the product which caused the plaintiff's injuries. Once a plaintiff has met her burden of joining the required defendants, they in turn may cross-complain against other manufacturers, not joined in the action, which they can allege might have supplied the injury-causing product. Under this approach, each manufacturer's (D) liability would approximate its responsibility for the injuries caused by its own products. It is acknowledged that it may be impossible to divide liability with mathematical exactitude, but, in such cases, the trier of fact will do the best it can. There also will be practical problems involved in defining the market and determining market share, but these are largely matters of proof. Reversed.

DISSENT: (Richardson, J.) A causal link between a plaintiff's injuries and a defendant's product is essential in products liability cases, and Sindell (P) fails to establish such a link. Thus, here, it remains wholly speculative and conjectural whether any of the named defendants actually caused Sindell's (P) injuries. The majority, while stating in its new rule that this element of actual causation can be satisfied by joining those manufacturers who produced a "substantial percentage" of the injurious product, does not define or provide guidance as to what constitutes a "substantial" share of the relevant market. Thus, not only does the majority ignore well-established precedent, it also lets plaintiffs pick and choose their defendants.

ANALYSIS

The California Supreme Court, which established the market share rule in *Sindell* held that each defendant could be held liable for the shares of absent or insolvent defendants no matter how small its share of the market. The court gradually stepped back from that holding, first holding in *Murphy v. E.R. Squibb & Sons, Inc.*, 710 P.2d

Continued on next page.

247, 255 (Cal. 1985), that the "substantial share" requirement of *Sindell* was not met when the plaintiff sued only one manufacturer with a 10 percent market share, and then holding, in *Brown v. Superior Court (Abbott Laboratories, RPI)*, 751 P.2d 470 (Cal. 1988), that a defendant was responsible only for its proportionate share of the loss, so that the entire loss could not be imposed on a defendant with an "insignificant" market share. These refinements to the initial rule were necessary because calculating market share in a case such as *Sindell* proved quite difficult, given that DES was marketed for multiple purposes and sold in different formats.

Quicknotes

ENTERPRISE LIABILITY Apportionment of liability between each participant in an industry equal to the participant's market share.

JOINT LIABILITY Liability owed to an injured party by two or more parties where each party has the right to insist that the other tortfeasors be joined to the matter.

MARKET SHARE LIABILITY The apportionment of liability between each participant in an industry equal to the participant's market share.

Herskovits v. Group Health Cooperative

Lung cancer victim (P) v. Medical group (D)

Wash. Sup. Ct., 664 P.2d 474 (1983)

NATURE OF CASE: Appeal from summary judgment denying damages for medical malpractice.

FACT SUMMARY: Herskovits (P) died of lung cancer after his chances of survival were reduced by Group Health Cooperative's (D) late diagnosis of his cancer.

RULE OF LAW

A defendant's conduct that increases the risk of death by decreasing the chances of survival is sufficient to take the issue of proximate cause to the jury.

FACTS: Herskovits (P) died of lung cancer. Herskovits's (P) chances of survival were reduced from 39 percent to 25 percent by Group Health Cooperative's (Cooperative's) (D) failure to diagnose his cancer on his first visit. After Herskovits (P) died, his estate sued Cooperative (D) for professional negligence on the basis that Cooperative's (D) late diagnosis reduced Herskovits's (P) chances for survival. Cooperative (D) moved for a judgment notwithstanding the verdict, contending that Herskovits (P) would have probably died of lung cancer even if his diagnosis had been made earlier. The motion was granted. Herskovits (P) appealed.

ISSUE: Is a defendant's conduct that increases the risk of death by decreasing the chances of survival sufficient to take the issue of proximate cause to the jury?

HOLDING AND DECISION: (Dore, J.) Yes. A defendant's conduct that increases the risk of death by decreasing the chances of survival is sufficient to take the issue of proximate cause to the jury. The criterion is whether Cooperative (D) deprived Herskovits (P) of a significant chance to survive rather than absolute proof that Cooperative's (D) conduct caused Herskovits's (P) death. A 36 percent reduction in Herskovits's (P) chances of survival is sufficient evidence of causation for a jury to consider the possibility that Cooperative's (D) failure to timely diagnose Herskovits's (P) illness was the proximate cause of his death. To decide otherwise would be a blanket release from liability anytime there was less than a 50 percent chance of survival, regardless how flagrant defendant's negligence. Reversed.

CONCURRENCE: (Pearson, J.) While the majority's decision is correct, its reasoning is not. A more rational approach would be to allow recovery even where the plaintiff could not ultimately prove that he was denied a cure but could prove he was denied a chance of a cure.

DISSENT: (Dolliver, J.) A better rule would be one that comports with the standard of proof of proximate cause, i.e., the plaintiff in a malpractice case must prove that defendant's negligence, in probability, proximately caused the death.

ANALYSIS

In an analogous case, *Jackson v. Johns-Manville Sales Corp.*, 781 F.2d 394 (5th Cir. 1986), the plaintiff had contracted asbestosis and sued the defendant for the over 50 percent probability that he would eventually contract cancer due to his earlier asbestos exposure. The defendant argued that the plaintiff could not recover for the loss since the development of cancer represented a future injury based on a present cause of action. The plaintiff countered that the cancer action had to be brought together with the asbestosis action because a suit for future cancer would be barred by the procedural rule that prevents splitting causes of action. The court held that it would allow recovery for "probable future consequences" of the plaintiff's exposure to asbestos.

Quicknotes

CAUSE IN FACT The event without which an injury would not have been incurred.

JUDGMENT N.O.V. A judgment entered by the trial judge reversing a jury verdict if the jury's determination has no basis in law or fact.

PROXIMATE CAUSE The natural sequence of events without which an injury would not have been sustained.

SUMMARY JUDGMENT Judgment rendered by a court in response to a motion by one of the parties, claiming that the lack of a question of material fact in respect to an issue warrants disposition of the issue without consideration by the jury.

General Electric Co. v. Joiner

Manufacturer (D) v. Electrician (P)

522 U.S. 136 (1997)

NATURE OF CASE: Writ of certiorari to determine appropriate standard of review.

FACT SUMMARY: General Electric Co. (D) sought to exclude scientific evidence introduced by Joiner (P) to support his expert testimony that his exposure to polychlorinated biphenyls (PCBs) caused his development of small-cell lung cancer.

RULE OF LAW

Abuse of discretion is the proper standard to be applied by an appellate court in reviewing a trial court's decision to admit or exclude scientific evidence.

FACTS: Joiner (P), an electrician, worked with electrical transformers, requiring him to often stick his hands and arms into the coolant to make repairs. It was later discovered that the coolant fluid of many transformers was contaminated with polychlorinated biphenyls (PCBs). Joiner (P) was diagnosed with small-cell lung cancer. He sued General Electric Co. (D), manufacturers of the transformers and coolant. Joiner (P) linked his development of cancer to his exposure to the PCBs and their derivatives. Joiner (P) had been a smoker for eight years, both his parents were smokers, and there was a history of lung cancer in his family. General Electric (D) removed to federal court and moved for summary judgment. The district court granted summary judgment for General Electric (D) because (1) there was no genuine issue as to whether Joiner (P) had been exposed to furans and dioxins, and (2) Joiner's (P) expert testimony failed to show a link between exposure to PCBs and small-cell lung cancer. The court of appeals reversed, holding the district court erred in excluding Joiner's (P) expert testimony. General Electric (D) appealed.

ISSUE: Is abuse of discretion the proper standard to be applied by an appellate court in reviewing a trial court's decision to admit or exclude scientific evidence?

HOLDING AND DECISION: (Rehnquist, C.J.) Yes. Abuse of discretion is the proper standard to be applied by an appellate court in reviewing a trial court's decision to admit or exclude scientific evidence. Application of this standard to this case indicates the district court did not abuse its discretion. Joiner (P) claimed that his exposure to PCBs promoted his development of lung cancer. In support of this claim he introduced expert testimony. The district court agreed with General Electric (D) that the experts' reliance on animal studies did not support Joiner's (P) contention that his exposure to PCBs contributed to his development of cancer. The issue here was not whether animal studies can ever be a proper foundation for expert testimony, but rather whether in this case the expert testimony was sufficiently supported by the animal studies relied upon. Since the studies relied upon by Joiner's (P) experts were so dissimilar from the facts in the case, the district court did not err in rejecting the experts' reliance on the studies. The court also concluded that the four epidemiological studies relied upon were not a sufficient basis for the experts' opinions. These studies did not support the experts' testimony either. A court may decide to exclude scientific evidence where the analytical gap is too great between the data and the opinion offered. Thus, the district court did not abuse its discretion in excluding the experts' testimony. Reversed and remanded.

CONCURRENCE: (Breyer, J.) Since modern life depends upon manufactured substances, judges must fulfill their *Daubert* gatekeeping functions to assure that litigation does not prohibit the production of certain chemicals.

CONCURRENCE AND DISSENT: (Stevens, J.) The court of appeals expressly decided that a "weight of the evidence" standard was acceptable. Under this standard an expert could have reasonably concluded that an inference was raised that PCBs promote lung cancer.

ANALYSIS

Here the court of appeals construed the decision in *Daubert v. Merrell Dow Pharmaceuticals, Inc.*, 509 U.S. 579 (1993), as altering the standard to be applied in deciding whether to admit or exclude scientific evidence. The Supreme Court, however, construed *Daubert* as maintaining the "gatekeeper" role of the trial court in screening scientific evidence under the Federal Rules of Evidence. This gatekeeper function has also been applied to the admission of technical evidence. *Kumho Tire Co. v. Carmichael*, 526 U.S. 137 (1999).

Quicknotes

SUMMARY JUDGMENT Judgment rendered by a court in response to a motion by one of the parties, claiming that the lack of a question of material fact in respect to an issue warrants disposition of the issue without consideration by the jury.

Ryan v. New York Central R.R.

Homeowner (P) v. Railroad (D)

N.Y. Ct. App., 35 N.Y. 210 (1866)

NATURE OF CASE: Action for damages for injury due to negligence.

FACT SUMMARY: Fire destroyed Ryan's (P) house. The fire started when a spark from New York Central Railroad's (D) train engine ignited a woodshed. The fire spread through several houses before reaching Ryan's (P).

RULE OF LAW

Damages can be awarded only when the injury is immediate and not the remote result of defendant's negligence.

FACTS: Ryan's (P) home in Syracuse was destroyed by a fire that spread from New York Central Railroad's (Central's) (D) woodshed, which had been ignited by a spark from Central's (D) train engine through either careless management or insufficient condition. Ryan's (P) house was 130 feet from the shed. Several other houses were also destroyed.

ISSUE: Can damages be awarded only when the injury is immediate and not the remote result of defendant's negligence?

HOLDING AND DECISION: (Hunt, J.) Yes. Damages can be awarded only when the injury is immediate and not the remote result of defendant's negligence. Liability would extend only to the owner of the first structure, that is, the structure upon which the spark lands. The result to be anticipated is that the structure upon which the spark lands will be damaged or destroyed. But the spread of the fire to other structures is not the necessary or usual result. The defendant has no control over that and cannot be responsible. The immediate result of the negligence was destruction of Central's (D) own woodshed. All other damage was remote. To hold defendant liable for all resulting damage would be to create a liability too great for any individual; all persons run some risk as to their neighbor's conduct. Affirmed.

ANALYSIS

Supposedly, a defendant is liable for damage that is the natural and probable consequence of his act. In New York, there has been created an arbitrary rule that the wrongdoer is liable for fire only to the first, adjoining property owner, as illustrated above. Here, as the first structure to be struck by sparks belonged to Central (D), Central (D) was not liable to anyone. Thus, it would not make any difference whether the adjoining structure was one large building or thirty small stores. Only the first, adjoining property owner could recover even if the fire covered the entire block, whereas with a series of small stores, the ones after the first on the same size block would not be covered. The court touched but did not rest its decision upon whether one should be liable for all damage from an intentionally set fire as opposed to a negligent set fire, where liability may be limited to the first, adjoining property.

Quicknotes

FORESEEABILITY A reasonable expectation that an act or omission would result in injury.

PROXIMATE CAUSE The natural sequence of events without which an injury would not have been sustained.

REMOTE DAMAGES Damages that are unexpected and unforeseeable, and over which the negligent party has no control.

Berry v. Sugar Notch Borough

Motorman (P) v. Railway company (D)

Pa. Sup. Ct., 43 A. 240 (1899)

NATURE OF CASE: Action for damages for negligence.

FACT SUMMARY: While driving the car in which he was a motorman in excess of the speed limit, Berry (P) was injured when a tree was blown down and fell on the roof of the car.

RULE OF LAW

A person's right to recover for injuries caused by the negligence of another is not automatically precluded because he was violating some ordinance at the time he was injured.

FACTS: An ordinance required that the cars run by the Wilkes-Barre and Wyoming Valley Traction Company not exceed a speed of eight miles per hour. Berry (P), a motorman for that line, was operating a car in excess of that speed during a windstorm when a tree was blown down and crashed into the roof of the car. Claiming that Sugar Notch (D), the borough where the accident occurred, had been negligent in permitting the tree to remain because it was diseased, Berry (P) brought suit to recover for his personal injuries. On appeal for a judgment in favor of Berry (P), Sugar Notch (D) continued to argue that his violation of the speed law precluded his recovery. It was asserted that Berry's (P) speed was the immediate cause of his injury because it was his particular speed that caused him to be at the place of the accident at the moment the tree blew down. Furthermore, urged Sugar Notch (D), even if the speed was not the sole efficient cause of the accident, it at least contributed to its severity and materially increased the damage.

ISSUE: Is a person's right to recover for injuries caused by the negligence of another automatically precluded because he was violating some ordinance at the time he was injured?

HOLDING AND DECISION: (Fell, J.) No. A person's right to recover for injuries caused by the negligence of another is not automatically precluded because he was violating some ordinance at the time he was injured. In this case, the speed did not cause or contribute to the accident. If it had, the appropriate ground for denying recovery in such a case would be that Berry (P) was guilty of contributory negligence and not that he had violated some ordinance. Turning to the argument that Berry's (P) speed placed him in the position where the tree could fall on his car, that was a matter of chance and something no foresight could have predicted. It could just as well have been that the fast speed would have carried him beyond the tree to a place of safety. So, in the sense argued, Berry's (P) speed was not the immediate cause of his injury. It may well be that the speed did add to the severity of the accident and the amount of damage; however, the jury has no way to make such a determination and no guide for differentiating between the injury actually suffered and what would have been suffered had the car been running at eight miles per hour or less. There is, therefore, no way to take such a factor into account, and recovery was properly granted. Affirmed.

ANALYSIS

Basically, Sugar Notch (D), in its defense, argued that the proximate cause of Berry's (P) injuries was his violation of the speed limit ordinance. The burden of proof is on the plaintiff to show the proximate cause of his injuries by presenting direct or circumstantial evidence that it is more probable than not that he was injured by the neglect of the defendant. In effect, Sugar Notch (D) attempted to show that Berry (P) was contributorily negligent, but there was no basis to show that his violation of the speed ordinance was a proximate cause.

Quicknotes

CONTRIBUTORY NEGLIGENCE Behavior on the part of an injured plaintiff falling below the standard of ordinary care that contributes to the defendant's negligence, resulting in the plaintiff's injury.

PROXIMATE CAUSE The natural sequence of events without which an injury would not have been sustained.

Brower v. New York Central & H.R.R.

Horse cart owner (P) v. Railroad (D)

N.J. Sup. Ct., 103 A. 166 (1918)

NATURE OF CASE: Suit to recover damages for loss of property.

FACT SUMMARY: The New York Central & H.R.R.'s (D) freight train collided with Brower's (P) cart at a grade crossing. The stunned driver was unable to prevent bystanders from stealing items that the cart had been carrying.

RULE OF LAW

A negligent party is liable for harm caused by the intervening acts of a third person if that person's acts should have been foreseen.

FACTS: A New York Central & H.R.R. (the Railroad) (D) freight train collided with Brower's (P) horse drawn cart at a grade crossing. The horse was killed, and the cart and harness were destroyed. The driver of the cart was stunned by the accident and thus was unable to prevent onlookers from stealing the contents of the cart, including empty barrels and a keg of cider. The train carried two detectives hired by the Railroad (D) to prevent theft, but neither made any effort to stop the people from stealing those articles. Brower (P) sued to recover damages from the Railroad (D) and won a judgment which included an award for the value of the stolen items. On appeal, the Railroad (D) denied liability for the purloined articles, arguing that their loss had resulted from the intervening acts of third persons.

ISSUE: Is a negligent party liable for harm caused by the intervening acts of a third person if that person's acts should have been foreseen?

HOLDING AND DECISION: (Swayze, J.) Yes. A negligent party is liable for harm caused by the intervening acts of a third person if that person's acts should have been foreseen. The Railroad's (D) negligence was responsible for the condition of the driver, and the loss of the items from the cart was a natural and probable consequence of the collision that stunned him. Obviously, the intervening acts of thieves were foreseeable, because the Railroad (D) placed two detectives on the train to guard against theft. Thus, the jury was entitled to find that the Railroad (D) should be held liable for the value of the stolen articles.

DISSENT: (Garrison, J.) The chain of causation between the original negligence and the loss of the contents of the cart was broken by the intervening criminal acts of the thieves. Their acts cannot be deemed foreseeable unless one accepts the proposition that crimes are a normal event and that lawful behavior is exceptional.

ANALYSIS

Intervening causes, whether natural or human, may break the chain of causation and relieve the original negligent actor of liability for the harm suffered by a plaintiff. Of course, the intervening force must be one over which the negligent party has no control if he is to be absolved of liability. Moreover, as the *Brower* court recognized, the chain of causation is not broken if the conduct of the intervening force could reasonably have been foreseen by the negligent actor. The rule of the *Brower* case is representative of the weight of authority and has been reiterated by countless courts.

Quicknotes

FORESEEABILITY A reasonable expectation that an act or omission would result in injury.

INTERVENING ACT An event whose occurrence breaks the causal chain between the tortfeasor's acts and the resulting injury.

PROXIMATE CAUSE The natural sequence of events without which an injury would not have been sustained.

Wagner v. International Ry.

Train passenger (P) v. Railroad (D)

N.Y. Ct. App., 133 N.E. 437 (1921)

NATURE OF CASE: Suit seeking damages for personal injuries.

FACT SUMMARY: Wagner's (P) cousin was thrown from an International Railway (D) car. Wagner (P) went searching for his cousin's body and was himself injured when he fell from a trestle.

RULE OF LAW

A party whose negligence has caused harm or the risk thereof is liable to all persons who are injured in the course of reasonable rescue attempts.

FACTS: Wagner (P) and his cousin Herbert boarded a crowded International Railway (D) (the Railroad) car. The conductor failed to close the doors of the car. The train was traveling at six to eight miles per hour when, without reducing speed, it rounded a bend. Herbert was pitched out of the car near a point at which the Railroad's (D) trestle changed to a bridge. The car crossed the bridge before stopping and Wagner (P), after disembarking, had to walk 445 feet to reach the site where his cousin had been thrown from the train. While atop the bridge, Wagner (P) lost his footing in the darkness, fell from the structure, and sustained injuries for which he later sued the Railroad (D). At trial, the judge instructed the jury that the Railroad's (D) negligence toward Herbert did not render it liable to Wagner (P) unless, as Wagner (P) maintained, the Railroad's (D) conductor had invited him to go to the bridge and had followed with a lantern. The jury returned a verdict in favor of the Railroad (D) and Wagner (P) appealed, contending that the charge to the jury had been improper.

ISSUE: Is a party whose negligence has caused harm or the risk thereof liable to all persons who are injured in the course of reasonable rescue attempts?

HOLDING AND DECISION: (Cardozo, J.) Yes. A party whose negligence has caused harm or the risk thereof is liable to all persons who are injured in the course of reasonable rescue attempts. To create a danger is to invite rescue efforts. It is natural and probable that rescue attempts will be undertaken. The negligent actor is liable to the rescuer, even to the one who has time to stop and reflect before acting. It is the negligence that creates the likelihood of the rescue, and since Wagner (P) acted reasonably and was not contributorily negligent, the Railroad (D) is liable for his injuries.

ANALYSIS

Wagner v. International Railway is consistent with the weight of authority. A tortfeasor may be held liable for the consequences of various foreseeable responses to his actions. The rule which makes the negligent actor liable for injuries sustained by a person engaged in a reasonable rescue attempt has been recognized and applied in a number of cases. It is based on assumption that it is reasonable to anticipate that, if a person is injured or imperiled by the conduct of another, some third party will likely endeavor to prevent or mitigate the potential harm. Of course, the tortfeasor will not be held liable for injuries suffered by a would-be rescuer whose efforts were patently foolhardy or unreasonable.

Quicknotes

FORESEEABILITY A reasonable expectation that an act or omission would result in injury.

PERIL OF RESCUERS An extension of the definition of foreseeable plaintiffs to include those persons who undertake to rescue the party put in danger by the tortfeasor; the tortfeasor thus owes a duty of care to any rescuers whom he has put in peril by exposing the plaintiff to injury.

In re Polemis & Furness, Withy & Co.

[Parties not identified.]

K.B., 3 K.B. 560 (1921)

NATURE OF CASE: Suit to recover damages for negligence.

FACT SUMMARY: The owners (P) of a ship chartered it to a business firm (D). One of the firm's (D) servants dropped a plank into a hold where benzine was stored, causing the ship to burn.

> **RULE OF LAW**
> **Once the negligence of a party has been established, he may be held liable for all the consequences, foreseeable or not, of his conduct.**

FACTS: The owners (P) of a ship chartered it to a firm (D) for use in transporting goods. One of the firm's (D) servants, while unloading cargo, negligently dropped a wooden plank into one of the ship's holds. The friction caused by the plank evidently created a spark, which ignited vapors from a quantity of benzine stowed in the hold. As a result, the ship burned. The owners (P) brought suit against the firm (D) that had chartered the vessel, and the matter was submitted to arbitration. The arbitrators found that the fire had been caused by the dropped plank, that the incident had been the result of negligence on the part of the firm's (D) servants, and that the charter agreement did not absolve the firm (D) from liability for losses attributable to its negligence. The arbitrators also found that it could not reasonably have been anticipated that the falling plank would cause a fire, but that the likelihood of some damage to the ship could have been anticipated. The court affirmed the award in favor of the owners (P), but the firm (D) appealed, arguing that liability should not attach because the particular harm that resulted from the dropped plank could not have been anticipated.

ISSUE: Once the negligence of a party has been established, may he be held liable for all the consequences, foreseeable or not, of his conduct?

HOLDING AND DECISION: (Lord Bankes, J.) Yes. Once the negligence of a party has been established, he may be held liable for all the consequences, foreseeable or not, of his conduct. The rule urged by the firm (D) has some support, but it clearly represents a minority position. The dropping of the plank constituted negligence, and it could have been anticipated that this act would cause some damage to the ship. The firm (D) is therefore liable, notwithstanding the fact that the nature and extent of the harm which actually occurred could not have been expected to result from the dropping of the board.

CONCURRENCE: (Lord Warrington, J.) The fact that some damage could have been anticipated renders the firm (D) guilty of negligence. Once this proposition has been established, it is clear the firm (D) is liable for all damages that were the direct consequence of its acts.

CONCURRENCE: (Lord Scrutton, J.) If an act could be expected to cause damage, the party performing that act is negligent and thus becomes liable for any and all consequences of his conduct. Since dropping the plank could have been expected to cause some damage, the firm (D) is liable for all the harm that actually occurred.

ANALYSIS

The rule of the *Polemis* case is a party is negligent only if his conduct could have been expected to cause some damage, but once his negligence has been established, a party is liable for all damage that actually occurred, whether or not the nature and extent of the harm were foreseeable. A majority of American jurisdictions still subscribe to the *Polemis* rule. Of course, under *Polemis* a negligent party is not liable for harm that resulted only because of a foreseeable efficient intervening cause, because such a force breaks the causal link between the original negligence and the harm ultimately suffered.

Quicknotes

FORESEEABILITY A reasonable expectation that an act or omission would result in injury.

REMOTE DAMAGES Damages that are unexpected and unforeseeable, and over which the negligent party has no control.

Overseas Tankship (U.K.) Ltd. v. Morts Dock & Engineering Co., Ltd. (Wagon Mound [No. 1])

Ship company (D) v. Dock owner (P)

P.C. Austl., A.C. 388 (1961)

NATURE OF CASE: Action for negligence.

FACT SUMMARY: A ship owned by Overseas Tankship Ltd. (D) spilled oil. The oil was later ignited and destroyed a dock owned by Morts Dock and Engineering Co., Ltd. (P).

RULE OF LAW
An injury must be reasonably foreseeable before liability for it can be imposed.

FACTS: When a ship owned by Overseas Tankship Ltd. (Overseas) (D) left Sydney harbor, it negligently discharged oil into the water. The oil floated around a dock owned by Morts Dock and Engineering Co., Ltd. (Morts) (P). Welding operations were suspended until it was determined that the oil was not flammable. Some molten metal dropped on a piece of material floating on some debris. This apparently ignited the oil and the dock burned. The court found that Overseas (D) was liable since its negligent oil spillage was the direct cause of Morts's (P) loss. Overseas (D) alleged that this was a freak accident that was totally unforeseeable.

ISSUE: Must an injury be reasonably foreseeable before liability for it can be imposed?

HOLDING AND DECISION: (Viscount Simonds, J.) Yes. An injury must be reasonably foreseeable before liability for it can be imposed. Not every direct cause of injury is actionable. The defendant must reasonably be able to foresee the risk of that particular injury. We reject the doctrine espoused in *Polemis*. It is not the act itself that is actionable, but the damage resulting from the incident. Where these damages cannot be foreseen they are not deemed actionable. The igniting of the oil was a freak incident and was totally unforeseeable. [Appeal allowed.]

ANALYSIS

See also *Doughly v. Turner Manufacturing Co., Ltd.*, 1 Q.B. 518 (1964), where it was not foreseeable that a cover which had fallen into a vat would explode and splash hot liquid on plaintiff. The foreseeability rule has not been extended to cover the "thin skull victim" rule. A plaintiff who is injured because of unforeseeable physical defects may still collect. A defendant takes his victim as he finds him. See *Smith v. Brain Leech and Co., Ltd.*, 2 Q.B. 405 (1962).

Quicknotes

CAUSATION The aggregate effect of preceding events that bring about a tortious result; the causal connection between the actions of a tortfeasor and the injury that follows.

THIN SKULL VICTIM RULE Defendant takes victim as he finds him.

Palsgraf v. Long Island R.R.

Train passenger (P) v. Railroad (D)

N.Y. Ct. App., 162 N.E. 99 (1928)

NATURE OF CASE: Action for damages for personal injury due to negligence.

FACT SUMMARY: Mrs. Palsgraf (P) was injured on Long Island R.R.'s (R.R's) (D) train platform when a guard helped a passenger aboard a moving train, jostling his package, causing it to fall to the tracks. The package, containing fireworks, exploded creating a shock, which tipped a scale onto Mrs. Palsgraf (P).

RULE OF LAW

The risk reasonably to be perceived defines the duty to be obeyed.

FACTS: Mrs. Palsgraf (P) purchased a ticket to Rockaway Beach from Long Island R.R. (R.R.) (D) and was waiting on the train platform. While standing on the platform, two men ran to catch a train that was pulling out from the platform. The first man jumped aboard but the second man, who appeared as if he might fall, was helped aboard by a guard who had kept the door open so they could jump aboard; a guard on the platform also helped by pushing him onto the train. The man was carrying a package wrapped in newspaper. In the process, the man dropped his innocent-looking package, which fell to the tracks. The package contained fireworks and exploded. The shock of the explosion was apparently of great enough strength to tip over some scales at the other end of the platform. The scales fell on Mrs. Palsgraf (P) and injured her. Mrs. Palsgraf (P) was awarded damages and R.R. (D) appealed.

ISSUE: Does the risk reasonably to be perceived define the duty to be obeyed?

HOLDING AND DECISION: (Cardozo, C.J.) Yes. The risk reasonably to be perceived defines the duty to be obeyed. If there was no foreseeable hazard as the result of an outwardly seeming innocent act with reference to the injured party, the act did not become a tort because it happened to be a wrong, though not to the injured party. Negligence is not enough upon which to base liability—there must be a duty to the injured party that could have been averted or avoided by observance of the duty. There can be no duty owed to an injured party when the wrong was committed toward someone else. The range of the duty is limited by the range of danger. There was nothing to suggest that the parcel from its appearance contained fireworks. Had the guard purposefully thrown down the package, he would have had no warning of a threat of harm to Mrs. Palsgraf (P). Just because the act was inadvertent does not impose liability. In the abstract, negligence itself is not a tort. To be a tort it must result in the commission of a wrong. A wrong imports the violation of a right. If the wrong was not willful it must be shown by the plaintiff that the act as to him had such great possibilities of danger, so many and so apparent, as to entitle him to protection against it though the harm was unintended. Had there been liability for the negligence toward Mrs. Palsgraf (P), she would recover for all injury "however novel or extraordinary." Accordingly, the judgment is reversed in favor of JR.R. (D).

DISSENT: (Andrews, J.) The concept that "there is no negligence unless there is in the particular case a legal duty to take care, and this duty must be one owed to the plaintiff himself and not to others" is too narrow. Negligence itself is a wrong. The rule of *In re Polemis*, 3 K.B. 560 (1921), is the correct statement of the law. A person who does a negligent act should be liable for its proximate results. Mrs. Palsgraf's (P) claim is for a breach of duty to herself and there cannot only be a duty when the harm is expected. Her right is not lesser to the right of the man with the parcel.

ANALYSIS

Cardozo states that negligence is a matter of relationship between the parties. That relationship must be based upon the foreseeability of harm to the person who is, in fact, injured. Just because defendant's act was negligent, it is not necessarily wrong to the injured party. The act must be negligent and wrong to the injured party to enable him to sue in his own right. If there is no duty to the injured party, there can be no violation of a right, so even if an act was negligent it could not have violated a wrong to the injured party. The dissent, on the other hand, states that each person owes a duty of due care to society at large. Each person must refrain from any act that unreasonably threatens the safety of others. Accordingly, any party injured by a negligent act would suffer a wrong, as the duty owed to each member of society at large would have been violated. A right of action must then arise despite the unforeseeability of the injury. The Restatement has accepted the view of this case that without any duty there can be no negligence, hence, never any liability to the unforeseeable injured party. Note that the determination on any question of duty is a question of law and never one for the jury. Cardozo, on the question of

Continued on next page.

duty, went even further by suggesting that the defendant could owe a duty to one particular interest of the injured party but not to a different interest of the same party. That is to say that there could be a duty to the injured party's property interest but not to his person. So, if defendant negligently sets afire plaintiff's unoccupied building and plaintiff is injured extinguishing the blaze, damages only to the building are recoverable, or vice versa, depending upon the original duty. This theory advanced in the dictum of Palsgraf was approved by the Restatement of Torts §281, but it has been widely opposed by most other courts. In fact, there is much authority against it and even Prosser has called this aspect of Cardozo's view "artificial." There are of course interests that, as a matter of public policy, should not be protected against certain types of wrongful conduct, but it does not follow from this that protection should always be limited to the interest which is threatened in advance.

Quicknotes

FORESEEABILITY A reasonable expectation that an act or omission would result in injury.

PROXIMATE CAUSE The natural sequence of events without which an injury would not have been sustained.

Marshall v. Nugent

Injured pedestrian (P) v. Car driver (D)

222 F.2d 604 (1st Cir. 1955)

NATURE OF CASE: For damages based on negligence.

FACT SUMMARY: Marshall (P) was struck by a car as he was attempting to warn oncoming traffic that a Socony-Vacuum Oil Co. (D) truck, driven by Prince, was blocking traffic.

RULE OF LAW

The defendant remains liable for the full consequences of his negligent act when the intervening force is one that a reasonable man would have foreseen as likely to occur under the circumstances, and the issue of foreseeability remains a question of fact for the jury.

FACTS: Prince, a truck driver for Socony-Vacuum Oil Co. (Socony) (D), intruded his truck into the ice-covered opposing traffic lane. He caused an oncoming car driven by Harriman—in which Marshall (P) was a passenger—to skid to a stop off the road. No injuries occurred. Prince stopped to assist, blocking his traffic lane with his truck. Upon Prince's suggestion, Marshall (P) began walking up the hill to warn oncoming traffic. Nugent's (D) car then came around the curve, swerved to avoid hitting the truck, skidded, and struck Marshall (P). Marshall (P) charged both Socony (D) and Nugent (D) as joint tortfeasors. Socony (D) argued that Prince's negligence, having caused no injury, was not the proximate cause of the subsequent injury when Nugent's (D) car hit Marshall (P) since the injury was not foreseeable. The jury found against Socony (D) for $25,000 and for Nugent (D). (This opinion concerns only the Socony appeal.)

ISSUE: Does the defendant remain liable for the full consequences of his negligent act when the intervening force is one that a reasonable man would have foreseen as likely to occur under the circumstances, and the issue of foreseeability remains a question of fact for the jury?

HOLDING AND DECISION: (Magruder, C.J.) Yes. The defendant remains liable for the full consequences of his negligent act when the intervening force is one that a reasonable man would have foreseen as likely to occur under the circumstances, and the issue of foreseeability remains a question of fact for the jury. In the development of the doctrine of proximate causation, the courts have attempted to confine the liability of the negligent actor to those harmful consequences that result from a risk, the foreseeability of which causes the defendant's conduct to be negligent. However, the term "proximate" does not mean that the defendant's act must be the immediate or next cause of the plaintiff's injury. Often the injury may be brought about by an intervening force of nature or act of a third person which seems quite remote in a chain of events (*e.g.*, proximate cause has been found where the plaintiff fainted, fracturing his skull, following a near collision). Many cases have held that a defendant whose negligence causes a traffic tie-up is liable for injuries and/or damages caused by an oncoming motorist. In the instant case, it was foreseeable that Marshall (P), having been delayed on a business journey by Prince's negligence, would get out on the highway and assist so that the journey might continue. The issue of the foreseeability of the risk and contributory negligence was a proper question of fact for the jury whose decision will stand. Affirmed.

ANALYSIS

The Restatement of Torts § 453(e) holds that the defendant is not liable for consequences which, looking backward after the incident, with complete knowledge of all that has occurred, would appear to be "highly extraordinary." The main requisite for liability—to be decided by the jury—is that the response to the defendant's negligent act be a normal one. An abnormal response breaks the chain of causality.

Quicknotes

CONTRIBUTORY NEGLIGENCE Behavior on the part of an injured plaintiff falling below the standard of ordinary care that contributes to the defendant's negligence, resulting in the plaintiff's injury.

FORESEEABILITY A reasonable expectation that an act or omission would result in injury.

PROXIMATE CAUSE The natural sequence of events without which an injury would not have been sustained.

Virden v. Betts and Beer Construction Co.

Injured worker (P) v. Construction company (D)

Iowa Sup. Ct., 656 N.W. 2d 805 (2003)

NATURE OF CASE: Appeal from reversal of summary judgment granted to defendant in negligence action.

FACT SUMMARY: Virden (P) contended that construction companies' (D) faulty installation of a ceiling was the proximate cause of his fall from a tall ladder he was using to repair the ceiling.

RULE OF LAW

As a matter of law, proximate cause is not established where a defendant's negligence is not a substantial factor in bringing about the plaintiff's injury.

FACTS: Virden (P), a high school maintenance worker, had to reinstall an angle iron that had fallen from the ceiling of the school's new wrestling room, which was built by Betts & Beer Construction and Stroh Corporation (the "construction companies") (D). As he was bolting the iron into place, he fell from the top of the 10-foot ladder on which he was standing. Neither Virden (P) nor the school contacted the construction companies (D) before he commenced work, nor did Virden (P) seek any assistance in securing the ladder, the placement of which was hampered by weight-lifting equipment. He sued the construction companies (D), claiming that their negligent construction proximately caused his fall. The trial court granted summary judgment to the construction companies (D), but the state's intermediate appellate court reversed. The state's highest court granted review.

ISSUE: As a matter of law, is proximate cause established where a defendant's negligence is not a substantial factor in bringing about the plaintiff's injury?

HOLDING AND DECISION: (Neuman, J.) No. As a matter of law, proximate cause is not established where a defendant's negligence is not a substantial factor in bringing about the plaintiff's injury. The construction companies' (D) duty was to ensure that users of the room were not injured by parts falling from the ceiling. A breach of that duty is only actionable negligence if it is also the proximate cause of an injury. To satisfy proximate causation, (1) the defendant's conduct must have in fact caused the damages; and (2) the policy of the law must require the defendant to be legally responsible for them. Regarding the first element, the plaintiff must, at a minimum, prove that the damages would not have occurred but for the defendant's negligence. Here, this but-for test is satisfied, because Virden (P) would not have had to get on the ladder but for the construction companies' (D) negligence. However, Virden (P) must also show that the construction companies' (D) negligence was a substantial factor in bringing about his injury. Because the duty to construct a solid ceiling is not to protect repairmen from perching on tall ladders but to prevent collapsing parts of the ceiling from falling on persons below, it was not foreseeable that a negligently welded angle iron would cause a ladder to tip or collapse—and here it is clear that the instrumentality of Virden's (P) injury was such a ladder, not the defective angle iron. Therefore, the trial court correctly granted summary judgment to the construction companies (D). Vacated.

ANALYSIS

The court noted that summary judgment on the question of proximate cause is rarely granted, since issues of proximate cause, like negligence, are generally left to the jury to resolve as fact matters. However, in exceptional circumstances, the issue of proximate cause may be decided as a matter of law on summary judgment where the material facts fail to show any causal link between the negligence and injury. The exception case is one where, after construing the evidence in its most favorable light and resolving all doubts in favor of the party seeking to establish proximate cause, the relationship between cause and effect nonetheless is so apparent and so unrelated to defendant's conduct that no reasonable jury could conclude defendant's fault was a proximate cause of plaintiff's injuries.

Quicknotes

ACTIONABLE Unlawful activity from which a cause of action may arise.

NEGLIGENCE Conduct falling below the standard of care that a reasonable person would demonstrate under similar conditions.

SUMMARY JUDGMENT Judgment rendered by a court in response to a motion made by one of the parties, claiming that the lack of a question of material fact in respect to an issue warrants disposition of the issue without consideration by the jury.

Hebert v. Enos

Neighbor (P) v. Neighbor (D)

Mass App. Ct., 806 N.E.2d 452 (2004)

NATURE OF CASE: Appeal from summary judgment for defendant in negligence action.

FACT SUMMARY: Hebert (P) contended that Enos's (D) faulty repairs of a second-floor toilet was a legal cause of the electrical shock and injuries Hebert (P) suffered when he went to water Enos's (D) flowers.

RULE OF LAW

A claim of negligence may be dismissed as a matter of law where the plaintiff cannot show that his injuries were a reasonably foreseeable consequence of the defendant's negligent conduct.

FACTS: Hebert (P) received a severe electrical shock when he went to water Enos's (D) flowers. Hebert (P) claimed that Enos's (D) faulty repairs of a second-floor toilet caused the toilet to overflow, and that the flooding water reacted with the home's electrical system, creating an electrical current that shocked and injured Hebert (P) when he touched the outside water faucet. Hebert (P) brought suit against Enos (D) for negligence, and Enos (D) moved for summary judgment, which the trial court granted on the ground that Hebert's (P) injuries were not a reasonably foreseeable consequence of Enos's (D) negligence. The state's intermediate appellate court granted review.

ISSUE: May a claim of negligence be dismissed as a matter of law where the plaintiff cannot show that his injuries were a reasonably foreseeable consequence of the defendant's negligent conduct?

HOLDING AND DECISION: (Kafker, J.) Yes. A claim of negligence may be dismissed as a matter of law where the plaintiff cannot show that his injuries were a reasonably foreseeable consequence of the defendant's negligent conduct. Hebert (P) established that Enos's (D) faulty toilet repair resulted in flooding, deterioration of electrical wiring inside the house, and, ultimately, severe electrical shock to Hebert (P) when he touched the outside faucet. Nonetheless, summary judgment is appropriate, despite this uninterrupted causal chain, if Hebert (P) cannot show that his injuries were a reasonably foreseeable result of Enos's (D) negligent conduct. Here, in light of the likelihood, character, and location of the harm, the injuries to Hebert (P) were a "highly extraordinary" consequence of a defective second-floor toilet, such that the law does not require a defendant in Enos's (D) position to guard against them. Merely because water and electricity are involved does not require a higher standard of care than is traditionally applied in negligence theory; the appropriate standard is whether the defendant exercised care that is reasonable in the circumstances. Because Enos (D) could not have reasonably foreseen the harm that befell Hebert (P), the unbroken causal chain that results from Enos's (D) negligence does not legally constitute proximate causation of Hebert's (P) injuries. Affirmed.

ANALYSIS

The issue of foreseeability is ordinarily a question of fact for the jury, but as this case demonstrates, a court may decide the issue as a matter of law in the absence of evidence that the risk that resulted in the plaintiff's injury should reasonably have been anticipated by the defendant. As a practical matter, in deciding the foreseeability question, it is not critical whether the court defines a duty as limited to guarding against reasonably foreseeable risk of harm or whether it defines the necessary causal connection between a breach of duty and some harm as one in which the harm was a reasonably foreseeable consequence of the breach of a duty.

Quicknotes

NEGLIGENCE Conduct falling below the standard of care that a reasonable person would demonstrate under similar conditions.

PROXIMATE CAUSE The natural sequence of events without which an injury would not have been sustained.

SUMMARY JUDGMENT Judgment rendered by a court in response to a motion made by one of the parties, claiming that the lack of a question of material fact in respect to an issue warrants disposition of the issue without consideration by the jury.

Mitchell v. Rochester Ry.

Pregnant train passenger (P) v. Railroad (D)

N.Y. Ct. App., 45 N.E. 354 (1896)

NATURE OF CASE: Appeal from decision in a negligence action.

FACT SUMMARY: Mitchell (P) sued Rochester Railway Co. (D) for negligence when Mitchell (P) was frightened by the horses pulling Rochester Railway Co.'s (D) horse car, causing her to faint and ultimately to have a miscarriage.

RULE OF LAW

A plaintiff is not entitled to recover for injuries, whether mental or physical, arising from the plaintiff's fright that is caused by a defendant's negligence.

FACTS: Mitchell (P) was standing at a crosswalk waiting to board one of Rochester Railway Co.'s (Rochester's) (D) cars. While just about to step aboard the car, one of Rochester's (D) horse cars came down the street. As the car drew near to Mitchell (P), the team of horses drawing the car turned to the right and came close enough to Mitchell (P) that she was standing between the horses' heads when they were stopped. Mitchell (P) testified that from fright and excitement caused by the proximity of the horses, she became unconscious and that the result was ultimately a miscarriage and consequent illness. Medical testimony was given to the effect that the mental shock Mitchell (P) received was sufficient to produce that result. At trial, Rochester (D) was held negligent, and Mitchell (P) was held free from all contributory negligence. Rochester (D) appealed.

ISSUE: Is a plaintiff entitled to recover for injuries, whether mental or physical, arising from the plaintiff's fright that is caused by a defendant's negligence?

HOLDING AND DECISION: (Martin, J.) No. A plaintiff is not entitled to recover for injuries, whether mental or physical, arising from the plaintiff's fright that is caused by a defendant's negligence. The single question presented here is whether Mitchell (P) is entitled to recover from Rochester's (D) negligence, which occasioned her fright and alarm and resulted in her injuries. Here, it cannot be properly said that Mitchell's (P) miscarriage was the proximate result of Rochester's (D) negligence. Mitchell's (P) injuries were plainly the result of an accident or unusual combination of circumstances, which could not have been reasonably anticipated and over which Rochester (D) had no control. Hence, her damages were too remote to justify a recovery in this action. No recovery can be had for injuries sustained by fright occasioned by the negligence of another, where there is no immediate personal injury. [Reversed and dismissed.]

ANALYSIS

Early cases required actual contact or "impact" to a plaintiff before that plaintiff was permitted to recover for negligently inflicted emotional distress. Resistance by the courts to recovery for emotional distress was based on the premise that such damages were too remote and, also, that many spurious suits would be brought if such recoveries were permitted. Many courts, however, did stretch the "impact" concept and allowed plaintiffs to recover for even the slightest impact, as long as some type of impact had occurred. For example, in *Kenney v. Wong Len*, 128 A. 343 (N.H. 1925), the plaintiff was allowed recovery when evidence revealed that a mouse hair in a spoonful of stew touched the inside of plaintiff's mouth. *Mitchell* was overruled in 1961 by *Battalla v. State*, 176 N.E.2d 729 (N.Y. 1961), which permitted recovery for the plaintiff's "severe emotional and neurological disturbances with residual physical manifestations," resulting from the plaintiff's fear, which was induced by the defendant's negligence. The court in *Battalla* concluded that it would be unjust, as well as opposed to experience and logic, to strictly adhere to the rule in *Mitchell*, observing that it is fundamental to our common-law system that one may seek redress for every substantial wrong.

Quicknotes

CONTRIBUTORY NEGLIGENCE Behavior on the part of an injured plaintiff falling below the standard of ordinary care that contributes to the defendant's negligence, resulting in the plaintiff's injury.

PROXIMATE CAUSE The natural sequence of events without which an injury would not have been sustained.

Dillon v. Legg

Mother of infant killed in car crash (P) v. Driver of car (D)

Cal. Sup. Ct., 441 P.2d 912 (1968) (en banc)

NATURE OF CASE: Action for emotional distress.

FACT SUMMARY: Dillon (P) saw her daughter get hit by Legg's (D) car.

RULE OF LAW

The zone of danger rule does not bar a recovery for negligent infliction of emotional distress where a close family member outside the zone views an accident causing an injury or death to another family member.

FACTS: Legg (D) negligently struck Dillon's (P) infant daughter with his vehicle, killing her. Both Dillon (P) and her other daughter (P) witnessed the accident. The daughter (P) saw it from a curb near the accident and Dillon (P) saw it from a distance. Both Dillon (P) and her daughter (P) brought an action for negligent infliction of emotional distress. The daughter's (P) claim was allowed, but Dillon's (P) was dismissed because she was not within the zone of danger created by Legg's (D) actions. Dillon (P) appealed.

ISSUE: Does the zone of danger rule bar a recovery for negligent infliction of emotional distress where a close family member outside the zone views an accident causing an injury or death to another family member?

HOLDING AND DECISION: (Tobriner, J.) No. The zone of danger rule does not bar a recovery for negligent infliction of emotional distress where a close family member outside the zone views an accident causing an injury or death to another family member. Whether or not a plaintiff who witnesses the negligent injury of a close family member is within the zone of danger should be irrelevant to the allowance of recovery for the shock and trauma suffered by viewing the accident. A defendant's duty should not be fixed by arbitrary rules such as the zone of danger. The harm complained of by Dillon (P) was foreseeable, and Legg (D) owed her a duty of care. As to the possibility of fraudulent and indefinable claims, the danger of such actions is no greater than in other cases involving emotional harm. The court would be avoiding its responsibility to separate fraudulent from legitimate claims by barring all plaintiffs alleging such an injury. As to indefinable claims, the tort concept of foreseeability may provide adequate limits to liability. Factors which may be considered are (1) was plaintiff near the scene of the accident; (2) was the shock or emotional trauma due to seeing or merely hearing about the accident; and (3) the closeness of the relationship between the plaintiff and the victim. Here, Dillon (P) saw the accident; the injuries were caused by the sight of the accident; and she was the parent of the victim. All these factors are clearly foreseeable, and she should be permitted to recover. Reversed.

DISSENT: (Traynor, C.J.) The zone of danger rule is correct.

DISSENT: (Burke, J.) Too many unanswered questions are left by the majority. Examples are emotional injury from a mistaken belief of injury; how near is "near;" how close a family member must the victim be for plaintiff to recover, etc.

ANALYSIS

Dillon is a minority holding. The zone of danger rule is applied in most jurisdictions and recovery is limited to fear for one's own safety or from physical manifestations of the trauma. What constitutes physical injury varies within the jurisdictions. In *Cosgrove v. Beymer*, 244 F. Supp. 824, (D. Del. 1965), dizziness, nervousness, and a mild headache were deemed insufficient. In *Daley v. LaCroix*, 384 Mich. 4, 179 N.W. 2d 390 (1970), emotional disturbances and traumatic neurosis were deemed to constitute physical injury.

Quicknotes

INTENTIONAL INFLICTION OF EMOTIONAL DISTRESS Intentional and extreme behavior on the part of the wrongdoer with the intent to cause the victim to suffer from severe emotional distress, or with reckless indifference, resulting in the victim's suffering from severe emotional distress.

NEGLIGENT INFLICTION OF EMOTIONAL DISTRESS Violation of the duty of care owed to another that occurs when an individual creates a foreseeable risk of injury to the other person which causes emotional distress resulting in some physical harm to that person.

CHAPTER 6

Affirmative Duties

Quick Reference Rules of Law

Buch v. Amory Manufacturing Co.

Injured child (P) v. Mill owner (D)

N.H. Sup. Ct., 44 A. 809 (1897)

NATURE OF CASE: Suit seeking damages for personal injuries.

FACT SUMMARY: Eight-year-old Buch (P) wandered into an Amory Manufacturing Co. (Amory) (D) mill and injured his hand when it was crushed by machinery. One of Amory's (D) overseers had observed Buch (P) but had not forced Buch (P) to leave the premises.

RULE OF LAW

A landowner has no duty to warn a trespasser of the existence of a dangerous condition or object even if the trespasser is a mere child.

FACTS: Eight-year-old Buch (P) was a trespasser in an Amory Manufacturing Co. (Amory) (D) mill. One of Amory's (D) overseers saw Buch (P) and told him to leave the premises, but this warning went unheeded because Buch (P) understood no English. The overseer made no other efforts to have Buch (P) removed, despite the fact potentially dangerous weaving machinery was being operated within the mill. Buch (P) crushed his hand in a machine his thirteen-year-old brother, an Amory (D) employee, was teaching him to run. Buch (P) later sued to recover damages and, after Amory's (D) motion for a directed verdict had been denied, the jury returned a verdict in Buch's (P) favor. Amory (D) then appealed.

ISSUE: Does a landowner have a duty to warn a trespasser of the existence of a dangerous condition or object even if the trespasser is a mere child?

HOLDING AND DECISION: (Carpenter, C.J.) No. A landowner has no duty to warn a trespasser of the existence of a dangerous condition or object even if the trespasser is a mere child. Moral obligations notwithstanding, Amory (D) was not bound to warn young Buch (P) of the dangerous machines or to protect him against harm. An adult trespasser need not be warned even of latent dangers. Similarly, a landowner has no duty to warn the child trespasser of an open and visible peril. The law recognizes a clear distinction between the duty to do no wrongful act and the duty to protect others against danger. The latter duty is moral only, and its breach has no legal significance. The situation is unchanged by the fact that the party choosing not to fulfill this moral duty is the owner of the property upon which harm occurs. No legal duty to protect a trespasser from harm exists, and for that reason judgment must be rendered in favor of Amory (D).

ANALYSIS

Buch v. Amory Manufacturing Co. illustrates the distinction, in terms of liability, between active and passive conduct. Active negligence subjects a party to liability for damages caused by his conduct. A failure to act, on the other hand, does not ordinarily make a party liable for any of the damages he could have prevented, no matter how easily he could have caused the harm to be averted. Thus, no one is required by law to act as a "Good Samaritan." Of course, where one party has created the danger with which another party is threatened, or the two enjoy some special relationship, a duty to warn of or protect against the peril may arise. Note that the facts of the *Buch* case would likely result in a different outcome today since the duties of landowners to trespassers, particularly to those whose presence has been discovered, has been expanded since *Buch* was decided.

Quicknotes

GOOD SAMARITAN LAW A statute relieving a bystander from tort liability for the attempted rescue of another.

TRESPASSERS Persons present on the land of another without the knowledge or express permission of the owner, and to whom only a minimum duty of care is owed for injuries incurred while on the premises.

Hurley v. Eddingfield

Decedent's estate (P) v. Family physician (D)

Ind. Sup. Ct., 59 N.E. 1058 (1901)

NATURE OF CASE: Appeal of judgment for the defendant in wrongful death action.

FACT SUMMARY: A decedent's estate (P) sued the decedent's family physician (D) when the physician (D) refused to come to the decedent's aid.

RULE OF LAW

A physician is not lawfully required to treat anyone who requests medical attention.

FACTS: Prior to dying, the decedent had sent a messenger to retrieve the decedent's licensed family physician (D). The physician (D) refused to render aid to the decedent and the decedent subsequently died. The decedent's estate (P) sued the physician (D) for wrongfully causing the death of his intestate. The lower court found in favor of the physician (D) and the estate (P) appealed.

ISSUE: Is a physician lawfully required to treat anyone who requests medical attention?

HOLDING AND DECISION: (Baker, J.) No. A physician is not lawfully required to treat anyone who requests medical attention. The physician (D) was not required to come to the decedent's aid. The act regulating the practice of medicine requires only that those who are licensed must meet certain qualifications, and subjects those who practice without a license to certain penalties. The State does not require those who are licensed to practice at all or according to certain terms against their will. Affirmed.

ANALYSIS

This case exemplifies the sense of individualism that pervaded the law at the time.

Quicknotes

WRONGFUL DEATH An action brought by the beneficiaries of a deceased person, claiming that the deceased's death was the result of wrongful conduct by the defendant.

Montgomery v. National Convoy & Trucking Co.

Injured car driver (P) v. Trucking company (D)

S.C. Sup. Ct., 195 S.E. 247 (1937)

NATURE OF CASE: Suit seeking damages for personal injuries.

FACT SUMMARY: Two National Convoy & Trucking Co. (D) trucks stalled on an icy highway, blocking it completely. Because no warning had been posted, Montgomery (P) saw the trucks too late to avoid a collision.

RULE OF LAW

A duty to warn of an existing danger must be carried out in a manner reasonably calculated to prevent harm.

FACTS: Two National Convoy & Trucking Co. (National) (D) trucks stalled on an icy highway, completely blocking the road. The trucks had stalled not far from a hill, and the drivers of the trucks knew, or should have known, that the icy conditions made it impossible for a car coming over the hill to avoid hitting the trucks if they were not seen until the car had actually started down the hill. Nevertheless, the drivers posted no warnings except for the truck lights and some highway flares which were placed at the site of the stalled vehicles. About 15 minutes after the trucks had stopped Montgomery's (P) car came over the hill and could not stop in time to prevent a collision. Montgomery (P) sustained injuries and ultimately won a judgment against National (D). On appeal, National (D) argued that the scope of its drivers' duty had not obligated them to post a warning at or before the top of the hill.

ISSUE: Must a duty to warn of an existing danger be carried out in a manner reasonably calculated to prevent harm?

HOLDING AND DECISION: (Baker, J.) Yes. A duty to warn of an existing danger must be carried out in a manner reasonably calculated to prevent harm. The drivers were guilty of no active negligence, but their failure to post an adequate warning constituted negligence by omission. The flares and lights were not effective to warn of the danger that drivers faced. Through no fault of their own, the drivers had created a traffic hazard, and they had a duty to warn other motorists of that danger. They did not adequately discharge that duty, because other drivers were not apprised of the peril in time to avoid contact. Since National's (D) drivers negligently failed to provide a sufficient warning, the judgment in favor of Montgomery (P) must be affirmed.

ANALYSIS

The rule of *Montgomery v. National Convoy & Trucking Co.* is supported by reason and logic and is declarative of the weight of authority. The duty to warn of impending danger may derive from various circumstances. But, in all contexts, it can be discharged only by providing a warning which promises to put parties on reasonable notice of the dangerous condition. It is expected that the party owing the duty to warn will, in effect, place himself in the position of those in need of the warning, and will then provide a notice that will be effective in light of all pertinent factors and circumstances.

Quicknotes

DUTY TO WARN An obligation owed by an owner or occupier of land to persons who come onto the premises to inform them of defects or active operations which may cause injury.

MISFEASANCE The commission of a lawful act in a wrongful manner.

NONFEASANCE The omission of, or failure to perform, an obligation.

Robert Addie & Sons (Collieries), Ltd. v. Dumbreck

Ash removal company (D) v. Father of deceased (P)

Scot. Ct. Sess., A.C. 358 (1929)

NATURE OF CASE: Damages for wrongful death.

FACT SUMMARY: Despite warnings to keep off the property of Robert Addie & Sons (Collieries), Ltd. (Addie) (D), Dumbreck's (P) four-year-old son went onto Addie's (D) land and was killed by a wheel which was part of a coal ash removal system.

RULE OF LAW

Although a landowner may not deliberately harm a trespasser, a landowner has no duty to protect a trespasser from risks or dangers.

FACTS: Robert Addie & Sons (Collieries), Ltd. (D) operated a coal ash removal system in an open field. The field was surrounded by a hedge, but gaps in the hedge enabled people to enter or traverse the field almost at will. Addie's (D) employees constantly warned both children and adults to keep off the premises, and a sign on one of the field's two gates warned that trespassers would be prosecuted. Nevertheless, people of all ages frequently crossed or played on the field. Part of Addie's (D) ash removal system consisted of a large wheel around which wound a heavy cable when the system's motor was in operation. The wheel was unprotected except for four boards that covered the top of the wheel but left a large space exposed at the bottom. Dumbreck's (P) four-year-old son was sitting on or near the boards covering the wheel when he was sucked into the mechanism by the pulley. Death resulted, and Dumbreck (P) sued Addie (D). Judgment was rendered in favor of Dumbreck (P), but on appeal Addie (D) argued that it had owed the child no duty of care since he had been a mere trespasser.

ISSUE: Although a landowner may not deliberately harm a trespasser, does a landowner have a duty to protect a trespasser from risks or dangers?

HOLDING AND DECISION: (Lord Hailsham, J.C.) No. Although a landowner may not deliberately harm a trespasser, a landowner has no duty to protect a trespasser from risks or dangers. The trespasser, unlike the invitee or the licensee, is owed no duty of care. Young Dumbreck was a mere trespasser, and the fact that Addie (D) knew that outsiders frequented its premises did not confer upon the child the status of a licensee. Addie (D) therefore owed young Dumbreck no duty of care and was entitled to judgment. Reversed.

CONCURRENCE: (Viscount Dunedin, J.) The legal distinctions between an invitee, a licensee, and a trespasser are clear and rigid, although disputes may arise when the facts of a case are analyzed in terms of these categories. A trespasser does not rise to the status of a licensee unless his presence has been permitted or willingly tolerated by the landowner. Addie (D) took every reasonable step to exclude outsiders. Thus, all intruders, including the unfortunate child, qualify as mere trespassers to whom no duty of care was or is owed.

ANALYSIS

Courts today are reluctant to apply the harsh common-law rule that no duty of care is owed to a trespasser. In this country, the common-law rule is often circumvented by elevating the apparent trespasser to the status of a licensee, or by holding that the trespasser had been "discovered" by the landowner, and thus was owed a duty of care.

Quicknotes

ATTRACTIVE NUISANCE DOCTRINE The assignment of liability to an owner or occupier of land who permits a dangerous instrumentality to remain on the property, knowing it is likely to attract children who have access to it, and who fails to take reasonable steps to prevent such injury.

INVITEE A person who enters upon another's property by an express or implied invitation and to whom the owner of the property owes a duty of care to guard against injury from those hazards that are discoverable through the exercise of reasonable care.

LICENSEES Persons known to an owner or occupier of land who come onto the premises voluntarily and for a specific purpose, although not necessarily with the consent of the owner.

TRESPASSERS Persons present on the land of another without the knowledge or express permission of the owner, and to whom only a minimum duty of care is owed for injuries incurred while on the premises.

Rowland v. Christian

Injured houseguest (P) v. Homeowner (D)

Cal. Sup. Ct., 443 P.2d 561 (1968)

NATURE OF CASE: Appeal from a motion for summary judgment.

FACT SUMMARY: Rowland (P), a licensee in the apartment of Christian (D), was injured by a broken water faucet handle. Christian (D) knew about the broken handle but did not warn Rowland (P).

RULE OF LAW

Where a land occupier is aware of a concealed condition involving, in the absence of precautions, an unreasonable risk of harm to those coming in contact with it and is aware that a person is about to come in contact with it, the failure to warn or to repair the condition constitutes negligence.

FACTS: Rowland (P), a social guest in Christian's (D) apartment, was injured by a cracked water faucet handle that broke in his hand. Rowland (P) asked permission to use the bathroom, and Christian (D) was aware of the cracked handle on the water faucet in the bathroom, having informed the landlord of the need to repair it. Christian (D) did not inform Rowland (P) of the danger, however. Rowland (P) brought an action for negligence against Christian (D), and Christian (D) moved for and was granted summary judgment. Rowland (P) appealed.

ISSUE: Where a land occupier is aware of a concealed condition on the land involving, in the absence of precautions, an unreasonable risk of harm to those coming in contact with it and is aware that a person is about to come in contact with it, does the failure to warn or to repair the condition constitute negligence?

HOLDING AND DECISION: (Peters, J.) Yes. Where a land occupier is aware of a concealed condition involving, in the absence of precautions, an unreasonable risk of harm to those coming in contact with it and is aware that a person is about to come in contact with it, the failure to warn or to repair the condition constitutes negligence. Common law has departed from the usual rules of negligence where persons have been injured after entering upon the land of another. In such cases, the courts, having developed out of a feudal society based upon land ownership, have looked to see first whether the injured was an invitee (business guest), a licensee (social guest), or a trespasser. These classifications have grown obsolete in a modern industrial society. "A man's life or limb does not become less worthy of protection by the law. . .because he has come upon the land of another without permission or with permission but without a business purpose." A guest should be reasonably entitled to rely upon a warning of the dangerous condition so that he, like the host, can be able to take special precautions against it. Reversed.

DISSENT: (Burke, J.) The court, by overturning centuries of tort law, has failed to provide guiding legal principles and has invaded the province of the legislature.

ANALYSIS

California was the first state to do away with the status of an entrant upon land. Few states have followed. Colorado now considers status to be just one factor in determining negligence but not determinative itself. The more common approach is to no longer distinguish between invitees and licensees but to retain the distinction as to the status of trespassers.

Quicknotes

FORESEEABILITY OF HARM An inquiry into the relatedness of events that contributed to the plaintiff's injury; whether the harm was foreseeable determines whether the tortfeasor's conduct was the proximate cause of the injury.

INVITEE A person who enters upon another's property by an express or implied invitation and to whom the owner of the property owes a duty of care to guard against injury from those hazards that are discoverable through the exercise of reasonable care.

LICENSEES Persons known to an owner or occupier of land who come onto the premises voluntarily and for a specific purpose, although not necessarily with the consent of the owner.

Coggs v. Bernard

Owner of brandy casks (P) v. Cask mover (D)

K.B., 92 Eng. Rep. 107 (1703)

NATURE OF CASE: Suit to recover for damages to property.

FACT SUMMARY: Bernard (D) agreed to move casks of brandy for Coggs (P), who allegedly gave no consideration in exchange for that service. While Bernard (D) was moving the casks, they became damaged.

RULE OF LAW

A party is liable for negligent acts committed in the course of performing a contract even if the contract itself, because of a lack of consideration, could not have been enforced.

FACTS: Bernard (D) agreed to move some casks of brandy for Coggs (P). The casks were damaged during the move, and Coggs (P) sued and won judgment. Bernard (D) moved for arrest of judgment, contending that it had not been alleged that he was a common porter or that he had received any reward or consideration.

ISSUE: Is a party liable for negligent acts committed in the course of performing a contract even if the contract itself, because of a lack of consideration, could not have been enforced?

HOLDING AND DECISION: (Sir Henry Gould, J.) Yes. A party is liable for negligent acts committed in the course of performing a contract even if the contract itself, because of a lack of consideration, could not have been enforced. Anyone who undertakes to carry another's goods is liable for harm caused by his negligence, and it makes no difference that he is not a common porter and received no consideration. Coggs (P) entrusted Bernard (D) with the casks, and it was because Bernard (D) began performance and ultimately acted negligently that damages were suffered. Therefore, the judgment in favor of Coggs (P) was appropriate.

CONCURRENCE: (Lord Holt, C.J.) The fact that Coggs (P) entrusted his goods to Bernard (D) was sufficient consideration to obligate Bernard (D) to take adequate care of them. If the contract had been purely executory, no action would lie against Bernard (D), but since Bernard (D) had begun performance, he is liable for the harm to Coggs's (P) property.

ANALYSIS

Coggs v. Bernard was illustrative of the confluence of tort law and contract law. More than a century later, in *Thorne v. Deas*, 4 Johns. Cas. 84 (N.Y. Sup. Ct. 1809), the court was confronted with a case by the co-owner of a ship who lost the vessel after the other co-owner had failed to fulfill his gratuitous promise to obtain insurance. The court denied recovery, noting that there had been no consideration and that the defendant's conduct had constituted mere nonfeasance. Had the defendant embarked upon performance, and thereafter been guilty of misfeasance, the plaintiff would have been entitled to recover, the *Thorne v. Deas* court reasoned. The plaintiffs in both *Coggs v. Bernard* and *Thorne v. Deas* might succeed today by invoking the doctrine of promissory estoppel.

Quicknotes

FAILURE TO WARN The failure of an owner or occupier of land to inform persons present on the property of defects or active operations that may cause injury.

MALFEASANCE The commission of an unlawful act.

MISFEASANCE The commission of a lawful act in a wrongful manner.

NEGLIGENCE PER SE Conduct amounting to negligence as a matter of law either because it is so contrary to ordinary prudence or it is in violation of statute.

PROMISSORY ESTOPPEL A promise that is enforceable if the promisor should reasonably expect that it will induce action or forbearance on the part of the promisee, and does in fact cause such action or forbearance, and it is the only means of avoiding injustice.

Erie R.R. v. Stewart

Railroad (D) v. Injured truck passenger (P)

40 F.2d 855 (6th Cir. 1930)

NATURE OF CASE: Suit seeking damages for personal injuries.

FACT SUMMARY: Stewart (P) was a passenger in a vehicle that was struck by a train. Erie Railroad (D) customarily maintained a watchman at the site, but he had provided no warning until too late to prevent the accident.

RULE OF LAW

A party who voluntarily assumes a duty not imposed upon him by law may be deemed negligent if, without proper notice, he discontinues his performance of that duty.

FACTS: Stewart (P) was a passenger in an automobile truck that was struck by an Erie R. R. (the Railroad) (D) train. The Railroad (D) customarily maintained a watchman at the crossing where the accident occurred, although no statute or ordinance required it to do so, and Stewart (P) was aware of the fact the watchman was ordinarily on duty. On the day of the accident, however, the watchman was in or near his shanty and provided no warning of the oncoming train until too late to prevent the collision. Stewart (P) sued the Railroad (D) to recover for injuries sustained in the accident, and at trial the jury was instructed that the watchman's absence, after a long period of having been stationed at the site to the knowledge of Stewart (P), would constitute negligence as a matter of law. The Railroad (D), appealing from a judgment in Stewart's (P) favor, argued that the jury instruction had been erroneous.

ISSUE: May a party who voluntarily assumes a duty not imposed upon him by law be deemed negligent if, without proper notice, he discontinues his performance of that duty?

HOLDING AND DECISION: (Hickenlooper, C.J.) Yes. A party who voluntarily assumes a duty not imposed upon him by law may be deemed negligent if, without proper notice, he discontinues his performance of that duty. The Railroad (D) had no statutory duty to post a watchman, but by doing so it invited motorists to proceed in reliance upon the implied assurance that any dangers would be made known in time to avert catastrophe. The Railroad (D) was not necessarily required to retain a watchman around the clock, but any time that the watchman's duties were not being carried out, the Railroad (D) had a responsibility to apprise the public of that fact. Its failure to do so was prima facie evidence of negligence, and in the absence of anything to rebut the allegation of negligence, the judgment in favor of Stewart (P) was appropriate. [Affirmed.]

CONCURRENCE: (Tuttle, J.) It is enough that the Railroad (D) had created a duty to post a watchman by virtue of having done so in the past. It should have assumed that the public at large would rely upon the existence of the watchman, and it is thus superfluous to show that Stewart (P) himself actually relied upon the presence of an adequate lookout.

ANALYSIS

Many other cases can be found in which negligence has been predicated upon the defendant's abandonment of a voluntary course of conduct that had been undertaken to promote the safety of the plaintiff. A large number of these cases seem to accept the proposition that liability will not attach unless actual reliance can be demonstrated. The reliance upon which liability depends need not always be that of the plaintiff, however. In some cases it has been deemed sufficient a third party refrained from acting on behalf of the plaintiff because of that third party's reliance upon the defendant's continuation of a custom.

Quicknotes

FAILURE TO WARN The failure of an owner or occupier of land to inform persons present on the property of defects or active operations that may cause injury.

NEGLIGENCE PER SE Conduct amounting to negligence as a matter of law either because it is so contrary to ordinary prudence or it is in violation of statute.

PRIMA FACIE EVIDENCE Evidence presented by a party that is sufficient, in the absence of contradictory evidence, to support the fact or issue for which it is offered.

Moch Co. v. Rensselaer Water Co.

Warehouse destroyed by fire (P) v. Water company (D)

N.Y. Ct. App., 159 N.E. 896 (1928)

NATURE OF CASE: Suit to recover for damage to property.

FACT SUMMARY: Rensselaer Water Co. (D) contracted to supply water to the city of Rensselaer. A fire destroyed a warehouse owned by Moch Co. (P). Adequate water service could have prevented the fire from spreading to the warehouse.

RULE OF LAW

A party whose performance of a contract incidentally confers a benefit upon third parties does not owe any duty to continue to perform in a manner that is satisfactory to those parties.

FACTS: Rensselaer Water Co. (Water Co.) (D) contracted to supply water for the city of Rensselaer. Water was to be furnished for sewer flushing, street sprinkling, and schools and other public buildings. Homeowners and businesses were to receive water at a reasonable rate, and water was to be supplied for service at fire hydrants. A fire broke out in the city, and eventually spread to a warehouse owned by the Moch Co. (P). Both the warehouse and its contents were destroyed. Moch (P) brought suit against Water Co. (D), alleging that Water Co. (D) had been notified of the fire, but had failed to supply water in adequate amounts and at satisfactory pressure to prevent the fire from spreading. Moch (P) claimed that the loss of its property had resulted from Water Co.'s (D) failure to fulfill its contract with the city. The trial court denied Water Co.'s (D) motion to dismiss the complaint, but the appellate division reversed. Moch (P) then appealed.

ISSUE: Does a party whose performance of a contract incidentally confers a benefit upon third parties owe any duty to continue to perform in a manner that is satisfactory to those parties?

HOLDING AND DECISION: (Cardozo, C.J.) No. A party whose performance of a contract incidentally confers a benefit upon third parties does not owe any duty to continue to perform in a manner that is satisfactory to those parties. The fact that one has begun to act does not always obligate him to continue to do so. If conduct has proceeded to such a state that its discontinuation would be likely to cause injury, a duty arises to continue that conduct. But to hold an actor liable to one party for failure to pursue his conduct toward another party with whom he has contracted, would be to unduly extend the common-law rules of tort liability. In fact, it would subject the parties to a contract to actions by a potentially infinite number of tort claimants. Moch (P) also cannot recover as a third-party beneficiary of the contract because Water Co. (D) obviously had no intention of being answerable to individual consumers. Nor does any statute enlarge Water Co.'s (D) duty to the extent that a third party may recover in tort for Water Co.'s (D) ineffectual performance. Therefore, the judgment in Water Co.'s (D) favor must be affirmed with costs.

ANALYSIS

Moch Co. v. Rensselaer Water Co. stands for the proposition that the failure to perform a contract can result in tort liability only if the party claiming damages was in privity with the breaching party. The earliest cases almost always excused water suppliers when their failure to provide enough water or sufficient pressure caused unnecessary damages as the result of a fire. The *Moch* case, however, seems inconsistent with the landmark case of *MacPherson v. Buick Motor Co.,* 217 N.Y. 382, III. N.E. 1050 (1916), in which it was held that the breach of a contractual obligation will result in liability to a third party if the injuries suffered by that individual were foreseeable.

Quicknotes

MISFEASANCE The commission of a lawful act in a wrongful manner.

NONFEASANCE The omission of, or failure to perform, an obligation.

PRIVITY OF CONTRACT A relationship between the parties to a contract that is required in order to bring an action for breach.

Kline v. 1500 Massachusetts Avenue Apartment Corp.

Renter (P) v. Landlord (D)

439 F.2d 477 (D.C. Cir. 1970)

NATURE OF CASE: Appeal from denial for damages for negligence.

FACT SUMMARY: Kline (P) sued 1500 Massachusetts Ave. Apartment Corporation (the Corporation) (D) for damages after she was attacked in a common area of the apartment building, contending the Corporation breached its duty to provide adequate security measures.

RULE OF LAW

A landlord is responsible for maintaining common areas of his property so as to minimize tenant exposure to an unreasonable risk of criminal attack.

FACTS: In 1959, Kline (P) rented an apartment from 1500 Massachusetts Ave. Apartment Corporation (the Corporation) (D). At the time, there were a doorman on duty 24 hours a day, an employee at the front desk observing all persons using the elevators, and two garage attendants regulating who entered the building from the garage. By 1966, no doorman was present, the front desk was unattended, the garage was left virtually unguarded, and an increased number of criminal assaults against the tenants were occurring in the common hallways of the building. Kline (P) and others had repeatedly informed the Corporation (D) of these attacks, but nothing was done. In September 1966, a female tenant was attacked in the hallway near Kline's (P) apartment, and two months later, Kline (P) was attacked in the same hallway. She sued, contending the Corporation (D) was liable for not providing adequate security measures. The district court held landlords have no such duty to protect their tenants. Kline (P) appealed.

ISSUE: Is a landlord responsible for maintaining the common areas of his property so as to minimize tenant exposure to an unreasonable risk of criminal attacks?

HOLDING AND DECISION: (Wilkey, J.) Yes. A landlord is responsible for maintaining the common areas of his property so as to minimize tenant exposure to an unreasonable risk of criminal attack. The landlord is the only party with control over the common areas of the property. Therefore, he, and not the tenants, is in a position to take necessary protective steps. The landlord is not an insurer of the tenant's safety, but he is obligated to minimize the risk of foreseeable harm. In this case, the standard of reasonable care is the amount of security protections maintained when Kline (P) rented the apartment. She was led to expect this level of care and relied on it in renting the apartment. Therefore, given the clear foreseeability of the attack and the lack of reasonable protective measures, the Corporation (D) was negligent. Reversed and remanded.

DISSENT: (MacKinnon, J.) Kline (P) presented no evidence that the attacker was not another tenant rather than an intruder. Therefore, if it were another tenant rather than an intruder, the lack of security measures would not be the proximate cause of the attack, and the Corporation (D) could not be held liable.

ANALYSIS

The recognition of a special duty owed by a landlord to a tenant has been adopted in other jurisdictions. In *Johnston v. Harris,* 387 Mich. 569, 198 N.W. 2d 409 (1972), a landlord was held liable for an attack on a tenant occurring in a dimly lit, unlocked vestibule of the apartment. In *Sampson v. Saginaw Professional Building Inc.*, 224 N.W. 2d 843 (1975), the Michigan Supreme Court extended the duty of the landlord to invitees of the tenant.

Quicknotes

DUTY OF A LANDLORD TO COMMON AREAS A landlord owes a duty to all persons injured as the result of defects present in shared areas of the leasehold accessible to the public.

DUTY TO PROTECT TENANTS Generally speaking, a landlord owes a duty to tenants for any defects or other injurious instrumentalities on the property, including those not located in common areas, which are known to the landlord and which he fails to repair, and which are otherwise not the result of the tenant's own negligence.

FORESEEABILITY A reasonable expectation that an act or omission would result in injury.

Tarasoff v. Regents of University of California

Parents of murder victim (P) v. Psychologist and university (D)

Cal Sup. Ct., 551 P.2d 334 (1976)

NATURE OF CASE: Action in damages for wrongful death.

FACT SUMMARY: Moore (D), a psychologist, failed to notify Tatiana (plaintiff's daughter) that one of his patients threatened to kill her.

RULE OF LAW

Where a person bears a special relationship to a party or others who may be the victim of the conduct, it is reasonably foreseeable that a legally cognizable duty arises to protect or control the third party.

FACTS: Poddar was a patient of Dr. Moore (D), a psychologist employed by the University of California at Berkeley (the University) (D). During a therapy session, Poddar told Moore (D) that he was going to kill Tatiana. Moore (D) informed the campus police who finally released Poddar since he appeared rational. Poddar killed Tatiana several days later. Tarasoff (P), Tatiana's parents, brought a wrongful death action against Powelson (D), Moore's superior, and the University (D) on the ground that they had negligently failed either to warn Tatiana or to restrain Poddar. The court sustained a general demurrer on the ground that the defendants did not owe a duty to Tatiana. Tarasoff (P) argued that the special relationship of doctor to patient created a duty to protect Tatiana.

ISSUE: Where a person bears a special relationship to a party or others who may be the victim of the conduct, is it reasonably foreseeable that a legally cognizable duty arises to protect or control the third party?

HOLDING AND DECISION: (Tobriner, J.) Yes. Where a person bears a special relationship to a party or others who may be the victim of the conduct, it is reasonably foreseeable that a legally cognizable duty arises to protect or control the third party. As a general rule a person is not liable for the conduct of another. An exception is created where a special relationship exists between the person and the actor or the person and a third party. These types of special relationships impose duties to prevent injury that may be caused by the actor or to protect a third party from injury. A doctor/patient relationship gives rise to this duty. Moore (D) had a duty to protect Tatiana from Poddar. The law recognizes certain conduct must be prevented or certain interests protected. In such cases right of action is granted or a penalty assessed. The basic tenet is whether there is a reasonably foreseeable likelihood of an unwarranted risk. Here the relationship exists; the right to life is deemed a protectible interest; and the risk was readily foreseeable. In such cases the law imposes a duty on the party to protect third parties from the actor's conduct. While the doctor/patient relationship requires the keeping of confidences, this privilege is outweighed by the need to protect human life. Affirmed in part, reversed in part, and remanded.

CONCURRENCE AND DISSENT: (Mosk, J.) I concur solely on the ground that Moore (D) had predicted that Poddar would kill. We are not concerned with whether he should have recognized whether the killing was likely to occur.

DISSENT: (Clark, J.) I dissent solely on the basis that the relationship required the keeping of confidences.

ANALYSIS

In *Bellah v. Greenson*, C.A. 1st, 1 Civ. 39770 (1977), the parents of a suicidal teenager who died from a self-inflicted overdose of sleeping pills relied on the above case in a wrongful death action against the girl's psychiatrist. The parents claimed that the psychiatrist had failed to personally take measures to prevent the suicide; that he had failed to warn others of her proclivity; and that he had also failed to warn them that their daughter was consorting with heroin addicts. The appellate court declined to extend the holding of *Tarasoff* to the case and distinguished it in that here there was a danger of self-inflicted harm rather than harm to others.

Quicknotes

DUTY TO PROTECT/AID A moral duty and not one imposed by law; no liability attaches to those persons who fail to undertake a rescue or otherwise aid a person in need absent a special relationship between them.

NEGLIGENT FAILURE TO PROTECT The breach of duty by a person with a special relationship or other fiduciary duty owed to the plaintiff to intercede and prevent a threatened injury.

PSYCHOTHERAPIST/PATIENT PRIVILEGE The right of a patient to refuse to reveal confidential information given during the course of a relationship with a physician entered into for the purpose of treatment.

SPECIAL RELATIONSHIP A relationship between two persons that imposes a fiduciary responsibility to act where one is threatened with injury, such as the relationship between a parent and child.

CHAPTER 7

Strict Liability

Quick Reference Rules of Law

CHAPTER 7

Intel Corporation v. Hamidi

Employer (P) v. Employee (D)

Cal. Sup. Ct., 71 P.3d 296 (2003)

NATURE OF CASE: Appeal of summary judgment in trespass to chattel action.

FACT SUMMARY: Intel Corporation (Intel) (P) sued Hamidi (D) for trespass to chattel when Hamidi (D) sent e-mails to current Intel (P) employees.

RULE OF LAW

The tort of trespass to chattel does not encompass an electronic communication that neither damages the recipient computer system nor impairs its functioning.

FACTS: Hamidi (D), a former Intel Corporation (Intel) (P) employee, sent six e-mails on Intel's (P) e-mail system, to up to 35,000 current Intel (P) employees, criticizing Intel's (P) employment practices. Although the content of Hamidi's (D) e-mails caused discussion among employees and managers, the messages did not damage Intel's (P) computer system or impair its functioning. Intel (P) sued, claiming that by communicating with its employees over the company's e-mail system, Hamidi (D) committed the tort of trespass to chattels. The trial court granted Intel's (P) motion for summary judgment and the court of appeal affirmed.

ISSUE: Does the tort of trespass to chattel encompass an electronic communication that neither damages the recipient computer system nor impairs its functioning?

HOLDING AND DECISION: (Werdegar, J.) No. The tort of trespass to chattel does not encompass an electronic communication that neither damages the recipient computer system nor impairs its functioning. This is because the e-mail does not interfere with the possessor's use or possession of the computer system itself. Intel's (P) claimed loss of productivity, caused by employees reading and reacting to Hamidi's (D) messages and its (P) efforts to block the messages, is not an injury to Intel's (P) interest in its computers because the computers worked as intended and were unharmed by the communications. The tort of trespass to chattels allows recovery for interferences with the possession of personal property that causes some injury. Even though Intel (P) was requesting only injunctive relief, it still had to prove actual harm. Intel's (P) workers were distracted from their work not because of the frequency of Hamidi's (D) messages, but because of the content of the e-mails and, therefore, it was not the functioning of Intel's (P) computer system that was allegedly harmed. The law of trespass to chattel should not be extended to cover an otherwise harmless e-mail whose contents are objectionable. Moreover, intangible intrusions on land are not actionable as trespass. Since Intel (P) did not claim that Hamidi's (D) e-mail physically damaged its servers, it could not prove trespass to land even if the computer were treated as a type of real property. Computers are personal, not real, property. Hamidi (D) had no tangible presence on Intel (P) property. Reversed.

CONCURRENCE: (Kennard, J.) Like a person who makes unwanted calls to a cell phone, Hamidi's (D) e-mails to Intel's (P) employees did not damage Intel's (P) computer system or impair its functioning and therefore the tort of trespass to chattels was not established.

DISSENT: (Brown, J.) The time required to review and delete Hamidi's (D) e-mails undermined the utility of Intel's (P) expensive computer system. Intel (P) objects to Hamidi's (D) use of Intel (P) property to display his message. Even if, however, Intel (P) objected only to the content of the e-mails, it still deserved an injunction.

DISSENT: (Mosk, J.) Hamidi's (D) actions are synonymous with someone intruding into a private office mailroom, taking the mail cart and dropping off unwanted mail on 30,000 desks. Hamidi's (D) actions did not occur in a public forum.

ANALYSIS

Trespass to chattels has successfully been used to hold spammers—senders of unsolicited commercial bulk e-mail—liable to Internet service providers because such e-mail overburdens the provider's computers and makes the system harder for recipients to use.

Quicknotes

TRESPASS TO CHATTELS Action for damages sustained as a result of defendant's unlawful interference with plaintiff's personal property.

Poggi v. Scott

Owner of wine barrels (P) v. Seller of wine barrels (D)

Cal. Sup. Ct., 139 P. 815 (1914)

NATURE OF CASE: Appeal from judgment of nonsuit in a conversion action.

FACT SUMMARY: Scott (D) inadvertently sold Poggi's (P) wine barrels and Poggi (P) sued for conversion.

RULE OF LAW

Conversion is exercising an unjustifiable and unwarranted dominion and control over another's property that causes injury to the property owner.

FACTS: Poggi (P) stored his wine in a basement space he rented initially from Mouser and then from Sanitary Laundry Company (Laundry Company). When Mouser sold the building to Scott (D), Mouser informed Scott (D) of Poggi's (P) lease with the Laundry Company. Scott (D) subsequently sold what he believed to be broken empty barrels stored in the basement. The barrels actually contained Poggi's (P) wine. The men to whom Scott (D) sold the barrels were subsequently arrested for theft of the wine. Poggi (P) sued Scott (D) to recover damages suffered as a result of Scott's (D) conversion of about two hundred barrels of Poggi's (P) wine. The jury found in favor of Scott (D) and Poggi (P) appealed.

ISSUE: Is Scott (D) liable for conversion because he exercised an unjustifiable and unwarranted dominion and control over another's property that causes injury to the property owner?

HOLDING AND DECISION: (Henshaw, J.) Yes. Scott (D) is liable for conversion because he exercised an unjustifiable and unwarranted dominion and control over another's property resulting in injury to the property owner. Neither knowledge, nor intent, nor negligence is necessary to prove conversion. An action for conversion rests upon the interference with the property of another resulting in injury. Conversion occurs when there is a breach of an absolute duty; the existence of bad faith is irrelevant. Scott (D) sold barrels that did not belong to him; it does not matter that he did not know the barrels contained wine. Moreover, Scott (D) had no right to sell the barrels whether they contained wine or not, and the fact he did so means he exercised an unjustifiable and unwarranted dominion and control over Poggi's (P) property. [Reversed.]

ANALYSIS

As this case demonstrates, conversion was initially considered a strict liability tort.

Quicknotes

ABATEMENT A decrease or lessening of something; in equity, a suspension or dismissal of a cause of action.

INJUNCTION A remedy imposed by the court ordering a party to cease the conduct of a specific activity.

INVERSE CONDEMNATION Taking of private property for public use so as to impair or decrease the value of property near or adjacent to, but not a part of, the property taken.

NUISANCE Use of property that interferes with the lawful use of another's property.

Moore v. Regents of the University of California

Cancer patient (P) v. University (D)

Cal. Sup. Ct., 793 P.2d 479 (1990)

NATURE OF CASE: Appeal from decision denying defendants' demurrer in a conversion action.

FACT SUMMARY: After the Medical Center of the University of California at Los Angeles (D) removed tissue from Moore's (P) body and, without Moore's (P) knowledge, developed a cell-line from the tissue capable of producing pharmaceutical products of great therapeutic value, financially benefiting from doing so, Moore (P) sued for conversion.

RULE OF LAW

Where plaintiff has neither title to the property alleged to have been converted nor possession thereof, plaintiff cannot maintain an action for conversion.

FACTS: Moore (P), a cancer patient with hairy-cell leukemia, sought medical treatment at the Medical Center of the University of California at Los Angeles (UCLA) (D). As part of the treatment, Moore's (P) spleen was removed. After removal of the spleen, and without Moore's (P) consent or knowledge, two UCLA (D) doctors discovered that Moore's (P) tissue was unique and, through genetic engineering, developed a cell-line capable of producing valuable pharmaceutical products. UCLA (D) then entered contracts with pharmaceutical companies and was paid hundreds of thousands of dollars pursuant to the contracts. UCLA (D) never informed Moore (P) about these happenings and continued to take tissue from Moore (P) for seven years after the removal of his spleen. Moore (P), after discovering that UCLA (D) had taken his tissue and profited financially thereby, sued UCLA (D) for conversion. The trial court sustained all UCLA's (D) demurrers to Moore's (P) complaint, and Moore (P) appealed. The court of appeals reversed the trial court and decided in Moore's (P) favor on the conversion issue. UCLA (D) appealed.

ISSUE: Where plaintiff has neither title to the property alleged to have been converted nor possession thereof, can plaintiff maintain an action for conversion?

HOLDING AND DECISION: (Panelli, J.) No. Where plaintiff has neither title to the property alleged to have been converted nor possession thereof, plaintiff cannot maintain an action for conversion. Since Moore (P) clearly did not expect to retain possession of his cells following their removal, in order to sue for their conversion, he must have retained an ownership interest in them. There are several reasons to doubt that he did retain such interest. First, no reported judicial decision supports Moore's (P) claim, either directly or by close analogy; second, California statutory law drastically limits any continuing interest of a patient in excised cells; third, the subject matters of UCLA's (D) patent—the patented cell-line and the products derived from it—cannot be Moore's (P) property. Also, there are three reasons why it is inappropriate to impose liability for conversion upon the allegations of Moore's (P) complaint. First, a fair balancing of relevant policy considerations counsels against extending the tort; second, problems in this area are better suited to legislative resolution; and third, the tort of conversion is not necessary to protect Moore's (P) rights since Moore (P) can base liability on existing disclosure obligations rather than rely on an unprecedented extension of the conversion tort. Reversed.

CONCURRENCE AND DISSENT: (Broussard, J.) Because Moore (P) alleged that UCLA (D) wrongfully interfered with his right to determine, prior to the removal of body parts, how these parts would be used after removal, Moore's (P) complaint states a cause of action under traditional common-law conversion principles.

DISSENT: (Mosk, J.) Acceptance of legislative dominance does not require judicial passivity in the application of traditional common-law principles of conversion to recent explosive growth in the commercialization of biotechnology. Here, Moore (P) also has argued a nondisclosure cause of action, which the court feels is adequate to solve the problem of this case. But the nondisclosure cause of action does not protect Moore's (P) right to participate in the benefits UCLA (D) will reap as a result of selling a product produced from Moore's (P) tissues. Therefore, the nondisclosure cause of action is not an adequate substitute for the conversion remedy, which does protect the right.

ANALYSIS

Justice Mosk's dissent in this case discussed at length the reasons that a nondisclosure cause of action could not adequately protect a person in Moore's (P) position. Mosk stated that the nondisclosure cause of action only gives a patient a right to refuse consent, *i.e.*, to prohibit commercialization of his tissue; it does not give him

Continued on next page.

the right to consent to that commercialization on the condition that he share in its proceeds. Also, the nondisclosure cause of action fails to reach a major class of defendants: all those outside the strict physician-patient relationship with the plaintiff.

Quicknotes

BREACH OF FIDUCIARY DUTY The failure of a fiduciary to observe the standard of care exercised by professionals of similar education and experience.

CONVERSION The act of depriving an owner of his property without permission or justification.

DEMURRER The assertion that the opposing party's pleadings are insufficient and that the demurring party should not be made to answer.

INFORMED CONSENT An individual's consent to a particular occurrence following full disclosure of the consequences of that decision.

Gehrts v. Batteen

Dog bite victim (P) v. Dog owner (D)

S.D. Sup. Ct., 620 N.W.2d 775 (2001)

NATURE OF CASE: Appeal of summary judgment in favor of Batteen (D) in dog bite action.

FACT SUMMARY: Nielsen's (D) dog bit Gehrts (P) and Gehrts (P) sued for damages.

RULE OF LAW

An owner of a domesticated animal may be liable for harm caused by his pet if the owner knows, or has reason to know, that the animal has abnormally dangerous propensities, regardless of the amount of care exercised by the owner. If an owner does not have actual knowledge, an action can still survive if an ordinary prudent person should have foreseen the event that caused the injury and taken steps to prevent the injury.

FACTS: Nielsen (D) left her St. Bernard, Wilbur, in the back of her (D) pickup truck when she went to visit Gerhts's (P) home. Wilbur was secured by a harness attached to a restraining device that allowed the dog to move freely between the sides of the pickup box but limited his movement between the front and back. Gehrts (P) attempted to pet Wilbur, with Nielsen's (P) permission, and received injuries to her nose and forehead as a result of Wilbur biting her. Gehrts (P) subsequently sued Nielsen (D) in negligence and strict liability and the trial court granted summary judgment in favor of Nielsen (D). Gehrts (P) appealed.

ISSUE: Was Nielsen (D) liable for the harm Wilbur caused?

HOLDING AND DECISION: (Gilbertson, J.) No. Nielsen (D) was not liable for the harm Wilbur caused because Nielsen (D) did not know, or have reason to know, that Wilbur had abnormally dangerous propensities, and an ordinary prudent person could not have foreseen the event that caused the injury and taken steps to prevent the injury. An owner of a domesticated animal may be liable for harm caused by his pet if the owner knows or has reason to know that the animal has abnormally dangerous propensities, regardless of the amount of care exercised by the owner. Absent an actual attack, barking, barring its teeth and straining at its leash is sufficient to establish such propensities. If an owner does not have actual knowledge, an action can still survive if an ordinary prudent person should have foreseen the event that caused the injury and taken steps to prevent the injury. In the present case, there is no evidence that Nielsen (D) had any knowledge that Wilbur had dangerous propensities. St. Bernards are by nature gentle dogs and Wilbur specifically had never growled, bared his teeth or acted aggressively toward any person. Furthermore, it was not proven that Nielsen (D) failed to use reasonable care in the circumstances because a prudent person would not have foreseen the danger. There was no evidence that Nielsen (D) was aware that Gehrts (P) owned a dog or that the scent of a dog would be on Gehrts (P) and that the scent of a strange dog would cause Wilbur to attack Gehrts (P). In addition, it is mere speculation to suggest that if Nielsen (D) restrained Wilbur in a different way while Gehrts (P) was petting him, Gehrts (P) would not have been bitten. Lastly, it is up to the legislature, not the courts, to adopt a strict liability standard for injuries caused by dogs. Affirmed.

DISSENT: (Sabers, J.) It is premature to say that the facts in this case warrant summary judgment. Precedent holds that summary judgment is not appropriate in negligence actions. There are numerous genuine issues of material fact in this case that should be resolved by a jury.

ANALYSIS

Other state legislatures, such as California, have mandated strict liability in dog bite actions.

Quicknotes

NEGLIGENCE Conduct falling below the standard of care that a reasonable person would demonstrate under similar conditions.

STRICT LIABILITY Liability for all injuries proximately caused by a party's conducting of certain inherently dangerous activities without regard to negligence or fault.

SUMMARY JUDGMENT Judgment rendered by a court in response to a motion by one of the parties, claiming that the lack of a question of material fact in respect to an issue warrants disposition of the issue without consideration by the jury.

Spano v. Perini Corp.

Garage owner (P) v. Construction company (D)

N.Y. Ct. App., 250 N.E.2d 31 (1969)

NATURE OF CASE: Property damage based on strict liability.

FACT SUMMARY: Blasting by Perini Corp. (D) on its own land wrecked Spano's (P) garage on nearby property.

RULE OF LAW

(1) One who engages in blasting is responsible for damage caused without any showing of fault.

(2) Proof of trespass is not necessary for recovery in strict liability.

FACTS: Spano (P) owns a garage that was wrecked by shock waves from a dynamite blast set off by Perini Corp. (D) on nearby property. There was no physical trespass caused by the blast nor was there any proof of negligence on the part of the defendant. In addition to the foregoing, suit was also brought for damages to an automobile that had been in the garage at the time of the blast. The two suits were consolidated and judgment was for Spano and Davis (P). Perini Corp. (D) appealed.

ISSUE:

(1) Is one who engages in blasting responsible for damage caused without any showing of fault?

(2) Is proof of trespass necessary for recovery in strict liability?

HOLDING AND DECISION: (Fuld, C.J.)

(1) Yes. One who engages in blasting is responsible for damage caused without any showing of fault. This case recognizes that under the doctrine of strict liability, an actor is liable for damage caused by abnormally dangerous activity without regard to fault. The rationale is that he who engages in an abnormally dangerous activity should bear the losses as opposed to the injured and innocent victim.

(2) No. Proof of trespass is not necessary for recovery in strict liability. The early common law would have distinguished between the physical invasion, which was a trespass, and the concussion, which would be in nuisance. For purposes of strict liability the distinction has been abandoned.

[Reversed and remanded.]

ANALYSIS

This case indicates the traditional approach to strict liability. If an activity cannot be made safe even by the exercise of utmost care, then strict liability applies. This is the majority view. In many jurisdictions the protection of strict liability has been extended to food, drugs, and products. In those jurisdictions, if a defect exists in the product when it left the manufacturer, the manufacturer will be absolutely liable.

Quicknotes

STRICT LIABILITY Liability for all injuries proximately caused by a party's conducting of certain inherently dangerous activities without regard to negligence or fault.

ULTRAHAZARDOUS ACTIVITIES Dangerous activities that give rise to strict liability by presenting a risk of serious harm to the community that cannot be removed through any exercise of due care.

Indiana Harbor Belt R.R. v. American Cyanamid Co.

Railroad (P) v. Chemical manufacturing company (D)

916 F.2d 1174 (7th Cir. 1990)

NATURE OF CASE: Appeal of damages awarded for injury to property.

FACT SUMMARY: American Cyanamid Co. (D), manufacturer of a dangerous chemical, was held strictly liable when a quantity of it spilled during transportation.

RULE OF LAW

Strict liability will not be imposed against the manufacturer of a toxic chemical for accidents occurring during transportation.

FACTS: American Cyanamid Co. (D), a chemical manufacturer, engaged a railroad car to transport 20,000 gallons of liquid acrylonitrile, a toxic substance, to a processing plant in New Jersey. While the car was sitting in a Chicago railroad yard owned by Indiana Harbor Belt R.R. (P), about 5,000 gallons spilled, which necessitated an evacuation of nearby homes and nearly $1 million in cleanup. Indiana Harbor Belt R.R. (P) filed suit against American Cyanamid (D) to recover the cost of cleanup, contending that the transportation of toxic chemicals was an ultrahazardous activity for which the manufacturer should be strictly liable. A district court, sitting in diversity, agreed and so instructed the jury. A verdict for damages was rendered, and American Cyanamid (D) appealed.

ISSUE: Will strict liability be imposed against the manufacturer of a toxic chemical for accidents occurring during transportation?

HOLDING AND DECISION: (Posner, J.) No. Strict liability will not be imposed against the manufacturer of a toxic chemical for accidents occurring during transportation. The Restatement (Second) of Torts, at § 520, lists six factors to be considered in determining whether an activity is ultrahazardous: (1) great probability of harm; (2) potentially serious level of harm; (3) the activity is not a matter of common usage; (4) harm cannot be prevented by utmost care; (5) the activity is inappropriate for the location; and (6) the social value of the activity is not sufficient to offset the risks. The basic purpose behind the ultrahazardous activity doctrine is to encourage the use of alternative methods when possible. In this case, no alternative exists to transport chemicals other than truck transport, which is not inherently safer. It would not be feasible to reroute the shipment of all hazardous materials around Chicago. Moreover, the negligence regime is perfectly adequate for deterring railway spills. Finally, the ultrahazardous activity doctrine concentrates on the activity, not the subject of the activity. American Cyanamid (D) is not considered to be engaged in an abnormally dangerous activity just because a product it manufactures becomes dangerous when handled. It is the transportation, not the manufacture of the chemical, which is under scrutiny. For these reasons, strict liability is inappropriate in this context. Reversed and remanded, with directions.

ANALYSIS

The classic case of ultrahazardous activity is dynamite blasting in an urban area. It entails a great risk of harm, and a less dangerous (albeit more expensive) method of building demolition exists—the wrecking ball. The ultrahazardous activity rule will make the demolisher strictly liable if he chooses the more dangerous method.

Quicknotes

STRICT LIABILITY Liability for all injuries proximately caused by a party's conducting of certain inherently dangerous activities without regard to negligence or fault.

ULTRAHAZARDOUS ACTIVITIES Dangerous activities that give rise to strict liability by presenting a risk of serious harm to the community that cannot be removed through any exercise of due care.

Vogel v. Grant-Lafayette Electric Cooperative

Farmers (P) v. Electric cooperative association (D)

Wis. Sup. Ct., 548 N.W.2d 829 (1996)

NATURE OF CASE: Suit for damages based on negligence on private nuisance.

FACT SUMMARY: On theories of negligence and private nuisance, the Vogels (P), dairy farmers, sought recovery for injuries sustained by their herd of cows as a result of stray voltage allegedly caused by Grant-Lafayette Electric Cooperative (D).

RULE OF LAW

Excessive stray voltage is actionable as a private nuisance if the trier of fact determines that such voltage unreasonably interferes with a person's interest in the private use and enjoyment of land.

FACTS: The Vogels (P) are dairy farmers and members of Grant-Lafayette Electric Cooperative (GLEC) (D). Shortly after the Vogels (P) built a new milking facility, their herd began exhibiting violent or erratic behavior while in the facility. The herd also suffered from excessive and chronic mastitis, and as a result, the Vogels (P) suffered a decline in their herd's milk production and cows were repeatedly culled from the herd. The Vogels (P) contacted GLEC (D) because they suspected the cows were suffering from the effects of excessive stray voltage. GLEC (D) installed an isolator at its transformer on the Vogels' (P) farm in order to reduce the risk of excessive stray voltage. After installation of the isolator, the behavior and other problems of the herd improved immediately. The Vogels (P) brought suit against GLEC (D) for negligence and nuisance. GLEC (D) denied the allegations and contended the Vogels (P) were contributorily negligent in the design, maintenance, and operation of their equipment. A jury found that GLEC (D) was negligent and that it had created a nuisance, and the Vogels (P) were found one-third negligent. A verdict was entered for $200,000. GLEC (D) appealed on the basis that stray voltage is not a private nuisance. The Vogels (P) appealed, claiming GLEC (D) committed an intentional nuisance and therefore the award could not be reduced for contributory negligence. The court of appeal held the trial court erred in submitting the nuisance claim to the jury and struck that portion of the award. The Vogels (P) appealed.

ISSUE: Is excessive stray voltage actionable as a private nuisance if the trier of fact determines that such voltage unreasonably interferes with a person's interest in the private use and enjoyment of land?

HOLDING AND DECISION: (Bradley, J.) Yes. Excessive stray voltage is actionable as a private nuisance if the trier of fact determines that such voltage unreasonably interferes with a person's interest in the private use and enjoyment of land. Private nuisance is defined as "a nontrespassory invasion of another's interest in the private use and enjoyment of land," Restatement (Second) of Torts § 821D. GLEC (D) argued that the term invasion constitutes a "unilateral encroachment." In other words, it constitutes an action by the defendant to which the plaintiff objects, not one which the plaintiff requested and facilitated. Thus, the Vogels' (P) act of requesting service and connecting its service to that of GLEC's (D) defeats their nuisance claim, and the court of appeals agreed. However, a request for electric service does not negate the element of invasion of nuisance. The Vogels' (P) request for electric service did not include excessive stray voltage. Such stray voltage is actionable if it unreasonably interferes with a person's interest in the private use and enjoyment of land. The Vogels (P) also argued that GLEC's (D) invasion was intentional under § 825(b) since it knew the stray voltage was substantially certain to result from its conduct under the basic laws of electricity. However, it is only unreasonable levels of stray voltage that may give rise to liability for an intentional invasion. The Vogels (P) failed to demonstrate evidence that GLEC (D) had knowledge of any unreasonable levels of stray voltage being released on their farm. The Vogels (P) also argued the invasion was intentional because it was continuing. This argument failed for the same reason. Reversed.

ANALYSIS

Many jurisdictions impose an "unreasonable" requirement in nuisance laws. Such jurisdictions only hold activity actionable if the interference with the plaintiff's use and enjoyment of his property is unreasonable. Whether an activity is unreasonable is determined by weighing the expected benefits of the conduct against their anticipated costs. Restatement (Second) of Torts § 826.

Quicknotes

CONTRIBUTORY NEGLIGENCE Behavior on the part of an injured plaintiff falling below the standard of ordinary care that contributes to the defendant's negligence, resulting in the plaintiff's injury.

NUISANCE Use of property that interferes with the lawful use of another's property.

Michalson v. Nutting

Property owner (P) v. Adjoining property owner (D)

Mass. Sup. Jud. Ct., 175 N.E. 490 (1931)

NATURE OF CASE: Appeal from dismissal of bill in equity seeking mandatory and permanent injunctions.

FACT SUMMARY: The plaintiffs (P) sought a court order requiring the defendants (D) to prevent the roots of their tree from encroaching on and causing injury to the plaintiffs' (P) property.

RULE OF LAW
A property owner is not liable for damage to the adjoining property of another that is caused by the roots of a tree growing on his land.

FACTS: The plaintiffs (P) brought a bill in equity alleging that roots from a poplar tree growing on the defendants' (D) property had penetrated the plaintiffs' (P) land and had filled up sewer and drain pipes there, causing damages, and also had grown under the cement cellar of the plaintiffs' (P) house, causing the cement to crack and crumble and threatening the house's foundation. The plaintiffs (P) sought a mandatory injunction compelling the removal of the roots, a permanent injunction restraining the defendants (D) from allowing the roots to encroach on plaintiffs' (P) land, and damages. The trial court ruled that the defendants (D) were not liable for the asserted damages and dismissed the bill with costs. The state's highest court granted review.

ISSUE: Is a property owner liable for damage to the adjoining property of another that is caused by the roots of a tree growing on his land?

HOLDING AND DECISION: (Wait, J.) No. A property owner is not liable for damage to the adjoining property of another that is caused by the roots of a tree growing on his land. It is well established that a property owner has the right to grow trees on his land and is not liable to an adjoining property owner for the shade or overhanging branches that emanate from a tree(s) on his land. There is no distinction in principle between damage caused by shade and overhanging branches and the penetration of roots onto adjoining property. The neighbor's recourse is not through the courts, but in his own hands: he can cut the overhanging limbs, as well as the penetrating roots. By leaving the neighbors to work out such annoyances between themselves, the law prevents the bringing of "innumerable and, in many instances, purely vexatious" actions. Affirmed.

ANALYSIS

The court in this case found that the injury at issue was "damnum absque injuria," which is Latin for harm without legal injury. While the tree roots caused real injury, this injury did not constitute actionable nuisance because the injured neighbor could resort to self-help and destroy the roots. Presumably, such destruction could kill the tree, in which case the owner of the tree would have no legal recourse for the tree's death.

Quicknotes

MANDATORY INJUNCTION An injunction that compels a defendant either to perform an act or to refrain from doing a particular act.

PERMANENT INJUNCTION A remedy imposed by the court ordering a party to cease the conduct of a specific activity until the final disposition of the cause of action.

Fontainebleau Hotel Corp. v. Forty-Five Twenty-Five, Inc.

Expanding hotel (D) v. Neighboring hotel (P)

Fla. Dist. Ct. App., 114 So. 2d 357 (1959)

NATURE OF CASE: Suit seeking injunctive relief.

FACT SUMMARY: The Fontainebleau Hotel Corp. (D) began construction of a building addition that threatened to cast a shadow upon the sunbathing area of a hotel owned by Forty-Five Twenty-Five, Inc. (P).

RULE OF LAW

A landowner may make reasonable and lawful use of his own property as long as he does not interfere with the legal rights of his neighbors or create a nuisance.

FACTS: The Fontainebleau Hotel, owned and operated by the Fontainebleau Hotel Corp. (D), commenced construction of a 14-story addition. Forty-Five Twenty-Five, Inc. (P), owner of the Eden Roc Hotel (Eden Roc), sought to enjoin the erection of the addition, claiming that it would cast a shadow on an area which Eden Roc guests used for sunbathing. Forty-Five Twenty-Five (P) alleged that the addition had been maliciously inspired and that it violated a building ordinance and interfered with various easements owned by Forty-Five Twenty-Five (P). A chancellor, after taking evidence, granted a temporary injunction. His memorandum opinion clearly stated that the sole basis for his ruling had been "the proposition that no one has a right to use his property to the injury of another." Fontainebleau Hotel Corp. (D) appealed from the order granting the temporary injunction.

ISSUE: May a landowner make reasonable and lawful use of his own property as long as he does not interfere with the legal rights of his neighbors or create a nuisance?

HOLDING AND DECISION: (Per curiam) Yes. A landowner may make reasonable and lawful use of his own property as long as he does not interfere with the legal rights of his neighbors or create a nuisance. Even at common law, a landowner enjoyed no legal right to the free flow of light and air across his neighbor's property. Thus, the fact that the Fontainebleau's addition may block sunlight that would otherwise reach the Eden Roc does not mean that there has been, or will be, an interference with a legal right belonging to Forty-Five Twenty-Five (P). No reason is suggested for departing from the rule stated, and if its operation proves to be offensive to public policy objectives, the only recourse is through appropriate ordinances. The order granting a temporary injunction must be reversed.

ANALYSIS

As the *Fontainebleau* court noted, American jurisdictions have consistently refused to recognize an easement for the air and light that pass through neighboring properties. Theoretically, conduct that interferes with air or light could nonetheless be characterized as a nuisance. Most courts, though, seem to think of nuisances as consisting of invasions rather than mere interferences. Thus, an activity that caused excessive bright lights at inopportune times of the day would be more likely to be abated than would conduct which prevented the transmittal of rays of sunlight. A further complication is the fact that courts are reluctant to find that a condition constitutes a nuisance if its only undesirable effect is to create aesthetic displeasure.

Quicknotes

DOCTRINE OF "ANCIENT LIGHTS" A doctrine descended from English common law that granted an interest in land for the unobstructed passage of light and air after 20 years of uninterrupted use.

EASEMENT OF "LIGHTS" An interest in land granted for the unobstructed passage of light and air, from English common law.

INJUNCTIVE RELIEF A court order issued as a remedy, requiring a person to do, or prohibiting that person from doing, a specific act.

NUISANCE Use of property that interferes with the lawful use of another's property.

SIC UTERE TUO UT ALIENUM NON LADEAS One's use of property should be done so as not to injure another.

Rogers v. Elliott

Sunstroke victim (P) v. Church custodian (D)

Mass. Sup. Jud. Ct., 15 N.E. 768 (1888)

NATURE OF CASE: Suit to recover damages for harm caused by an alleged nuisance.

FACT SUMMARY: Elliott (D), the custodian of a church, insisted upon ringing the church bell despite notice from a physician that the noise from the bell caused Rogers (P) to suffer physical harm.

RULE OF LAW

Whether or not a particular activity constitutes a nuisance depends upon the way in which it would affect a person of ordinary sensitivity and temperament.

FACTS: Elliott (D) was custodian and manager of a Roman Catholic Church in a small Massachusetts town. One of his activities consisted of ringing a bell in the church each day. In a house not far from the church, Rogers (P) was recovering from a severe case of sunstroke. After Elliott (D) rang the bell on Saturday, Rogers (P) suffered convulsions that his physician attributed to the noise from the bell. The doctor visited Elliott (D) and informed him that the ringing of the bell the next day would again affect Rogers's (P) physical condition, but Elliott (D) replied that he had no love for Rogers (P) and would continue to ring the bell even if his own mother were sick. The following day, Elliott's (D) ringing of the bell caused further damage to Rogers (P), who sued Elliott (D) on the theory that the bell ringing constituted a nuisance.

ISSUE: May the hypersensitivity of one particular complainant be taken into account in determining whether or not an activity constitutes a nuisance?

HOLDING AND DECISION: (Knowlton, J.) No. Whether or not a particular activity constitutes a nuisance depends upon the way in which it would affect a person of ordinary sensitivity and temperament. Property may be put to legitimate and proper use, and what is a lawful use must be determined by reference to an objective standard. If the effects upon unusually sensitive individuals were taken into account, the permissibility of a particular land use might be subject to daily change, depending upon the identities and levels of tolerance of the people who were to be found in the vicinity at a given moment. Obviously, no semblance of certainty or continuity can be achieved unless it is the effect upon a normal person that is used as a standard for measuring the propriety of an activity. The presence of express malice may have a bearing on the issue, but this case presents insufficient facts from which to infer express malice. Thus, the case involves merely the protests of a single hypersensitive individual who is not entitled to relief in the absence of a showing that the conduct complained of was unreasonably objectionable even to the average person. Judgment on the verdict.

ANALYSIS

The rule ordinarily applied in tort cases is that the defendant "takes the plaintiff as he finds him." In other words, the defense that the plaintiff was hypersensitive or was particularly susceptible to injury usually is unavailing. In the context of nuisance cases, however, the rule of *Rogers v. Elliott* is almost always recognized and applied. The *Rogers v. Elliott* holding seems particularly appropriate in those cases where the individual of normal sensibilities need not be a merely imaginary creature because several such people actually exist in close proximity to the hypersensitive plaintiff and the defendant and have offered no objection to the defendant's conduct.

Quicknotes

HYPERSENSITIVE PLAINTIFFS In tort law, a plaintiff who has the potential to suffer a greater degree of unforeseeable injury than an ordinary person due to their unique or individual nature (*i.e.*, the eggshell-skull plaintiff) thus increasing the damages owing to defendant, who will be held liable for the entire range of injury; put another way, the defendant "takes the plaintiff as he finds him."

MALICE The intention to commit an unlawful act without justification or excuse.

NUISANCE Use of property that interferes with the lawful use of another's property.

Ensign v. Walls

Homeowner (P) v. Dog breeder (D)

Mich. Sup. Ct., 34 N.W.2d 549 (1948)

NATURE OF CASE: Suit to enjoin an alleged nuisance.

FACT SUMMARY: Ensign (P) and others (P) claimed that Walls's (D) dog-breeding business constituted a nuisance. Walls (D) had operated the business for years before most of those protesting had moved into the neighborhood.

RULE OF LAW

The fact that an alleged nuisance existed long before those objecting to it moved into the vicinity does not necessarily prevent a court from ordering it abated.

FACTS: For some years, Walls (D) had bred St. Bernard dogs in the city of Detroit. Ensign (P) and other nearby property owners (P) sued for an injunction preventing Walls (D) from continuing to operate. It was alleged that her business created noise, offensive odors, and a vermin problem, and that dogs occasionally escaped and wandered around the neighborhood. Walls (D) denied that her activities constituted a nuisance, and also claimed that an injunction should not issue since she had operated her business since 1926 and had invested considerable money in it, while many of those who objected to her activities had only recently moved into the neighborhood. The lower court ruled that an injunction should issue, and Walls (D) appealed.

ISSUE: Does the fact that an alleged nuisance existed long before those objecting to it moved into the vicinity necessarily prevent a court from ordering it abated?

HOLDING AND DECISION: (Carr, J.) No. The fact that an alleged nuisance existed long before those objecting to it moved into the vicinity does not necessarily prevent a court from ordering it abated. That the nuisance predated the appearance of the protestors is but one factor to be considered in determining whether the condition should be abated. It is appropriate to note that an activity that presents no problems in an isolated locale may become offensive when the surrounding neighborhood becomes more densely populated. In such circumstances, public policy mandates that operations injurious to health and comfort are to be excluded from populous areas. Ample evidence supports the conclusion that Walls's (D) business constituted a nuisance, and it was within the discretion of the trial judge to grant injunctive relief. Walls (D) argued that a complete shutdown of her operations was an unnecessarily drastic measure, but no evidence has been presented, which tends to show that Walls (D) could conduct her business without causing a nuisance. Therefore, the decree affording injunctive relief must be affirmed.

ANALYSIS

The result of *Ensign v. Walls* is consistent with that reached by numerous other courts. That is, the defense that the plaintiff "came to the nuisance" rarely prevails. A minority of courts reason that if the nuisance predated the arrival of the plaintiff, relief should be denied on the theory that the plaintiff knowingly assumed whatever hardships result from the nuisance. The majority rule, however, is rooted in the notion that a landowner enjoys a right to the use and control of his property and can never be deprived of that right even by a neighbor whose unreasonable land use began long ago.

Quicknotes

DAMNUM ABSQUE INJURIA When an injury is sustained but the law affords no means of recovery.

INJUNCTIVE RELIEF A court order issued as a remedy, requiring a person to do, or prohibiting that person from doing, a specific act.

NUISANCE Use of property that interferes with the lawful use of another's property.

Boomer v. Atlantic Cement Co.

Landowner (P) v. Cement plant (D)

N.Y. Ct. App., 257 N.E.2d 870 (1970)

NATURE OF CASE: Action for an injunction to enjoin maintenance of a nuisance and for damages.

FACT SUMMARY: Property owners (P) sued a cement plant (D), alleging that pollution emanating from the plant had injured their lands. The trial court refused an injunction, but did authorize successive actions for damages.

RULE OF LAW

Although a nuisance will be enjoined even when a marked disparity is shown in economic consequence between the effect of the injunction and the effect of the nuisance, if the practical effect of the injunction will be to close a production plant, a court will condition on equitable grounds the continuance of the injunction on the payment of permanent damages.

FACTS: Atlantic Cement Co., Inc. (Atlantic) (D) operated a large cement plant near Albany, New York, in which it had invested $45,000,000 and employed over 300 workers. A group of neighboring landowners (P) brought actions for injunction and damages against Atlantic (D), alleging injury to their property from dirt, smoke, and vibration emanating from the plant. The trial court held that a nuisance existed but denied the issuance of an injunction. Rather, it awarded the landowners (P) damages up to the time of trial, thus permitting them to maintain successive actions at law for damages thereafter as further injury was incurred. Atlantic (D) appealed.

ISSUE: If the practical effect of an injunction will be to close a production plant, will a court condition on equitable grounds the continuance of the injunction on the payment of permanent damages?

HOLDING AND DECISION: (Bergan, J.) Yes. If the practical effect of an injunction will be to close a production plant, a court will condition on equitable grounds the continuance of the injunction on the payment of permanent damages. Courts should be wary of using a decision in private litigation as a purposeful mechanism to achieve direct public objectives greatly beyond the rights and interests before the court. The judicial establishment is neither equipped in the limited nature of any judgment it can pronounce nor prepared to lay down and implement an effective policy for the elimination of air pollution. This is a problem government alone is to resolve. Although an injunction should not be denied because the damage to a plaintiff is slight as compared to the defendant's expense of abating a nuisance, to follow this rule literally in this case would have the immediately drastic effect of closing the plant. One alternative would be to grant the injunction but postpone its effect to a specified future date to give opportunity for technical advances to permit Atlantic (D) to eliminate the nuisance. However, it is unlikely that Atlantic (D) by itself will be able to eliminate its pollution in the near future. The rate of the research is simply beyond its control. A better alternative would be to grant the injunction unless Atlantic (D) pays the landowners (P) permanent damages as may be fixed by the court. An amount of $185,000 would fairly compensate the landowners (P) for all past and future injury they have and will suffer. Reversed and remitted.

DISSENT: (Jasen, J.) The majority has in effect licensed a continuing wrong. Furthermore, once permanent damages are assessed and paid, the incentive to alleviate the wrong would be eliminated. Moreover, Atlantic (D) should not be allowed, as a private party, inverse condemnation; the public is not being benefited. Finally, the landowners (P) are being forced to accept servitude on their land for the benefit of a private party.

ANALYSIS

In determining whether or not to enjoin a nuisance, a court "may take into consideration the relative economic hardship which will result to the parties from the granting or denial of the injunction, the good faith or intentional misconduct of each, and the interest of the general public in the continuation of the defendant's enterprise." Prosser, *Law of Torts* (1971 4th ed.) ch. 15, §90 p. 604. Another factor, as this case illustrates, is the financial investment each party has made in his land.

Quicknotes

ABATEMENT A decrease or lessening of something; in equity, a suspension or dismissal of a cause of action.

INJUNCTION A remedy imposed by the court ordering a party to cease the conduct of a specific activity.

INVERSE CONDEMNATION The taking of private property for public use so as to impair or decrease the value of property near or adjacent to, but not a part of, the property taken.

NUISANCE Use of property that interferes with the lawful use of another's property.

Anonymous

[Parties not identified.]

Y.B. Mich. 27 Hen. 8, f. 27, pl. 10 (1536)

NATURE OF CASE: Action for damages arising from an obstruction in the road preventing passage.

FACT SUMMARY: The plaintiff sued the defendant for obstructing the King's highway.

RULE OF LAW

Complaints regarding an obstruction on the King's highway are to be brought to the King, not the courts, for resolution.

FACTS: The plaintiff sued the defendant for causing an obstruction on the King's highway that prevented the plaintiff from passing through, whereas previous to the obstruction the plaintiff was able to pass.

ISSUE: Did the plaintiff bring his case to the proper venue?

HOLDING AND DECISION: (Baldwin, C.J.) No. The plaintiff did not bring his action to the proper venue. It is up to the King to resolve matters involving nuisances on his highways, not the courts. Many people could be harmed by the defendant's actions. Therefore, if we allow the plaintiff's action, the defendant could theoretically be punished 100 times over for the same malfeasance. The plaintiff needs to go tell the King about his concerns. Judgment for the defendant.

DISSENT: (Fitzherbert, J.) If an individual is harmed, above and beyond the normal harm that everyone experiences by such a nuisance on the King's highway, then that individual is entitled to bring a private action. The plaintiff in the present action was inconvenienced more than any other person and he, therefore, should be allowed to have this action for his special harm.

ANALYSIS

In present day, public nuisances are still usually resolved via administrative regulation, and private actions are maintainable only for special harms.

Quicknotes

PUBLIC NUISANCE An activity that unreasonably interferes with a right common to the overall public.

Burgess v. M/V TAMANO

Class action representative (P) v. Oil tanker (D)

370 F. Supp. 247 (D. Me. 1973)

NATURE OF CASE: Motion to dismiss certain class actions for damages for negligence, unseaworthiness, trespass, and nuisance arising from an oil spill.

FACT SUMMARY: After 100,000 gallons of oil spilled from the oil tanker M/V TAMANO (D), several groups of plaintiffs, including commercial fishermen (P), commercial clam diggers (P), and owners of beach businesses (P), brought class actions against the tanker (D), its owners (D), the state of Maine (D), and a variety of other defendants for damages. The M/V TAMANO (D) and other defendants moved to dismiss the actions of these particular classes on the grounds their economic interests were not legally cognizable.

RULE OF LAW

A plaintiff may recover in tort for the invasion of a public right only if the plaintiff has suffered damage different in kind from that sustained by the public generally.

FACTS: After striking an outcropping, the oil tanker M/V TAMANO (D) discharged around 100,000 gallons of oil into the coastal waters of Maine (D) that also washed onto beaches. Several groups of plaintiffs, including commercial fishermen (P), commercial clam diggers (P), and owners of beach businesses (P) that depended on tourist trade brought class actions in federal district court against the tanker (D), its owners (D), the state of Maine (D), and a variety of other defendants for damages, asserting liability on theories of negligence, unseaworthiness, trespass, and nuisance. The M/V TAMANO (D) and other defendants moved to dismiss the actions of these particular classes on the grounds that their economic interests were not legally cognizable because none of the classes had any property interest in the coastal waters and marine life or shores that claimed to have been injured by the spill.

ISSUE: May a plaintiff recover in tort for the invasion of a public right only if the plaintiff has suffered damage different in kind from that sustained by the public generally?

HOLDING AND DECISION: (Gignoux, J.) Yes. A plaintiff may recover in tort for the invasion of a public right only if the plaintiff has suffered damage different in kind from that sustained by the public generally. Here, the title to the affected coastal waters and marine life is vested in Maine (D), and individual citizens have no separate property interest therein. Additionally, the right to fish or to harvest clams in Maine's (D) coastal waters is not the private right of any individual but is a public right held by Maine (D) in trust for the common benefit of the people. It is well-established law that a private individual can recover in tort for invasion of a public right only if the individual has suffered damage particular to that individual, i.e., damage different in kind, rather than simply in degree, from that sustained by the public generally. Applying these principles to the case at bar, it is clear the commercial fishermen (P) and clam diggers (P) have alleged such "particular" damage, whereas the owners of beach businesses only indirectly affected by the spill have not. The fishermen (P) and clam diggers (P) have a special interest, apart from that of the public generally, to take fish and harvest clams from Maine's (D) coastal waters. Their injury has resulted from the oil spill's alleged interference with their direct exercise of the public right to fish and to dig clams. By contrast, the owners of beach businesses (P) do not assert such direct interference. Instead, they complain of losing customers, which results only indirectly from the pollution of the coastal waters and beaches in which they do not have a property interest. Although in some instances their damage may be greater in degree, the injury of which they complain, which is derivative from that of the public at large, is common to all businesses and residents of the beach area. Accordingly, the motion is granted as to the owners of beach businesses (P) but denied as to the commercial fishermen (P) and clam diggers (P).

ANALYSIS

In this case, as in numerous other cases in which commercial fishermen using public waters have sought damages for the pollution or other tortious invasion of those waters, and have been permitted to recover, the court applies the general principle that a pecuniary loss to a plaintiff will be regarded as different in kind where the plaintiff has an established business making a commercial use of the public right with which the defendant interferes. Thus, to the extent they can establish their pecuniary losses, the commercial fishermen (P) and clam diggers (P) should be entitled to recover for the same.

Continued on next page.

Quicknotes

CLASS ACTION A suit commenced by a representative on behalf of an ascertainable group that is too large to appear in court, shares a commonality of interests, and will benefit from a successful result.

NEGLIGENCE Conduct falling below the standard of care that a reasonable person would demonstrate under similar conditions.

NUISANCE An unlawful use of property that interferes with the lawful use of another's property.

PECUNIARY LOSS Loss of money or the loss of something of monetary value.

TRESPASS Unlawful interference with, or damage to, the real or personal property of another.

City of New York v. Chevron Corp.

Municipality (P) v. Multinational oil company (D)

993 F.3d 81 (2d Cir. 2021)

NATURE OF CASE: Appeal from dismissal of state-law nuisance action seeking to hold oil companies liable for damages resulting from greenhouse gas emissions and global warming.

FACT SUMMARY: The City of New York (the City) (P) sought, under state nuisance law, to hold multinational oil companies (the Producers) (D) liable for damages resulting from greenhouse gas emissions and global warming. The Producers (D) asserted that such a state tort action would conflict with federal common law, which, in turn, was displaced in this area by the Clean Air Act, so that the City's (P) state law claim had to be dismissed.

RULE OF LAW

A plaintiff is precluded by federal common law from bringing a state-law nuisance action to hold an oil company liable for damages resulting from greenhouse gas emissions and global warming.

FACTS: It is almost undisputed by scientists that the use of fossil fuels, and the concomitant emissions of greenhouse gases, has contributed greatly to global warming. In turn, the rise in the Earth's surface temperatures has led to rising sea levels, among other environmental impacts. A city like the City of New York (the City) (P), which has a 520-mile coastline, is exceptionally vulnerable to such rising sea levels. In an effort to mitigate this impact, and other global-warming impacts, the City (P) launched a $20 billion-plus climate resiliency program meant to protect the public and its property. Notwithstanding that every person who uses gas and electricity contributes to global warming, the City (P) brought suit pursuant to New York state nuisance law against the largest fossil fuel producers worldwide since the mid-nineteenth century (collectively, the Producers) (D)), asserting that its taxpayers should not have to shoulder the burden of financing the City's (P) preparations to mitigate the effects of global warming, and suggesting the Producers (D) were primarily responsible for global warming and should bear the brunt of these costs. The City (P) also asserted that the Producers (D) have known for decades that their fossil fuel products pose a severe risk to the planet's climate, and the City (P) alleged that, despite that knowledge, the Producers (D) downplayed the risks and continued to sell massive quantities of fossil fuels, which has caused and will continue to cause significant changes to the City's (P) climate and landscape. Although the Producers (D) have done nothing illegal by producing and selling fossil fuels, the City (P) believes that it is appropriate to shift the costs of protecting the City (P) from climate change impacts back onto the companies that have done nearly all they could to create this "existential threat." The Producers (D) defended, in part, by moving to dismiss on the grounds that the City's state-law claims were displaced by federal common law, and that even though federal common law in this area was displaced as to domestic greenhouse gas emissions by the federal Clean Air Act, an intricate regulatory regime intended to protect and enhance the quality of the nation's air resources and administered by the Environmental Protection Agency (EPA), the Clean Air Act's displacement of federal common law did not resuscitate the City's (P) state-law claims. [The federal district court granted the Producers' (D) motions to dismiss.] The Second Circuit Court of Appeals granted review.

ISSUE: Is a plaintiff precluded by federal common law from bringing a state-law nuisance action to hold an oil company liable for damages resulting from greenhouse gas emissions and global warming?

HOLDING AND DECISION: (Sullivan, J.) Yes. A plaintiff is precluded by federal common law from bringing a state-law nuisance action to hold an oil company liable for damages resulting from greenhouse gas emissions and global warming. Federal common law exists in only the few and restricted enclaves where a federal court is compelled to consider federal questions that cannot be answered from federal statutes alone, and, once Congress speaks directly to those questions, the need for such an unusual exercise of lawmaking by federal courts disappears. Federal common law, in other words, is a "necessary expedient" that permits federal courts to address issues of national concern until Congress provides a more permanent solution. Where federal common law exists, state law cannot be used. For over a century, a mostly unbroken string of cases has applied federal law to disputes involving interstate air or water pollution. This is because such quarrels often implicate two federal interests that are incompatible with the application of state law. Here, the City (P) does not seek to hold the Producers (D) liable for the effects of emissions released in New York, or even in New York's neighboring states. Instead, the City (P) seeks to hold the Producers (D) liable, under New York law, for the effects of emissions made around the globe over the past several hundred years. Such a sprawling case is simply beyond the limits of state law. First, a substantial damages award like the one requested by the City (P) would effectively regulate the Producers'

Continued on next page.

(D) behavior far beyond New York's borders because any actions the Producers (D) would have to take to mitigate their liability would have to take effect in every state and every country on the planet. Because this would implicate the conflicting rights of states and the nation's relations with foreign nations, this case is a quintessential example of a case that should be decided under federal common law. The City (P) protests that it is not seeking to regulate the Producers (D) at all; however, such an assertion ignores economic reality and that a damages award of the magnitude sought by the City (P) is effective, de facto, regulation. Undoubtedly, even though such an award would regulate cross-border emissions in an indirect and roundabout manner, it would regulate them nonetheless by forcing them to either cease global production altogether, or to develop a new means of pollution control. For these reasons, the City's (P) claims must be brought under federal common law. However, this conclusion itself is problematic, because the Clean Air Act preempts federal common-law claims concerned with domestic greenhouse gas emissions, as Congress addressed in that legislation the issues raised in this dispute concerning domestic emissions. Given that the Clean Air Act preempts federal common law in this area, the City (P) argues that its state-law action is revived unless specifically preempted by the Clean Air Act. However, this position is difficult to square with the fact that federal common law governed this issue in the first place. Affirmed.

ANALYSIS

In reaching its conclusion that the Clean Air Act displaces the federal common law of nuisance, the Second Circuit observed that Congress's choosing to preempt the federal common law of nuisance with a well-defined and robust statutory and regulatory scheme of environmental law was by no means surprising, given that numerous courts have bemoaned the "vague" and "indeterminate" standards attached to nuisance law. In *Int'l Paper Co. v. Ouellette*, 479 U.S. 481, 496 (1987), for example, the U.S. Supreme Court observed that "[t]here is perhaps no more impenetrable jungle in the entire law than that which surrounds the word 'nuisance'" (quoting W. Keeton et al., *Prosser and Keeton on Law of Torts* 616 (5th ed. 1984)). And, in *North Carolina ex rel. Cooper v. Tenn. Valley Auth.*, 615 F.3d 291, 302 (4th Cir. 2010), the court reasoned that "while public nuisance law doubtless encompasses environmental concerns, it does so at such a level of generality as to provide almost no standard of application." The Second Circuit, agreeing that such an elastic standard is especially ill-suited to address a technically complex area of the law such as environmental law, observed that it made far more sense to entrust the complex balancing of interests that climate change demands to an expert agency such as the EPA.

Quicknotes

FEDERAL COMMON LAW A body of law developed through the judicial decisions of the federal courts as opposed to the legislative process.

NUISANCE An unlawful use of property that interferes with the lawful use of another's property.

PREEMPTION Doctrine holding that matters of national interest take precedence over matters of local interest; federal law takes precedence over state law where federal law exists, as in federal common law, or where the clear and manifest purpose of Congress in a statute is to displace state law.

City & County of San Francisco v. Purdue Pharma L.P.

Municipality (P) v. Pharmaceutical company (D)

620 F. Supp. 3d 936 (N.D. Cal. 2022)

NATURE OF CASE: Action for public nuisance.

FACT SUMMARY: The City of San Francisco (San Francisco) (P), plagued by the ravages of the opioid epidemic, contended that Walgreens (D), the largest retail pharmacy chain in the city, contributed to San Francisco's (P) opioid crisis by failing to conduct adequate due diligence when its pharmacies dispensed prescription opioids, and, therefore, contributed to the opioid public nuisance.

RULE OF LAW

A retail pharmacy chain contributes to a municipality's opioid public nuisance by failing to conduct adequate due diligence when dispensing opioid prescriptions in that municipality.

FACTS: The City of San Francisco (San Francisco) (P) has been plagued by the ravages of an opioid epidemic, defined by high rates of opioid abuse and addiction throughout the city, with the number of people abusing, and dying from, opioids accelerating. This has strained San Francisco's (P) hospitals, has forced streets, parks, and public spaces to close, has exacerbated crime and homelessness, and has forced San Francisco (P) to devote significant resources to a multiprong fight against the opioid epidemic. Walgreens (D) is the largest retail pharmacy chain in San Francisco (P). For 15 years, Walgreens (D) distributed and dispensed over one hundred million prescription opioid pills in the city. The federal Controlled Substances Act (CSA) and its implementing regulations impose duties on distributors and dispensers of prescription opioids. In exchange for the privilege of distributing and dispensing prescription opioids, Walgreens (D) has regulatory obligations to take reasonable steps to prevent the drugs from being diverted and harming the public. San Francisco (P) brought an action for abatement of a public nuisance against Walgreens (D) in federal district court, alleging that Walgreen (D) breached those duties by failing to conduct adequate due diligence, as required by the CSA, and, thereby, contributed to the city's opioid crisis, a public nuisance. San Francisco (P) adduced evidence that showed that for 15 years Walgreens (D) did not provide its pharmacists with sufficient time, staffing, or resources to perform due diligence on opioid prescriptions, and that pharmacists experienced constant pressure to fill prescriptions as quickly as possible as well as a shortage of resources to review them before dispensing. The district court considered the merits of the case.

ISSUE: Does a retail pharmacy chain contribute to a municipality's opioid public nuisance by failing to conduct adequate due diligence when dispensing opioid prescriptions in that municipality?

HOLDING AND DECISION: (Breyer, J.) Yes. A retail pharmacy chain contributes to a municipality's opioid public nuisance by failing to conduct adequate due diligence when dispensing opioid prescriptions in that municipality. San Francisco (P) proved that the opioid epidemic, defined by high rates of opioid abuse, addiction, and overdoses, constitutes a public nuisance. It further proved that the opioid epidemic interferes with all five categories of public rights recognized by the state's highest court—"the public health, the public safety, the public peace, the public comfort or the public convenience." In this regard, to succeed on its public nuisance claim, San Francisco (P) had the burden of proving by a preponderance of the evidence that Walgreens (D) had knowledge that its unreasonable conduct caused a substantial interference with a right common to the public. As to unreasonable conduct, conduct encompasses any action that assists in creating a system that causes an interference with a public right. Conduct is unreasonable if it violates a statute, ordinance, or administrative regulation, and is also unreasonable if the gravity of the harm outweighs the social utility of the defendant's conduct. San Francisco (P) proved that Walgreens (D) violated the CSA for 15 years, and, thereby engaged in unreasonable conduct sufficient to support a public nuisance claim. The CSA and its implementing regulations strike a bargain with registrants. In exchange for the privilege of dispensing powerful controlled substances, pharmacies are required to take reasonable steps to prevent those substances from being diverted and harming the public. Here, Walgreen (D) failed to take those reasonable steps. Further, Walgreens (D) acted with knowledge of the harm resulting from its unreasonable conduct. The CSA regulations that applied to Walgreens (D) were put in place precisely because of the harms that result when opioids are diverted. Based on the regulatory scheme alone, it is reasonable to infer that Walgreens "must have known" that failing to prevent diversion of opioids would result in harm in San Francisco (P). Walgreen's (D) unreasonable conduct was a substantial factor in bringing about the public nuisance—the city's opioid

Continued on next page.

epidemic. With regard to factual causation, San Francisco (P) presented sufficient evidence to permit inferences that support a finding of causation in fact. Regarding proximate causation, San Francisco (P) proved that the numerous forms of harm resulting from Walgreens' (D) unlawful dispensing of illegitimate opioid prescriptions were foreseeable; it is well known that a lack of reasonable care in the handling, distribution, and administration of controlled substances can foreseeably harm the individuals who take them. In fact, that's why those substances are controlled in the first place—overuse or misuse can lead to addictions and long-term health problems. Because Walgreens (D) substantially interfered with public rights, it is susceptible to San Francisco's (P) public nuisance claim. A public nuisance is one that affects at the same time an entire community or neighborhood, or any considerable number of persons, although the extent of the annoyance or damage inflicted upon individuals may be unequal. In other words, public nuisances are offenses against, or interferences with, the exercise of rights common to the public. Here, it is clear that Walgreens (D) significantly contributed to the public opioid nuisance and ensuing public harms, including interference with public peace, comfort, and convenience. Walgreens (D) argued that a public nuisance claim requires a plaintiff to identify discrete conduct or conditions that are abatable, and that every state public nuisance decision involved well-defined conduct like emitting noxious odors or a well-defined hazardous condition like water pollution or lead paint in home. Thus, Walgreens (D) argued that to be actionable, a nuisance claim must involve discrete conduct or conditions that can be remedied through abatement. The court rejected this argument, observing that the state courts had repeatedly rejected the "ability to abate" argument made by Walgreens (D), and that those courts held that liability for nuisance did not hinge on whether the defendant owned, possessed, or controlled the property, nor on whether the defendant was in a position to abate the nuisance; instead, the critical question was whether the defendant created or assisted in the creation of the nuisance. For all these reasons, San Francisco (P) has proven by a preponderance of the evidence that Walgreens substantially contributed to the public nuisance in San Francisco (P). A subsequent trial will be held to determine the extent to which Walgreens (D) must abate the public nuisance that it helped to create.

ANALYSIS

Courts in other jurisdictions have expressed concerns about extending the law of nuisance to the sale or distribution of opioids. These courts have reasoned that nuisance law traditionally applies only in the context of conduct that interferes with public property or resources, and these courts have also expressed the concern that applying the law of public nuisance to the sale, marketing, and distribution of products would invite litigation against any product with a known risk of harm. The district court in this case rejected those concerns, noting that unlike nuisance law in other states, California law (which the district court is required to apply) has never imposed such a requirement that there be some form of injury to land or property. The court also observed that California common law consistently has defined nuisance in broad terms that encompass injuries to health, or acts that are indecent or offensive to the senses or obstructions to the free use of property in any manner that might interference with the comfortable enjoyment of life or property. The court further concluded that this case did not raise concern that "floodgates" of litigation would open against a company that sells any product with a known risk of harm, reasoning that San Francisco's (P) case against Walgreens (D) was not based on dispensing controlled substances with known risks of harm—but instead was based on Walgreens' (D) multi-year violation of federal regulations that were put in place to prevent the controlled substances that Walgreens (D) dispenses from causing harm. Thus, in the court's view, it was Walgreens' (D) conduct in dispensing opioids—not the opioids themselves—that was the fundamental cause of the harm.

Quicknotes

CAUSE IN FACT The event without which an injury would not have been incurred.

CONTROLLED SUBSTANCE A drug whose medical distribution is regulated by the federal government; certain classifications are unlawful.

NUISANCE An unlawful use of property that interferes with the lawful use of another's property.

PROXIMATE CAUSE The natural sequence of events without which an injury would not have been sustained.

PUBLIC NUISANCE An activity that unreasonably interferes with a right common to the overall public.

Ira S. Bushey & Sons, Inc. v. United States

Drydock owner (P) v. Coast Guard (D)

398 F.2d 167 (2d Cir. 1968)

NATURE OF CASE: Appeal in an action for damages based on employer's vicarious liability.

FACT SUMMARY: While returning to his docked United States Coast Guard ship, Lane, an intoxicated seaman, opened the drydock valves, causing both the ship and Ira S. Bushey & Sons, Inc.'s (P) drydock to partially sink.

RULE OF LAW

An employer is vicariously liable for the reasonably foreseeable conduct of its employees performed within the scope of employment, even when such conduct was not motivated by a purpose of serving the employer.

FACTS: Lane, an intoxicated seaman, was returning at night from shore leave to his ship, a United States Coast Guard vessel in drydock. However, before going aboard, Lane opened a valve that controlled the flooding of the drydock tanks. As a result, both the ship and the Ira S. Bushey & Sons, Inc. (Bushey) (P) drydock were damaged. Bushey (P) sought damages based on the Government's (D) vicarious liability for Lane's actions. The Government (D) denied liability, relying on § 228(1) of the Restatement (Second) of Agency, which stated that the conduct of a servant is within the scope of his employment only if it is actuated at least in part by a purpose to serve the master. However, the trial court rejected that argument and held that an expansion of the employer's liability would serve the public policy of a more intensive screening of employees and allocation of resources. The Government (D) appealed.

ISSUE: Is an employer vicariously liable for the reasonably foreseeable conduct of its employees within the scope of their employment, even when such conduct was not motivated by a purpose of serving the employer?

HOLDING AND DECISION: (Friendly, J.) Yes. An employer is vicariously liable for the reasonably foreseeable conduct of its employees performed within the scope of employment, even when such conduct was not motivated by a purpose of serving the employer. Although courts have traditionally gone to great lengths to find that the motive of the negligent employee was to serve the master, we believe that this "motive test" can be highly artificial. In the instant case, while surely Lane was not serving the Government (D) in his destructive action, nevertheless his conduct was not so "unforeseeable" as to make it unfair to charge the Government (D) with responsibility. It was surely foreseeable that sailors will return to their ships in an intoxicated state and that intoxicated crew members, in crossing the drydock, might intentionally or negligently damage it. Such an allocation of a reasonably foreseeable risk is fair, and the Government (D) must bear the loss. Affirmed.

ANALYSIS

Although the doctrine of respondeat superior enjoys a virtually unquestioned acceptance in all common-law jurisdictions, nevertheless, writers have usually been unable to identify and to defend its precise rationale. Much effort has been expended to place the stringent rules of respondeat superior within the traditional negligence framework. Young B. Smith, "Frolic and Detour," 23 *Colum. L. Rev.* 444, 445-456 (1923), listed nine rationales for vicarious liability: control, profit, revenge, carefulness and choice, identification, evidence, indulgence, danger, and satisfaction. However, he then concluded that none of them could account for the doctrine. The profit rationale would seem to be the most reasonable. Simply stated, it holds that just as the employer gains from his worker's activities, so too should he bear the losses from those activities.

Quicknotes

FORESEEABILITY A reasonable expectation that an act or omission would result in injury.

VICARIOUS LIABILITY The imputed liability of one party for the unlawful acts of another.

Search v. Uber Technologies, Inc.

Rideshare service passenger (P) v. Rideshare company (D)

128 F. Supp. 3d 222 (D.D.C. 2015)

NATURE OF CASE: Motion to dismiss causes of action for, inter alia, negligent hiring, training, and supervision; and negligence under respondeat superior and apparent-agency theories.

FACT SUMMARY: After Erik Search (P) was stabbed multiple times by Yohannes Deresse (D), the driver of a car that Search (P) had requested using Uber Technologies, Inc.'s (Uber's) (D) rideshare app on his phone, Search (P) contended that Deresse (D) was Uber's (D) employee and agent, and Search (P) sought to hold Uber (D) liable for the injuries inflicted by Deresse (D) under several tort theories. Uber (D) contended that Deresse (D) was not Uber's (D) employee, but, instead, was an independent contractor.

RULE OF LAW

(1) To state a claim for negligent hiring, a plaintiff must allege specific facts from which an inference can be drawn that the employer did not conduct a reasonable background investigation, and that such an investigation would have uncovered a reason not to hire the alleged tortfeasor.

(2) A plaintiff states a claim for vicarious liability under the doctrine of respondeat superior by alleging specific facts from which an inference can be drawn that there was an employer-employee relationship between the party sought to be held liable and the alleged tortfeasor, and that the tortfeasor committed a tortious act within the scope of the tortfeasor's employment.

(3) A plaintiff states a claim for apparent agency by alleging specific facts from which an inference can be drawn that an independent contractor, as an agent of the principal that hired the independent contractor, had "apparent authority" as a consequence of the principal's placing the agent in such a position as to mislead third persons into believing that the agent was clothed with authority that in fact the agent did not possess.

FACTS: Using Uber Technologies, Inc.'s (Uber's) (D) ride-share app on his phone, Erik Search (P) requested a car to transport him and his friends. The car that arrived was driven by Yohannes Deresse (D). Immediately following the group's entry into the car, Deresse (D) began to act erratically. Uncomfortable with Deresse's (D) behavior, Search (P) and his companions exited the vehicle and began walking away. Deresse (D) followed them out of the car and began to verbally harass them. In response, Search (P) told Deresse (D) to leave them alone, and that they did not feel safe riding with him. Deresse (D) then pulled out a knife and stabbed Search (P) multiple times in his chest and arm. Search (P) sustained severe injuries during the course of the brutal attack, requiring him to undergo CT scans, x-rays, surgical exploration of the chest wound, diagnostic laparoscopy, cauterization, and muscle reconstruction with sutures and staples, and, in addition, Search (P) suffered pain, mental anguish, humiliation, and indignity as a result of the assault. Search (P) brought suit against Deresse (D) and Uber (D) in state court, alleging various state-law tort claims, including negligent hiring, training, and supervision; and negligence under respondeat superior and apparent-agency theories. Uber (D) removed the suit to federal court and moved to dismiss all causes of action brought by Search (P). Uber (D) denied that Deresse (D) was its employee or agent, asserting instead that it is not a transportation company but a technology company that acts as a conduit between transportation providers and passengers. Uber (D) also claimed that Deresse (D) was an independent contractor who provided transportation. In support of his claim, Search (P) alleged that Uber (P) screens new drivers, dictates the fares they may charge, and pays such drivers weekly. He also alleged that upon threat of termination, Uber (D) subjects its drivers to a host of specific requirements, including, inter alia, the use of the Uber (D) app, standards for the cleanliness and mechanical functioning of their cars, rules regarding tipping, minimum timeframes and acceptance rates for ride requests, and display of the Uber (D) logo. Search(P) also alleged that Uber (D), through several forms of media, such as its mobile app and its website, represented to customers that Uber (D) was "your private driver," that it subjected its drivers to rigorous screening procedures before hiring them, and that it continued to monitor those drivers after they were hired. Uber (D), relying entirely on its User Agreement, responded that it could not have been clearer that Deresse (D) was not its agent and that it was unreasonable for Search (P) to believe otherwise, since the agreement included an exculpatory provision whereby Uber (D) clearly, unequivocally, and specifically stated that Deresse (D) was not its agent. The district court considered and decided Uber's (D) motion to dismiss.

Continued on next page.

ISSUE:

(1) To state a claim for negligent hiring, must a plaintiff allege specific facts from which an inference can be drawn that the employer did not conduct a reasonable background investigation, and that such an investigation would have uncovered a reason not to hire the alleged tortfeasor?

(2) Does a plaintiff state a claim for vicarious liability under the doctrine of respondeat superior by alleging specific facts from which an inference can be drawn that there was an employer-employee relationship between the party sought to be held liable and the alleged tortfeasor, and that the tortfeasor committed a tortious act within the scope of the tortfeasor's employment?

(3) Does a plaintiff state a claim for apparent agency by alleging specific facts from which an inference can be drawn that an independent contractor, as an agent of the principal that hired the independent contractor, had "apparent authority" as a consequence of the principal's placing the agent in such a position as to mislead third persons into believing that the agent was clothed with authority that in fact the agent did not possess?

HOLDING AND DECISION: (Boasberg, J.)

(1) Yes. To state a claim for negligent hiring, a plaintiff must allege specific facts from which an inference can be drawn that the employer did not conduct a reasonable background investigation, and that such an investigation would have uncovered a reason not to hire the alleged tortfeasor. Here, Search (P) merely repeated a quote from Uber's (D) website where Uber (D) promised to conduct "a rigorous background check" of "[a]ll Uber ridesharing and livery partners." However, Search (P) failed to make any factual allegation that Uber (D) did not actually conduct a background check consistent with this promise prior to hiring Deresse (D). Furthermore—and fatally for his claim—Search (P) did not allege either that these background-investigation procedures were not reasonably calculated to discover a "red flag" in Deresse's (D) past, or even that any such "red flag" existed. Nor did he identify any particular measures that Uber (D) did not take that could have prevented the hiring of Deresse (D). For these reasons, Search's (D) allegations are merely conclusory and do not recite any facts from which the court can infer that Uber (D) was negligent in hiring and supervising Deresse (D). Accordingly, the motion to dismiss as to this claim is granted.

(2) Yes. A plaintiff states a claim for vicarious liability under the doctrine of respondeat superior by alleging specific facts from which an inference can be drawn that there was an employer-employee relationship between the party sought to be held liable and the alleged tortfeasor, and that the tortfeasor committed a tortious act within the scope of the tortfeasor's employment. A claim for vicarious liability under a respondeat superior theory consists of two prongs: an employer-employee relationship and a tortious act committed by the employee within the scope of employment. In this jurisdiction, the question of whether an employer-employee relationship exists is governed by a five-factor test that examines: (1) involvement in the selection and engagement of the employee; (2) payment of wages; (3) power to discharge; (4) power to control the employee's conduct; and (5) whether the employee's work is part of the regular business of the employer. Under this test, the fourth factor—the right to control an employee, rather than the actual exercise of control or supervision—is usually the determinative factor. Here, Search (P) adduced facts from which a reasonable factfinder could conclude that Uber (D) exercised control over Deresse (D) in a manner evincing an employer-employee relationship. These included the facts that Uber (D) controlled the rate of refusal of ride requests, the timeliness of the drivers' responses to requests, the display on vehicles of its logo, the frequency with which drivers were permitted to contact passengers, the drivers' interactions with passengers (including how they accepted tips and collected fares), and the quality of drivers via its rating system. Regarding the fourth and "determinative" factor: whether Uber (D) controlled Deresse's (D) day-to-day operations or merely exercised general supervision over his activities, Uber (D) contended that an entity that monitors, evaluates, and improves the results of a worker's performance is not necessarily an employer. Although Uber (D) is correct that the right to inspect and the right to set standards are not necessarily indicia of control but may be indicative of a contractual relationship between an employer and independent contractor, it is the parties' actual relationship that is dispositive. And here, as indicated, Search (P) alleged sufficient facts from which such a relationship could be inferred. Thus, assuming that such existed between Uber (D) and Deresse (D), the next question is whether Deresse's (D) stabbing of Search (P) outside the scope of his employment. If an employee's conduct is different in kind from that authorized, far beyond the authorized time or space limits, or too little actuated by a purpose to serve the employer, that conduct falls outside the scope of employment. Accordingly, Uber (D) maintains that a violent attack could not conceivably be one of a limousine driver's job duties, and it is therefore always outside the scope of employment. However, the scope of employment inquiry is not this narrow. In fact, if there is evidence that the assault grew out of a

Continued on next page.

job-related controversy, an assault may very well fall within the scope of the perpetrator's employment. Here, Search (P) has alleged facts suggesting that the dispute giving rise to Deresse's (D) attack grew out of an encounter related to Uber's (D) business. Scope of employment is ordinarily a question for the jury, and here it cannot be concluded that, as a matter of law, Deresse's (D) alleged stabbing was an act outside such employment. Therefore, the motion to dismiss as to this claim is denied.

(3) Yes. A plaintiff states a claim for apparent agency by alleging specific facts from which an inference can be drawn that an independent contractor, as an agent of the principal that hired the independent contractor, had "apparent authority" as a consequence of the principal's placing the agent in such a position as to mislead third persons into believing that the agent was clothed with authority that in fact the agent did not possess. Even if Deresse (D) and Uber (D) were not bound by an actual employer-employee relationship, Search (P) argued in the alternative that Uber (D) represented to customers, including Search (P), that its drivers were its agents and that it screened and managed them accordingly. Apparent authority depends on the third-party's perception of the agent's authority, which may be based upon written or spoken words or any other conduct of the principal that, reasonably interpreted, causes the third person to believe that the principal consents to have the act done on her behalf by the apparent agent. The purpose of this doctrine is to prevent a defendant principal from denying any liability for the torts of its independent contractors while it profits from the image and good will created by the company's general business reputation. Here, Search (P) alleged that Uber (D), through several forms of media such as its mobile app and its website, represented to customers that it was "your private driver," that it subjects its drivers to rigorous screening procedures before hiring them, and that it "continues to monitor" those drivers after they are hired. Uber (D) responds by pointing to its User Agreement, where it expressly stated that Deresse (D) was not its agent. However, whatever its exculpatory effect, the User Agreement is material outside the complaint, offered to disprove the facts as alleged therein, and the Court thus cannot consider it in resolving the motion to dismiss. Accordingly, the motion to dismiss as to this claim is denied.

ANALYSIS

In many jurisdictions, employers operating public businesses are generally bound to use reasonable care to select employees or agents competent and fit for the work assigned to them and to refrain from retaining the services of an unfit employee or agent. When an employer has disregarded this duty and, as a result, injury is occasioned to a third person, liability may be imputed to the employer through a claim for negligent hiring, notwithstanding that the injury was brought about by the willful act of the employee or agent that was beyond the scope of employment. A master-servant relationship need not underlie a claim of negligent hiring, and an entity may also be liable for the negligent hiring of an independent contractor. Thus, for a negligent-hiring claim, it is irrelevant whether the tortfeasor (here, Deresse (D)) was an independent contractor or an employee. Moreover, as this case illustrates, the direct-liability theory of negligent hiring is distinct from negligence based on the vicarious-liability doctrine of respondeat superior.

Quicknotes

APPARENT AUTHORITY The authority granted to an agent to act on behalf of the principal in order to effectuate the principal's objective, which may not be expressly granted but which is inferred from the conduct of the principal and the agent.

INDEPENDENT CONTRACTOR A party undertaking a particular assignment for another while retaining control over the manner in which the assignment is executed.

NEGLIGENT HIRING Doctrine that holds an employer liable for an employee's or agent's unlawful acts during the course or scope of employment when the employer knew or should have known that the employee or agent posed an undue risk to others but failed to conduct a reasonable background investigation of the employee or agent prior to hiring the employee or agent that would have uncovered such risk.

RESPONDEAT SUPERIOR Rule that the principal is responsible for tortious acts committed by its agents in the scope of their agency or authority.

VICARIOUS LIABILITY The imputed liability of one party for the unlawful acts of another.

CHAPTER 8

Products Liability

Quick Reference Rules of Law

CHAPTER 8

Winterbottom v. Wright

Injured coachman (P) v. Coach supplier (D)

Ex., 152 Eng. Rep. 402 (1842)

NATURE OF CASE: Action for damages based on negligence.

FACT SUMMARY: Winterbottom (P) was injured while driving a defective mail coach which the government had bought from Wright (D) pursuant to a supply-maintenance contract.

RULE OF LAW

A contracting party, unless he has undertaken a public duty, has no liability to third parties who are injured as a result of a breach of the contract.

FACTS: Wright (D) agreed to supply and maintain mail coaches for the use of the Postmaster General. Atkinson also had a contract with the Postmaster General to supply horses and coachmen to operate the mail coaches. Winterbottom (P), one of Atkinson's coachmen, was injured when one of the coaches supplied by Wright (D) broke down. Winterbottom (P) brought suit against Wright (D), contending that his injuries were the result of Wright's (D) negligent performance of the contract with the Postmaster General.

ISSUE: Does a contracting party, unless he has undertaken a public duty, have liability to third persons who are injured as a result of a breach of the contract?

HOLDING AND DECISION: (Baron Abinger, J.) No. A contracting party, unless he has undertaken a public duty, has no liability to third parties who are injured as a result of a breach of the contract. Parties to a contract are liable only to each other for breaches of the contract, and any third party not in privity with the contracting parties in respect of the contract may not sue any party to the contract for the contract's breach. If such an action were permitted, contracting parties would be exposed to a potentially unlimited number of suits by strangers to the contract, even in the situation where the breach has been excused or waived. Winterbottom (P) was not privy to the contract between the Postmaster General and Wright (D), and therefore may not maintain an action against him.

ANALYSIS

The harsh *Winterbottom* decision was followed by the majority of courts in the United States during the second half of the 19th century, but a number of exceptions developed. The New York court in *Thomas v. Winchester*, 6 N.Y. 397 (1852), allowed a negligence action by a woman who was poisoned against a chemist who had sold the falsely labeled poison to her druggist. The court's rationale was that the poison was an "imminently dangerous" article, while the defective mail coach in *Winterbottom* was not. Other applications of the "imminently dangerous" exception proved difficult, however, and the New York court, in *MacPherson v. Buick Motor Co.*, 217 N.Y. 382 (1916), finally formulated a general rule of liability of remote manufacturers which eliminated privity as a requirement.

Quicknotes

LATENT DEFECTS A defect that cannot be discovered upon ordinary examination.

NUISANCE Use of property that interferes with the lawful use of another's property.

PRIVITY OF CONTRACT A relationship between the parties to a contract that is required in order to bring an action for breach.

MacPherson v. Buick Motor Co.

Injured car owner (P) v. Car manufacturer (D)

N.Y. Ct. App., 111 N.E. 1050 (1916)

NATURE OF CASE: Action for damages for negligence.

FACT SUMMARY: MacPherson (P) purchased a car for his wife (P), who was injured when a defective wheel collapsed.

RULE OF LAW

A manufacturer will be strictly liable for injury caused by his product where, if negligently made, it will be dangerous to the life of any potential user.

FACTS: MacPherson (P) purchased a Buick for his wife (P), telling the salesman of this fact. A wheel on the car collapsed because it was negligently manufactured. Buick Motor Co. (Buick) (D) obtained the wheels from another manufacturer, but the defect could have easily been discovered by a reasonable inspection. MacPherson (P) and his wife (P) brought suit for property damage and personal injury resulting from the accident. Buick (D) defended on the grounds that an automobile was not a dangerous instrument, therefore strict liability was inappropriate, and that no privity existed between it and the wife (P) since the car was purchased by Mr. MacPherson (P). Judgment was rendered for MacPherson (P) on the ground that negligence in the manufacture of an automobile rendered it dangerous to life and property, and it was foreseeable that Mrs. MacPherson (P) might use the car.

ISSUE: Will a manufacturer be strictly liable for injury caused by his product where, if negligently made, it will be dangerous to the life of any potential user?

HOLDING AND DECISION: (Cardozo, J.) Yes. A manufacturer will be strictly liable for injury caused by his product where, if negligently made, it will be dangerous to the life of any potential user. Buick (D) knew or should have known that if its car tires were made negligently, severe injury would be likely to result. Buick (D) had a duty to inspect the tires before selling the car to the public. Since it was foreseeable that others might use the product and be injured thereby, privity is not required. Affirmed.

DISSENT: (Bartlett, C.J.) The defective wheel was not imminently dangerous to human life. The manufacturer should not be liable except where there is an imminent danger that the negligence will cause serious injury.

ANALYSIS

After *MacPherson*, every jurisdiction abandoned the privity requirement where the product was likely to cause death or serious injury. In *Hanna v. Fletcher*, 231 F.2d 469 (D.C. Cir. 1956), the court held a contractor liable where a third party was later injured when part of a building collapsed due to faulty construction. No privity was required.

Quicknotes

DUTY TO INSPECT Regarding products liability, the examination of a product for defects prior to releasing the product to a consumer precludes product liability claims from being imposed under a negligence theory, unless those defects arose as the result of manufacturing or design defects.

NEGLIGENCE Conduct falling below the standard of care that a reasonable person would demonstrate under similar conditions.

STRICT LIABILITY Liability for all injuries proximately caused by a party's conducting of certain inherently dangerous activities without regard to negligence or fault.

Escola v. Coca Cola Bottling Co. of Fresno

Injured waitress (P) v. Cola manufacturer (D)

Cal. Sup. Ct., 150 P.2d 436 (1944)

NATURE OF CASE: Suit to recover damages for personal injuries.

FACT SUMMARY: Escola (P), a waitress in a restaurant, was injured when a Coca Cola Bottling Co. of Fresno (D) bottle exploded while being placed in a refrigerator.

RULE OF LAW

The manufacturer of a defective product should be held strictly liable for any injuries that result from the use of the product.

FACTS: Escola (P) was a waitress in a restaurant that served a soft drink manufactured by the Coca Cola Bottling Co. of Fresno (Coca Cola) (D). Escola (P) was in the process of refrigerating bottles of Coca-Cola that had been delivered to the restaurant at least 36 hours before. As the fourth bottle was being placed in the refrigerator, it exploded, causing severe injuries to Escola (P). In her suit for damages, Escola (P) alleged negligence on the part of Coca Cola (D) and successfully relied on the doctrine of res ipsa loquitur. Coca Cola (D) appealed, arguing that its negligence had not been established.

ISSUE: Should the manufacturer of a defective product be held strictly liable for any injuries that result from the use of the product?

HOLDING AND DECISION: (Gibson, J.) [In an opinion not fully reprinted in the casebook, the majority of the court affirmed Escola's (P) judgment, basing its affirmance on the doctrine of res ipsa loquitur.]

CONCURRENCE: (Traynor, J.) Yes. The manufacturer of a defective product should be held strictly liable for any injuries that result from the use of the product. In the modern commercial setting, a consumer rarely has opportunity to inspect the items which he purchases, yet it is imperative that defective merchandise be prevented from reaching potential users. Public policy mandates that liability be imposed upon the manufacturer, who is best able to prevent defects and is at the same time singularly able to spread the costs of bearing the risk of harm. And the liability of the manufacturer should not depend upon proof of his negligence, because it will be a rare case in which an injured party, unfamiliar with the manufacturer's production process, will be able to ascertain the precise nature of that negligence. Where foodstuffs are involved, strict criminal liability is imposed by statute upon producers of defective goods, and the potential injuries which may result from the use of products other than food justifies application of the strict liability doctrine to civil actions against manufacturers of all products. A retailer always owes his customer an implied warranty of safety, but since the retailer usually can recover from the manufacturer for judgments obtained by injured consumers, it makes sense to impose liability upon the manufacturer directly. Consumers are constantly bombarded with representations concerning a product's utility and worth, and justifiably rely upon the manufacturer's assertions in that regard. It is, therefore, fair that when defective products do reach the market, the manufacturer should be held strictly liable for injuries to any party who uses such products properly. Clearly, the facts of this case compel the conclusion that the judgment in favor of Escola (P) should be affirmed.

ANALYSIS

Justice Traynor's concurring opinion in *Escola v. Coca Cola Bottling Co. of Fresno* was one of the earliest and most thorough arguments in favor of strict liability in products liability cases. Today, of course, strict liability is widely accepted as the appropriate standard in such cases. Note that the plaintiff must establish that the defect in the product manufactured by the defendant was the legal cause of his injuries. And, liability will not attach if it is proved that the defect that caused the plaintiff's injuries was not present when the product left the control of the defendant. Recovery will also be denied upon a showing that the plaintiff was injured only because he chose to use the product in a manner other than the producer intended or could have anticipated.

Quicknotes

DUTY TO INSPECT Regarding products liability, the examination of a product for defects prior to releasing the product to a consumer precludes product liability claims from being imposed under a negligence theory, unless those defects arose as the result of manufacturing or design defects.

NEGLIGENCE Conduct falling below the standard of care that a reasonable person would demonstrate under similar conditions.

RES IPSA LOQUITUR A rule of law giving rise to an inference of negligence where the instrument inflicting the injury is in the exclusive control of the defendant and where such harm could not ordinarily result in the absence of negligence.

STRICT LIABILITY Liability for all injuries proximately caused by a party's conducting of certain inherently dangerous activities without regard to negligence or fault.

Casa Clara Condominium Assn., Inc. v. Charley Toppino & Sons, Inc.

Homeowner association (P) v. Concrete supplier (D)

Fla. Sup. Ct., 620 So. 2d 1244 (1993)

NATURE OF CASE: Appeal from dismissal of a negligence action to recover economic losses.

FACT SUMMARY: Casa Clara Condominium Association, Inc. (P) sued Charley Toppino & Sons, Inc. (Toppino) (D) in negligence to recover economic losses suffered after building its homes with defective concrete supplied by Toppino (D).

RULE OF LAW

The economic loss rule prohibits tort recovery when a product damages itself, causing economic loss, but does not cause personal injury or damage to any property other than itself.

FACTS: Casa Clara Condominium Association, Inc. (Casa Clara) (P) sued Charley Toppino & Sons, Inc. (Toppino) (D) in an action for negligence after Toppino (D) supplied concrete to Casa Clara (P) for the construction of condominiums. The concrete (which contained a high salt content) caused the reinforcing steel in the condos to rust, which, in turn, caused the concrete to break off. Casa Clara's (P) claims against Toppino (D) included breach of common-law implied warranty, products liability, negligence, and violation of the building code. The circuit court dismissed all counts against Toppino (D) in each case. The district court, on appeal, applied the economic loss rule and held that, because no person was injured and no other property damaged, Casa Clara (P) had no cause of action against Toppino (D) in tort.

ISSUE: Does the economic loss rule prohibit tort recovery when a product damages itself, causing economic loss, but does not cause personal injury or damage to any property other than itself?

HOLDING AND DECISION: (McDonald, J.) Yes. The economic loss rule prohibits tort recovery when a product damages itself, causing economic loss, but does not cause personal injury or damage to any property other than itself. This rule is the fundamental boundary between contract law, which is designed to enforce the expectancy interests of the parties, and tort law, which imposes a duty of reasonable care and thereby encourages citizens to avoid causing physical harm to others. Economic loss has been defined as damages for inadequate value, costs of repair, and replacement of the defective product or consequent loss of profits—without any claim of personal injury or damage to other property. In other words, economic losses are disappointed economic expectations, which are protected by contract law, rather than tort law. Here, Casa Clara (P) finds a tort remedy attractive because it permits the recovery of greater damages than an action in contract and may avoid the conditions of the contract. However, Casa Clara (P) homeowners are seeking purely economic damages—no one has sustained any physical injury, and no property other than the structures built with Toppino's (D) concrete has sustained any damage. Casa Clara (P) argues that holding it to contract remedies is unfair and homeowners in general should be exempted from the operation of the economic loss rule. But there are protections for home buyers, such as statutory warranties, the general warranty of habitability, and the duty of sellers to disclose defects, as well as the ability of the house buyer to inspect a house for defects. Coupled with the home buyers' power to bargain over price, these protections are sufficient when compared to the mischief that could be caused by allowing tort recovery for purely economic losses. Affirmed.

CONCURRENCE AND DISSENT: (Barkett, C.J.) Here, although Casa Clara (P) homeowners assert that their homes are literally crumbling around them because Toppino's (D) concrete was negligently manufactured, the courts have said "too bad!" That answer is unacceptable in light of the principle underlying Florida's Access to Courts provision: absent compelling countervailing public policies, wrongs must have remedies.

CONCURRENCE AND DISSENT: (Shaw, J.) Under negligence theory, purely economic loss cannot be recovered by parties to a contract when the loss is to property that is the subject of the contract. However, the logic of this restriction is inapplicable in this instance. The rationale of the economic loss rule is that parties who have bargained for the distribution of risk of loss should not be permitted to circumvent their bargain after loss occurs. But the economic loss theory was never intended to defeat tort causes of action that would otherwise lie for damages to a third party by a defective product.

ANALYSIS

The *Casa Clara* rule has been adopted as the law by most courts. A strong minority of courts, however, takes the position the strict liability rule of Restatement §402A should prevail over warranty disclaimers even in circumstances where there has been only economic loss. Some courts take the middle ground and apply §402A only when there has been "sudden" damage to the product, resulting in personal injury.

Continued on next page.

Quicknotes

ECONOMIC LOSS RULE For products liability losses, economic losses can include repair and replacement costs as well as lost profits and the commercial value lost due to inadequate use.

WARRANTY OF HABITABILITY An implied warranty owed by a landlord to a tenant to provide leased premises in properly maintained in a habitable condition prior to leasing the premises and during the duration of the lease.

Loomis v. Amazon.com LLC

Consumer (P) v. Online marketplace operator (D)

Cal. Ct. App. 277 Cal. Rptr. 3d 769 (2021)

NATURE OF CASE: Appeal from grant of summary judgment to defendant in action for strict products liability.

FACT SUMMARY: Kisha Loomis (P) contended that Amazon.com LLC (Amazon) (D), an online marketplace operator, should be held strictly liable for injuries Loomis (P) suffered from an allegedly defective hoverboard, notwithstanding that a third party had sold the hoverboard through Amazon's (D) website. Amazon (D) countered that it could not be held liable, because it was merely providing an "online storefront" for third parties to sell their wares, rather than serving as a retailer or distributor of consumer goods.

RULE OF LAW

(1) An entity that is a direct link in the vertical chain of distribution of a consumer product purchased from a third-party vendor through the entity's website is liable in strict products liability when the product is defective and causes injury to the consumer that purchased the product.

(2) An entity that participates in the stream of commerce for a product for its financial benefit may be held liable in strict products liability when the product is defective and causes injury to the consumer that purchased the product.

FACTS: Kisha Loomis (P) ordered a hoverboard on the website of Amazon.com LLC (Amazon) (D), an online marketplace operator. The hoverboard was sold by a third-party seller named TurnUpUp through the Amazon (D) website. When the hoverboard was plugged into charge, it created a fire, and Loomis (P) suffered burns as a result of fighting the fire. She brought a state strict products liability suit against Amazon (D), contending that it should be held strictly liable for her injuries. Amazon (D) countered that it could not be held liable, because it was merely providing an "online storefront" for third parties to sell their wares, rather than serving as a retailer or distributor of consumer goods—which it does in cases where it sells its own wares. Where Amazon (D) is the seller of a product, it is identified as the seller on its website's product detail page. However, where a third party is the seller, it is identified as such on the product detail page and again on the order confirmation page before the user places the order. The third-party sources the product, sets the price, and holds title to it. All third-party sellers operate under the Amazon (D) services business solutions agreement (BSA). Amazon (D) processes the payment for a third-party sale, transmits the order to the third party, and remits payment to the third-party after deducting Amazon's (D) fees, including a 15 percent referral fee based on the total sale price. Amazon (D) also prohibits third-party vendors from communicating directly with consumers who buy their products through the Amazon (D) website. Amazon (D) also imposed safety certification, indemnification, and insurance requirements on third-party sellers. The state trial court reviewed the case.

ISSUE:

(1) Is an entity that is a direct link in the vertical chain of distribution of a consumer product purchased from a third-party vendor through the entity's website liable in strict products liability when the product is defective and causes injury to the consumer that purchased the product?

(2) May an entity that participates in the stream of commerce for a product for its financial benefit be held liable in strict products liability when the product is defective and causes injury to the consumer that purchased the product?

HOLDING AND DECISION: (Ohta, J.)

(1) Yes. An entity that is a direct link in the vertical chain of distribution of a consumer product purchased from a third-party vendor through the entity's website is liable in strict products liability when the product is defective and causes injury to the consumer that purchased the product. Here, Amazon's (D) third-party business model under the BSA, and Amazon's (D) business practices, make it a direct link in the vertical chain of distribution and, therefore, subject to strict liability. Contrary to Amazon's (D) assertion that it merely provided an online storefront for TurnUpUp and others to sell their wares, it is undisputed Amazon (D) placed itself squarely between TurnUpUp, the seller, and Loomis (P), the buyer, in the transaction at issue. Amazon's (D) business model and practices undermine its characterization of its marketplace as an online mall providing online storefronts for sellers. Owners of malls typically do not serve as conduits for payment and communication in each transaction between a buyer and a seller. Moreover, they do not typically charge a per-item fee rather than a fixed amount to rent their storefronts. Instead, these actions—(1) interacting with the customer, (2) taking the order, (3) processing the order

Continued on next page.

to the third-party seller, (4) collecting the money, and (5) being paid a percentage of the sale—are consistent with a retailer or a distributor of consumer goods. For these reasons, Amazon (D) is susceptible to being held strictly liable in this action, and the trial court erred in granting summary judgment to Amazon (D).

(2) Yes. An entity that participates in the stream of commerce for a product for its financial benefit may be held liable in strict products liability when the product is defective and causes injury to the consumer that purchased the product. A defendant may be strictly liable under the stream of commerce approach if: (1) the defendant received a direct financial benefit from its activities and from the sale of the product; (2) the defendant's role was integral to the business enterprise such that the defendant's conduct was a necessary factor in bringing the product to the initial consumer market; and (3) the defendant had control over, or a substantial ability to influence, the manufacturing or distribution process. Here, the 15 percent referral fee Amazon (D) receives from third-party vendors satisfies the first factor. The second factor here is triable because there was no evidence presented as to Amazon's (D) role in bringing TurnUpUp's hoverboards to market. Finally, the third factor is satisfied because Amazon exerted influence over the process thanks to its ability to require safety certification, indemnification, and insurance before it agreed to list any product. For these reasons, the trial court erred in granting summary judgment to Amazon (D).

Regardless of whether Amazon (D) has a direct link in the vertical chain of distribution for products sold through its website, or is a participant in the stream of commerce for a product for its profit, policy considerations support imposing strict liability on Amazon (D) in cases such as the one at bar. The relevant public policy considerations are: (1) whether Amazon (D) may play a substantial part in ensuring that the product is safe or may be in a position to exert pressure on the manufacturer to that end, (2) whether Amazon (D) may be the only member in the distribution chain reasonably available to the injured plaintiff, and (3) whether Amazon (D) is in a position to adjust the costs of compensating the injured plaintiff amongst various members in the distribution chain. Here, Amazon (D) can take limited, cost-efficient steps to ensure product safety, so the first factor is satisfied. As to the second factor, the record shows that Amazon (D) may be the only member of the distribution chain reasonably available for an injured consumer to recover damages. Finally, as to the third factor—loss spreading—Amazon (D) may be the only member of the distribution chain reasonably available for an injured consumer to recover damages. Therefore, the application of strict liability to Amazon's (D) third-party seller business model is supported by these relevant public policy considerations. Reversed.

CONCURRENCE: (Wiley, J.) This case exemplifies the application of tort law principles to evolving technologies. Judges have long had the impulse, through the use of strict products liability, to minimize the social cost of accidents, which makes this case an easy one to decide. When efforts to minimize accident costs are relatively inexpensive and apt to be effective, courts impose tort duties. Amazon (D) has cost-effective options for minimizing accident costs. Amazon (D) therefore has a duty in strict liability to the buyers from its site, including Loomis (P) here. In fact, Amazon (D) claims it already is taking such cost-effective measures, and imposing liability on Amazon (D) in cases such as the one at bar create financial incentives that back up Amazon's (D) assertions that it is concerned for customer safety. Although some commentators have suggested that considerations of moral justice can compete with tort law's calculus of social benefit, even if they do in some cases, moral justice and cost-benefit analyses do not conflict in this case.

ANALYSIS

Although Judge Ohta and Judge Wiley emphasize the tort-law principle that strict liability will be imposed on entities that act as sellers and distributors of consumer products where those entities have cost-effective options for minimizing accident costs, the corollary of that principle is that courts will refrain from imposing tort duties where measures to avoid accidents are burdensome and unlikely to be cost-effective. This notion means that courts do not seek to avoid accidents at all costs. Thus, for example, courts and society permit the use of planes and cars rather than safer, slower means of travel, because, at some point, a quest for perfect safety becomes irrationally expensive.

Quicknotes

CHAIN OF DISTRIBUTION LIABILITY All parties involved in creating and selling a product, from the manufacturer, to all distributors, to the end retailer, may be held liable under strict products liability when the product is deemed to be defective and causes injury.

STREAM OF COMMERCE LIABILITY Any individual or entity that participates in the stream of commerce for a product, including manufacturers, suppliers, assemblers of component parts, lessors, distributors, and others, may be held liable under strict products liability when the product is deemed to be defective and causes injury.

STRICT PRODUCTS LIABILITY Liability of a manufacturer or seller of a product for injuries sustained as a result of any defects without the necessity of a showing of negligence.

Speller v. Sears, Roebuck and Co.

Fire victim (P) v. Manufacturer and retailer (D)

N.Y. Ct. App. 790 N.E.2d 252 (2003)

NATURE OF CASE: Appeal of summary judgment in favor of Sears, Roebuck and Co. (D) in a products liability action.

FACT SUMMARY: Speller (P) sued Sears, Roebuck and Co. (Sears) (D) after her (P) decedent, Sandra, died and Sandra's (P) son was injured in a fire allegedly caused by a defective refrigerator, which Sears (P) sold.

RULE OF LAW

The circumstantial approach to proving a product liability action requires proof that the product did not perform as intended and all other causes for the product's failure, that are not attributable to the defendants, must be excluded.

FACTS: Speller's (P) decedent, Sandra, died in a house fire that also injured Sandra's (P) seven-year-old son. The fire originated in the kitchen. Speller (P) sued Sears, Roebuck and Co. (Sears) (D), Whirlpool Corporation (D), and the property owner alleging negligence, strict products liability, and breach of warranty. Speller (P) asserted that the fire was caused by defective wiring in the refrigerator, which was manufactured by Whirlpool (D) and sold by Sears (D). Sears (D) and Whirlpool (D) moved for summary judgment on the basis of a report by the New York City Fire Marshal concluding that a stovetop grease fire was the cause of the fire. In opposition, Speller (P) presented three expert opinions that contradicted the Fire Marshal's findings and placed blame for the fire on the defective refrigerator. Sears (D) was granted summary judgment, and Speller (P) appealed.

ISSUE: Does the circumstantial approach to proving a product liability action require proof that the product did not perform as intended and all other causes for the product's failure, that are not attributable to the defendants, must be excluded?

HOLDING AND DECISION: (Graffeo, J.) Yes. The circumstantial approach to proving a product liability action requires proof that the product did not perform as intended and all other causes for the product's failure, that are not attributable to the defendants, have been excluded. Speller (P) raised a triable issue of fact concerning whether the defective refrigerator caused the fire because she proved that all other causes for the product's failure, that were not attributable to the defendant, had been excluded. A product manufacturer or others in the distribution chain will be liable if someone is injured as a result of a defective product if the defect was a substantial factor in causing the injury. In the present case, the wiring of the refrigerator was not tested because it was consumed in the fire. Speller (P) had to prove her claim circumstantially by establishing that the refrigerator caused the house fire and therefore it did not perform as intended. The circumstantial approach is a viable route to prove a products liability case. However, in addition to proving that the product did not perform as intended, all other causes for the product's failure that are not attributable to the defendants must be excluded. Sears's (D) motion argued that the injuries were not caused by their product, but by a grease fire that began on the stove. Speller (P), however, came forward with competent evidence, in the form of three expert witnesses, excluding the stove as the origin of the fire, and concluding that the fire originated in the refrigerator. The three expert witnesses were an electrical engineer, a fire investigator, and a former Deputy Chief of the New York City Fire Department. Their testimony regarding the source of the fire raised a triable question of fact, which, if credited by the jury, was sufficient to rebut Sears's (D) alternative cause evidence. Based on Speller's (P) proof, a reasonable jury could conclude that Speller (P) excluded all other causes of the fire. [Reversed.]

ANALYSIS

The holding in this case is consistent with the Restatement (Third) of Torts: Product Liability §3 (1998).

Quicknotes

PRODUCT LIABILITY The legal liability of manufacturers and sellers for damages and injuries suffered by buyers, users, and even bystanders because of defects in goods purchased.

SUMMARY JUDGMENT Judgment rendered by a court in response to a motion by one of the parties, claiming that the lack of a question of material fact in respect to an issue warrants disposition of the issue without consideration by the jury.

Campo v. Scofield

[Parties not identified.]

N.Y. Ct. App. 95 N.E.2d 802 (1950)

NATURE OF CASE: [Nature of case not stated in casebook excerpt.]

FACT SUMMARY: [Facts not stated in casebook excerpt.]

RULE OF LAW
A manufacturer will not be liable if it does everything necessary to make a machine function properly for the purpose for which it was designed, if the machine is without any latent defect, and if the machine's functioning creates no danger that is not known to the user.

FACTS: [Facts not stated in casebook excerpt.]

ISSUE: Will a manufacturer be liable if it does everything necessary to make a machine function properly for the purpose for which it was designed, if the machine is without any latent defect, and if the machine's functioning creates no danger that is not known to the user?

HOLDING AND DECISION: (Fuld, J.) No. A manufacturer will not be liable if it does everything necessary to make a machine function properly for the purpose for which it was designed, if the machine is without any latent defect, and if the machine's functioning creates no danger that is not known to the user. A manufacturer does not have to furnish a machine that does not wear out in order to guard against injury resulting from deterioration. A manufacturer, therefore, has no duty to guard against an injury from a patent peril or from a source manifestly dangerous because the very nature of the product puts the user on notice of the possible dangers surrounding it.

ANALYSIS

The court is inferring here that a manufacturer is not required to make a machine accident-proof or foolproof.

Quicknotes

LATENT DEFECTS A defect that cannot be discovered upon ordinary examination.

Volkswagen of America, Inc. v. Young

Car manufacturer (D) v. Car crash victim (P)

Md. Ct. App., 321 A.2d 737 (1974)

NATURE OF CASE: Suit seeking damages for wrongful death.

FACT SUMMARY: Young's (P) decedent was killed when the back seat of his Volkswagen of America, Inc. (D) car tore loose following a collision with another vehicle.

RULE OF LAW

An automobile manufacturer may be held liable for injuries sustained in a so-called second collision if those injuries were the result of the manufacturer's negligent design of the vehicle.

FACTS: Young's (P) decedent stopped his 1968 Volkswagen of America, Inc. (Volkswagen) (D) car at a traffic light and was struck from behind by a negligently driven Ford. He suffered fatal injuries when he was tossed into the rear of his car after colliding with the back seat. This so-called second collision resulted when the bracketing pieces and seat adjustment mechanisms of the back seat tore loose from the body of the car. Young (P) brought suit in federal district court, alleging that the Volkswagen (D) Beetle had been so designed and manufactured as to be hazardous, not merchantable, and not fit for its intended purpose. Upon motion of Volkswagen (D), the federal court certified to the Maryland Court of Appeals the question of whether a vehicle's intended use included its involvement in an accident, and whether a manufacturer could be held liable for injuries caused by improper design and manufacture of a vehicle even though the defect did not contribute to the occurrence of the accident from which the injuries resulted.

ISSUE: May an automobile manufacturer be held liable for injuries sustained in a so-called second collision if those injuries were the result of the manufacturer's negligent design of the vehicle?

HOLDING AND DECISION: (Eldridge, J.) Yes. An automobile manufacturer may be held liable for injuries sustained in a so-called second collision if those injuries were the result of the manufacturer's negligent design of the vehicle. In *Evans v. General Motors Corporation*, 359 F.2d 822 (7th Cir. 1966), it was held that a manufacturer is not liable in such a case since an automobile's intended use does not include its involvement in accidents. But the modern trend is clearly to follow the rule of *Larsen v. General Motors Corporation*, 391 F.2d 495 (8th Cir. 1968), wherein it was held that injuries resulting from a second collision are the responsibility of the manufacturer if those injuries occurred because of the faulty design of the vehicle. The *Larsen* court emphasized that automobile manufacturers should anticipate that their products will be involved in accidents and are therefore obligated to make vehicles that will be reasonably safe even if collisions occur. Economy of manufacture, attractiveness, and utility of the vehicle are factors to be considered in determining whether a reasonably safe product has been created, and the manufacturer cannot be held liable for dangerous design features that are obvious and apparent. But traditional principles of negligence dictate that liability should attach when latent design defects cause a second collision or otherwise exacerbate injuries. Imposition of liability in such cases does not make the manufacturer an insurer, nor does it obligate the manufacturer to produce cars that are injury proof. And, it cannot seriously be contended that the result reached in this case should be imposed only pursuant to legislative mandate. While this type case is not one in which strict liability should be imposed, to hold automobile manufacturers liable under the circumstances of this case is wholly consistent with the evolution of negligence law.

ANALYSIS

The thoughts articulated by the Maryland Court of Appeals in *Volkswagen of America, Inc. v. Young* are consistent with the results reached in most recent second collision cases. For instance, there appears to be little opposition to the important proposition that accidents are within the scope of an automobile's intended use. It is worthwhile to note that, although the *Young* decision expressly rejects the strict liability standard, strict liability was imposed in a California case that involved facts strikingly similar to those of the *Young* case. See *Cronin v. J.B.E. Olson Corp.*, 8 Cal. 3d 121, 501 P.2d 1153, 104 Cal. Rptr. 433 (1972).

Quicknotes

DESIGN DEFECT A defect that exists in a product regardless of the method of manufacture or amount of due care exercised by those in the commercial chain of distribution, but instead as the result of flaws in the product's design.

NEGLIGENCE Conduct falling below the standard of care that a reasonable person would demonstrate under similar conditions.

STRICT LIABILITY Liability for all injuries proximately caused by a party's conducting of certain inherently dangerous activities without regard to negligence or fault.

Barker v. Lull Engineering Co.

Injured construction worker (P) v. Manufacturer of construction loader (D)

Cal. Sup. Ct., 573 P.2d 443 (1978)

NATURE OF CASE: Appeal from denial of damages in products liability action.

FACT SUMMARY: Barker (P) sought to recover under a strict liability theory for injuries sustained while operating a machine manufactured by Lull Engineering Co. (D), claiming that the defective design of the machine proximately caused these injuries.

RULE OF LAW

A product is defectively designed (1) if it does not perform as safely as the ordinary consumer would expect, when used in an intended or reasonably foreseeable manner, or (2) if the benefits of the product's design are outweighed by the risk of danger inherent in such design.

FACTS: Lull Engineering Co. (Lull) (D) manufactured a "high-lift loader," designed for use on level terrain. In August 1970, while operating the machine on uneven terrain in order to lift some lumber, Barker (P) felt the loader vibrate. Jumping off the loader to escape harm, he was struck by a heavy piece of lumber and seriously injured. When Barker (P) brought suit, the trial court instructed the jury that "strict liability for a defect in design of a product is based on a finding that the product was unreasonably dangerous for its intended use." Following a verdict for Lull (D), Barker (P) appealed, claiming that the trial court erred in giving this instruction.

ISSUE: Is a product defectively designed (1) if it does not perform as safely as the ordinary consumer would expect, when used in an intended or reasonably foreseeable manner, or (2) if the benefits of the product's design are outweighed by the risk of danger inherent in such design?

HOLDING AND DECISION: (Tobriner, C.J.) Yes. A product is defectively designed (1) if it does not perform as safely as the ordinary consumer would expect, when used in an intended or reasonably foreseeable manner, or (2) if the benefits of the product's design are outweighed by the risk of danger inherent in such design. In *Cronin v. J.B.E. Olson Corp.*, 8 Cal.3d 121, 501 P.2d 1153, 104 Cal. Rptr. 433 (1972), the California Supreme Court rejected the use of the "unreasonably dangerous" standard for defining "defect" in product liability actions. The "unreasonably dangerous" terminology suggested that recovery should be permitted only if a product is more dangerous than contemplated by the average consumer. Often, however, the consumer cannot know what to expect, as he has no idea how safe the product could be made. Thus, a manufacturer's liability should not be so circumscribed. While *Cronin* involved a "manufacturing defect," the rationale of the case is equally applicable to "design defects." Furthermore, with respect to the risk-benefit standard, once the plaintiff makes a prima facie showing that the injury was proximately caused by the product's design, the manufacturer has the burden of proving the design is not defective. Here, the trial court did not instruct the jury properly but, rather, used the "unreasonably dangerous" standard. In light of the *Cronin* decision, this is prejudicial error. Reversed.

ANALYSIS

Barker v. Lull Engineering Co. is a major expansion of the concept of product defect. Other states have likewise rejected the Restatement's "unreasonably dangerous" terminology, *e.g., Azzarello v. Black Bros. Co., Inc.,* 480 Pa. 547, 391 A. 2d 1020 (1978). Furthermore, at least one case has squarely adopted the standard developed by the California Supreme Court in *Barker v. Lull: Caterpillar Tractor Co. v. Beck*, 593 P.2d 871 (Alaska 1979).

Quicknotes

DESIGN DEFECT A defect that exists in a product regardless of the method of manufacture or amount of due care exercised by those in the commercial chain of distribution, but instead as the result of flaws in the product's design.

PROXIMATE CAUSE The natural sequence of events without which an injury would not have been sustained.

STRICT LIABILITY Liability for all injuries proximately caused by a party's conducting of certain inherently dangerous activities without regard to negligence or fault.

MacDonald v. Ortho Pharmaceutical Corp.

Birth control pill users (P) v. Pharmaceutical manufacturer (D)

Mass. Sup. Jud. Ct., 475 N.E.2d 65 (1985)

NATURE OF CASE: Appeal from decision granting judgment notwithstanding the verdict.

FACT SUMMARY: MacDonald (P) appealed from the court's decision granting Ortho Pharmaceutical Corp.'s (Ortho) (D) motion for judgment notwithstanding the verdict in favor of MacDonald (P), contending that as a manufacturer of an oral contraceptive, Ortho (D) had a direct duty to MacDonald (P), the consumer, to warn her of inherent dangers.

RULE OF LAW

The manufacturer of birth control pills owes a direct duty to the consumer to warn her of the dangers inherent in the use of the pill.

FACTS: Ortho Pharmaceutical Corp. (Ortho) (D) manufactured birth control pills eventually prescribed to MacDonald (P). Ortho (D) provided a booklet outlining the dangers inherent in the use of the pill to MacDonald's (P) gynecologist. The individual pill dispenser also contained warnings in compliance with United States Food and Drug Administration (FDA) requirements. Neither warning mentioned a "stroke," though each mentioned blood clotting and possible fatal consequences. MacDonald (P), who suffered a stroke and permanent brain damage, sued Ortho (D), alleging essentially the failure to warn properly. The jury found Ortho (D) negligent for failure to give sufficient warnings of the dangers inherent in the pill's use. Upon motion by Ortho (D), the court entered a judgment in favor of Ortho (D) notwithstanding the jury's verdict, finding that Ortho's (D) duty to warn was satisfied by giving adequate warnings to the physician. MacDonald (P) appealed.

ISSUE: Does the manufacturer of birth control pills owe a direct duty to the consumer to warn her of the dangers inherent in the use of the pill?

HOLDING AND DECISION: (Abrams, J.) Yes. The manufacturer of birth control pills owes a direct duty to the consumer to warn her of the dangers inherent in the use of the pill. While noting that this is a departure from the ordinary "prescription drug" rule, the prescription of oral contraceptives differs from the ordinary prescription drug situation in the following ways. The consumer is much more involved in the decision to use the pill. There are substantial risks associated with the pill, and direct warnings from the manufacturer are feasible. There is limited participation (annually) by the physician, and there may be inadequate communication between physician and patient regarding the dangers inherent in the use of the pill. Given these distinctions, Ortho (D) cannot rely on warnings issued to physicians to satisfy its common-law duty to warn. (The court went on to determine that the dispenser warning, although in compliance with FDA regulations, was not sufficient as a matter of law, and upheld the jury's decision that the warning was not unreasonable as a matter of law.) Reversed and remanded.

DISSENT: (O'Connor, J.) Adequate warning to the physician in compliance with FDA regulations is sufficient as a matter of law to comply with Ortho's (D) duty to warn.

ANALYSIS

The expanded liability recognized in the present case has been expanded to other areas. In *Lauperi v. Sears, Roebuck & Co.*, 787 F.2d. 726 (1st Cir. 1986), the *MacDonald* reasoning was used to expand the scope of liability to the manufacturer of smoke alarms for the failure to adequately warn the consumer.

Quicknotes

JUDGMENT NOTWITHSTANDING THE VERDICT A judgment entered by the trial judge reversing a jury verdict if the jury's determination has no basis in law or fact.

NEGLIGENCE Conduct falling below the standard of care that a reasonable person would demonstrate under similar conditions.

Vassallo v. Baxter Healthcare Corp.

Breast implant recipient (P) v. Manufacturer (D)

Mass. Sup. Jud. Ct., 696 N.E.2d 909 (1998)

NATURE OF CASE: Products liability action.

FACT SUMMARY: Vassallo (P) brought suit, seeking recovery of damages for injuries sustained as a result of the rupturing of her silicone breast implants on the basis that the implants were negligently designed and that the manufacturer negligently failed to provide adequate warnings in breach of the implied warranty of merchantability.

RULE OF LAW

A defendant is not liable under the implied warranty of merchantability for failure to warn or to provide instructions about risks that were not reasonably foreseeable at the time of sale or that could not have been reasonably discovered through reasonable testing prior to the marketing of the product.

FACTS: Vassallo (P) underwent breast implant surgery. About 15 years later, she underwent a mammogram after suffering from chest pains under her left armpit. The mammogram showed that the breast implants had possibly ruptured. The silicone gel implants were removed and replaced with saline implants. During the surgery the surgeon noted severe, permanent scarring of Vassallo's (P) pectoral muscles that was attributed to the silicone gel. The left implant had ruptured, and the right had several pinholes through which the silicon could escape. Testimony revealed that there was knowledge regarding the possible adverse long-term consequences of leaking silicone into the body; however, Heyer-Schulte Corp. (D), the manufacturer, conducted few animal and no clinical studies regarding the safety of its silicone gel implants. While Heyer-Schulte (D) did furnish warnings to doctors, they did not address the possibility of gel bleed, ruptures, or the consequences of silicone gel escaping into the body. Vassallo (P) brought suit for damages on the basis that the implants were negligently designed, accompanied by negligent product warnings, and in breach of the implied warranty of merchantability, resulting in her injuries. The jury found in favor of Vassallo (P). The judge entered a separate memorandum of decision in favor of Vassallo (P). Baxter Healthcare Corp. (Baxter) (D) appealed.

ISSUE: Is a defendant liable under the implied warranty of merchantability for failure to warn or to provide instructions about risks that were not reasonably foreseeable at the time of sale or that could not have been reasonably discovered through reasonable testing prior to the marketing of the product?

HOLDING AND DECISION: (Greaney, J.) No. A defendant is not liable under the implied warranty of merchantability for failure to warn or to provide instructions about risks that were not reasonably foreseeable at the time of sale or that could not have been reasonably discovered through reasonable testing prior to the marketing of the product. The manufacturer will be held accountable to the standard of knowledge of an expert in the relevant field and is subject to a continuing duty to warn consumers of risks discovered following the sale of the particular product. Baxter (D) argued that products liability law regarding the implied warranty of merchantability should be reformulated to adopt a "state of the art" standard conditioning the manufacturer's liability on the actual or constructive knowledge of the risks. The duty to warn under the implied warranty of merchantability presumes that a manufacturer is fully informed of all the risks associated with a product, regardless of the state of the art at the time of sale. Thus, the manufacturer is strictly liable for failure to warn of associated risks. The majority of states follow the Restatement (Second) of Torts § 402A comment j principle that the seller must warn against a danger "if he has knowledge, or by the application of reasonable, developed human skill and foresight should have knowledge of, the danger." This state follows the minority rule, which applies a hindsight analysis to the duty to warn. The rationale for the hindsight rule in strict liability jurisdictions is that the goal of providing an incentive to manufacturers to take reasonable measures for consumer protection would not be advanced if liability were imposed with respect to risks that were incapable of being discovered. In light of the modern trend regarding the duty to warn in products liability cases and the Restatement (Third) of Torts, the law in Massachusetts is revised to state that a defendant will not be held liable under an implied warranty of merchantability for failure to warn or provide instructions about risks that were not reasonably foreseeable at the time of sale or could not have been reasonably discovered through reasonable testing prior to the marketing of the product. The manufacturer will be held accountable to the standard of knowledge of an expert in the relevant field and is subject to a continuing duty to warn consumers of risks discovered following the sale of the particular product. This standard applies to all claims

Continued on next page.

on which a final judgment has not yet been entered, or to which an appeal is pending or the appeal period has not yet expired, and to all claims commenced after this ruling. [Affirmed.]

ANALYSIS

The majority of jurisdictions follow the Restatement (Second) of Torts § 402A comment j rule requiring a warning if the seller has knowledge, or if "by the application of reasonable, developed human skill and foresight should have knowledge of the danger." Restatement (Third) of Torts: Products Liability § 2(c) comment m ratifies this rule and clarifies that the manufacturer has a duty to perform testing prior to marketing a product to discover risks. Furthermore, a seller of the product is also charged with knowledge of the risks as discovered by the reasonable testing.

Quicknotes

FAILURE TO WARN The failure of an owner or occupier of land to inform persons present on the property of defects or active operations that may cause injury.

IMPLIED WARRANTY OF MERCHANTABILITY An implied promise made by a merchant in a contract for the sale of goods that such goods are suitable for the purpose for which they are purchased.

REASONABLE FORESEEABILITY A reasonable expectation that an act or omission would result in injury.

Hood v. Ryobi America Corp.

Injured consumer (P) v. Manufacturer (D)

181 F.3d 608 (4th Cir. 1999)

NATURE OF CASE: Appeal from summary judgment for defendant.

FACT SUMMARY: Hood (P) alleged that Ryobi America Corp. (D) failed to adequately warn of dangers of using an allegedly defectively designed saw.

RULE OF LAW

A manufacturer may be liable for placing a product on the market that bears inadequate instructions and warnings or that is defective in design.

FACTS: Hood (P) purchased a saw manufactured by Ryobi America Corp. (Ryobi) (D) to use for home repairs. The saw itself warned that the saw blade guards that were attached to the saw should never be removed. The owner's manual also contained similar warnings. Disregarding the warnings, Hood (P) removed the saw blade guards and was later seriously injured when the spinning saw blade flew off the saw. Hood claimed that Ryobi's (D) warnings were not adequate because they were not specific enough, and that the saw had been defectively designed. Hood (P) sued under negligence, strict liability, and breach of warranty. The district court granted Ryobi's (D) motion for summary judgment and Hood (P) appealed.

ISSUE: May a manufacturer be liable for placing a product on the market that bears inadequate instructions and warnings or that is defective in design?

HOLDING AND DECISION: (Wilkinson, C.J.) Yes. A manufacturer may be liable for placing a product on the market that bears inadequate instructions and warnings or that is defective in design. A warning need only be one that is reasonable under the circumstances. Ryobi's (D) warnings were clear and unequivocal. Ryobi (D) placed three labels on the saw itself and at least four warnings in the owner's manual. The warnings were adequate as a matter of law. Affirmed.

ANALYSIS

The court declined to hold the manufacturer liable because of the affirmative misuse by Hood (P). The additional warnings Hood (P) had claimed were necessary were found by the court to be more confusing and unnecessary. Some courts rule on the issue of the adequacy of the warnings as a matter of law. Other courts leave this issue for the jury to decide.

Quicknotes

DUTY TO WARN An obligation owed by an owner or occupier of land to persons who come onto the premises, to inform them of defects or active operations which may cause injury.

NEGLIGENCE Conduct falling below the standard of care that a reasonable person would demonstrate under similar conditions.

PRODUCT LIABILITY The legal liability of manufacturers and sellers for damages and injuries suffered by buyers, users, and even bystanders because of defects in goods purchased.

STRICT LIABILITY Liability for all injuries proximately caused by a party's conducting of certain inherently dangerous activities without regard to negligence or fault.

Air & Liquid Systems Corp. v. DeVries

Manufacturer of equipment used on Navy ships (D) v. Relative of deceased Naval veteran (P)

139 S. Ct. 986 (2019)

NATURE OF CASE: Appeal in action for negligent failure to warn.

FACT SUMMARY: In an action brought by relatives of Naval veterans (P) who had died from exposure to asbestos on Navy ships, manufacturers (D) of equipment used on the ships that required asbestos parts to be added to the equipment contended that they did not have a duty to warn about the dangers of those parts, since they themselves were not the parts manufacturers.

RULE OF LAW

In the maritime tort context, a product manufacturer has a duty to warn when (1) its product requires incorporation of a part, (2) the manufacturer knows or has reason to know that the integrated product is likely to be dangerous for its intended uses, and (3) the manufacturer has no reason to believe that the product's users will realize that danger.

FACTS: Manufacturers (D) produced equipment such as pumps, blowers, and turbines for Navy ships. The equipment required asbestos insulation or asbestos parts in order to function as intended. Those parts were later integrated into the equipment by the Navy. When used on the ships, the equipment released asbestos fibers into the air. Two Navy veterans who were exposed to asbestos on the ships developed cancer and later died. The veterans' families (P) sued the equipment manufacturers (D), claiming that the manufacturers were negligent in failing to warn of the dangers of asbestos. The manufacturers (D) contended that they were entitled to the common-law "bare-metal defense," which holds that a manufacturer is not liable for harms caused by later-added third-party parts. The United States Supreme Court granted certiorari in the case.

ISSUE: In the maritime tort context, does a product manufacturer have a duty to warn when (1) its product requires incorporation of a part, (2) the manufacturer knows or has reason to know that the integrated product is likely to be dangerous for its intended uses, and (3) the manufacturer has no reason to believe that the product's users will realize that danger?

HOLDING AND DECISION: (Kavanaugh, J.) Yes. In the maritime tort context, a product manufacturer has a duty to warn when (1) its product requires incorporation of a part, (2) the manufacturer knows or has reason to know that the integrated product is likely to be dangerous for its intended uses, and (3) the manufacturer has no reason to believe that the product's users will realize that danger. Tort law imposes a duty to exercise reasonable care on those whose conduct presents a risk of harm to others. That includes a duty to warn when a manufacturer knows or has reason to know that its product is or is likely to be dangerous for the use for which it is supplied and has no reason to believe that the product's users will realize that danger. Three approaches have emerged on how to apply that "duty to warn" principle when a manufacturer's product requires later incorporation of a dangerous part in order for the integrated product to function as intended. The first—the foreseeability rule—provides that a manufacturer may be liable when it was foreseeable that its product would be used with another product or part, even if the manufacturer's product did not require use or incorporation of that other product or part. The second—the bare-metal defense—provides that if a manufacturer did not itself make, sell, or distribute the part or incorporate the part into the product, the manufacturer is not liable for harm caused by the integrated product, even if the product required incorporation of the part and the manufacturer knew that the integrated product was likely to be dangerous for its intended uses. A third approach, falling between those two, imposes on the manufacturer a duty to warn when its product requires incorporation of a part and the manufacturer knows or has reason to know that the integrated product is likely to be dangerous for its intended uses. The third approach is the most appropriate for maritime cases such as the one at bar. The foreseeability rule would sweep too broadly, imposing a difficult and costly burden on manufacturers, while simultaneously overwarning users. The bare-metal defense ultimately goes too far in the other direction, since both a manufacturer that supplies a product that is dangerous in and of itself, and a manufacturer that supplies a product that requires incorporation of a part that the manufacturer knows or has reason to know is likely to make the integrated product dangerous for its intended uses, know or have reason to know that the product is or is likely to be dangerous for the use for which it is supplied. In the latter case, the product manufacturer will often be in a better position than the parts manufacturer to warn of the danger, because the product manufacturer knows the nature of the ultimate integrated product. Requiring a warning in these circumstances will not impose a significant burden on manufacturers, who already have a duty to warn of the dangers

Continued on next page.

of their own products. Nor will it result in substantial uncertainty about when product manufacturers must provide warnings, because the rule requires a manufacturer to warn only when its product requires a part for the integrated product to function as intended. Moreover, there have not been any substantial overwarning problems in those jurisdictions that have adopted this middle-of-the-road approach. Finally, because this rule will arise only in certain narrow circumstances, it will not require a plethora of new warnings. [Affirmed.]

DISSENT: (Gorsuch, J.) The traditional common-law approach, rather than the one adopted by the Court, should be the one applied in cases such as the one at bar. That is because a product manufacturer is best situated to understand and warn users about its risks, and, by placing the duty to warn on the manufacturer, the manufacturer is forced to internalize the full cost of any injuries resulting from inadequate warnings. Under the Court's approach, the manufacturer's duty to warn is diluted when other parties are required to share that duty and the costs that come with it.

ANALYSIS

As the Court itself emphasizes, its holding is limited to maritime tort cases, and does not purport to define the proper tort rule outside of the maritime context. Indeed, the Court acknowledges that it has created its new standard in part because of the solicitude for sailors that is a unique feature of the federal courts' maritime tort jurisdiction, pursuant to which federal courts act as common-law courts. Thus, nothing in the Court's opinion compels courts operating outside the maritime context to apply the test announced by the Court. In other tort cases, courts remain free to accept the "bare-metal" defense. As Justice Gorsuch observes in his dissent, this will better accord with consumer and manufacturer expectations, since encouraging manufacturers to offer warnings about other people's products risks long, duplicative, fine print, and conflicting warnings that will leave consumers less sure about which to take seriously and more likely to disregard them all. Thus, for example, a company that sells smartphone cases will not have be concerned with whether it needs to warn about the risk of exposure to cell phone radiation, and a seller of hot dog buns will not have to be concerned about providing warnings about the health risks of consuming processed meat. Ostensibly, not mandating a social insurance policy in which everyone must pay for everyone else's mistakes will keep product costs down and encourage the output of socially productive products.

Quicknotes

COMMON LAW A body of law developed through the judicial decisions of the courts as opposed to the legislative process.

FORESEEABILITY A reasonable expectation that an act or omission would occur.

MARITIME LAW That area of law pertaining to navigable waters.

Daly v. General Motors Corp.

Fatal car accident victim (P) v. Car manufacturer (D)

Cal. Sup. Ct., 575 P.2d 1162 (1978)

NATURE OF CASE: Appeal from denial of damages in products liability action.

FACT SUMMARY: After decedent sustained fatal injuries when thrown from his car, which was manufactured by General Motors Corp. (D), Daly (P) claimed the defective design of the door lock caused decedent to be thrown. But General Motors (D) contended that decedent was ejected through his failure to use the car's safety devices.

RULE OF LAW

A plaintiff's negligent conduct will reduce his recovery in strict products liability by an amount proportionate to his fault.

FACTS: In October 1970, decedent was driving his Opel on the freeway when it hit the metal divider. Thrown from the car, he sustained fatal head injuries. Daly (P), on behalf of the widow and children, alleged defective product design, claiming that the exposed pushbutton of the door lock was forced open in the collision, causing decedent to be ejected. General Motors Corp. (D) introduced evidence that the car contained a seat belt harness and a door lock, either of which would have prevented decedent's ejection and, further, that decedent was intoxicated and failed to use these protections. Daly (P) appealed from a verdict for General Motors (D).

ISSUE: Will a plaintiff's negligent conduct reduce his recovery in strict products liability by an amount proportionate to his fault?

HOLDING AND DECISION: (Richardson, J.) Yes. A plaintiff's negligent conduct will reduce his recovery in strict products liability by an amount proportionate to his fault. Strict liability is imposed on manufacturers in order to avoid placing the burden of loss on injured persons who are unable to protect themselves from manufacturing defects. But that part of a plaintiff's damages which results from his own fault should not be apportioned to others. Thus, comparative principles should apply to proportionately reduce his recovery in strict liability. This principle is not retroactive, however. In this case, since the issue of comparative fault was first raised on appeal, there was no basis for having the jury evaluate the evidence under comparative fault principles. The principles will apply in the event of retrial, however. Reversed.

CONCURRENCE AND DISSENT: (Jefferson, J.) The jury cannot accurately measure or compare a defendant's strict liability with a plaintiff's negligence; thus, it will be unable to fairly apportion liability.

DISSENT: (Mosk, J.) Negligence is a concept foreign to products liability. The issues are whether a product is defective and whether the defect caused the injury; the victim's conduct is irrelevant to these issues.

ANALYSIS

As a general rule contributory negligence (failure to guard against or discover defects) is not a defense to a strict products liability action, while assumption of the risk is a defense. Some states, California now among them, have extended the concept of comparative fault to strict products liability actions, e.g., *Butand v. Suburban Marine & Sporting Goods, Inc.*, 555 P. 2d 42 (Alaska 1976). In these states, assumption of the risk has merged with comparative principles and is no longer a separate defense.

Quicknotes

DESIGN DEFECT A defect that exists in a product regardless of the method of manufacture or amount of due care exercised by those in the commercial chain of distribution, but instead as the result of flaws in the product's design.

STRICT LIABILITY Liability for all injuries proximately caused by a party's conducting of certain inherently dangerous activities without regard to negligence or fault.

Geier v. American Honda Motor Co.

Injured driver (P) v. Manufacturer (D)

529 U.S. 861 (2000)

NATURE OF CASE: Review of dismissal of tort claims.

FACT SUMMARY: Geier (P) was seriously injured when her car struck a tree, and she sued American Honda Motor Co. (D) for allegedly negligently and defectively designing a car without a driver's side airbag.

RULE OF LAW

A "no airbag" lawsuit conflicts with the objectives of a Federal Motor Vehicle Safety Standard and is therefore preempted.

FACTS: Geier (P), who was injured when her car hit a tree, alleged that American Honda Motor Co. (Honda) (D) was negligent in not equipping the car with air bags or other passive restraint devices. The district court dismissed the suit, claiming it was preempted by federal standards that gave manufacturers a choice as to whether to install airbags. The court of appeals affirmed. Geier (P) appealed. The United States Supreme Court granted certiorari.

ISSUE: Does a "no airbag" lawsuit conflict with the objectives of a Federal Motor Vehicle Safety Standard, and is it therefore preempted?

HOLDING AND DECISION: (Breyer, J.) Yes. A "no airbag" lawsuit conflicts with the objectives of a Federal Motor Vehicle Safety Standard and is therefore preempted. Ordinary preemption principles apply to this case. The National Traffic and Motor Vehicle Safety Act authorized the promulgation of federal standards and preempted state law safety standards. [Affirmed.]

DISSENT: (Stevens, J.) An interim regulation, motivated by the Secretary of Transportation's desire to foster gradual development of a variety of passive restraint devices, should not deprive state courts of jurisdiction over claims of negligence or defective design. Honda (D) has not overcome the presumption against preemption in this case.

ANALYSIS

The dissent would have permitted preemption of tort claims only if they created a special burden on the federal regulatory scheme. The preemption was based on inferences from regulatory history and commentary alone. The majority deferred to the Department of Transportation's own interpretation of the federal standards.

Quicknotes

DEFECTIVE DESIGN A product that is manufactured in accordance with a particular design; however, such design is inherently flawed so that it presents an unreasonable risk of injury.

FEDERALISM A scheme of government whereby the power to govern is divided between a central government and localized governments.

NEGLIGENCE Conduct falling below the standard of care that a reasonable person would demonstrate under similar conditions.

PREEMPTION Judicial preference recognizing the presumption in favor of federal legislation over state legislation of the same subject matter.

Wyeth v. Levine

Drug manufacturer (D) v. Drug recipient (P)

555 U.S. 555 (2009)

NATURE OF CASE: Appeal, on grounds that certain federal regulations preempt state tort law, from state's highest court's affirmance of a jury verdict for a plaintiff in a product liability action.

FACT SUMMARY: Levine (P) contended that notwithstanding the federal Food and Drug Administration's approval of Wyeth's (D) warning label for Wyeth's (D) drug Phenergan, the warning label was inadequate by state tort law standards. Wyeth (D) asserted that state tort law was preempted by federal regulatory law in this area.

RULE OF LAW

Federal regulatory law does not preempt state tort law where the state law does not frustrate the achievement of congressional objectives.

FACTS: Wyeth (D) manufactured the antinausea drug Phenergan. The warnings on Phenergan's label had been deemed sufficient by the federal Food and Drug Administration (FDA) when it approved Wyeth's (D) new drug application in 1955 and when it later approved changes in the drug's labeling. After a clinician injected Levine (P) with Phenergan by the "IV-push" method, whereby a drug is injected directly into a patient's vein, the drug entered Levine's (P) artery, she developed gangrene, and doctors amputated her forearm. Levine (P) brought a state-law damages action on theories of common-law negligence and strict liability, alleging, inter alia, that Wyeth (D) had failed to provide an adequate warning about the significant risks of administering Phenergan by the IV-push method. Although Phenergan's labeling warned of the danger of gangrene and amputation following inadvertent intra-arterial injection, Levine (P) alleged that the labeling was defective because it failed to instruct clinicians to use the IV-drip method of intravenous administration instead of the higher risk IV-push method. More broadly, she alleged that Phenergan is not reasonably safe for intravenous administration because the foreseeable risks of gangrene and loss of limb are great in relation to the drug's therapeutic benefits. A state jury ruled for Levine (P), and the state's highest court affirmed. Wyeth (D) appealed, claiming that federal regulatory law preempted the state's tort law in this area, and the United States Supreme Court granted certiorari.

ISSUE: Does federal regulatory law preempt state tort law where the state law does not frustrate the achievement of congressional objectives?

HOLDING AND DECISION: (Stevens, J.) No. Federal regulatory law does not preempt state tort law where the state law does not frustrate the achievement of congressional objectives. The argument that Levine's (P) state-law claims are preempted because it is impossible for Wyeth (D) to comply with both the state law duties underlying those claims and its federal labeling duties is rejected. Although a manufacturer generally may change a drug label only after the FDA approves a supplemental application, the agency's "changes being effected" (CBE) regulation permits certain pre-approval labeling changes that add or strengthen a warning to improve drug safety. Pursuant to the CBE regulation, Wyeth (D) could have unilaterally added a stronger warning about IV-push administration, and there is no evidence that the FDA would ultimately have rejected such a labeling change. Wyeth (D) is incorrect in its understanding that the FDA, rather than the manufacturer, bears primary responsibility for drug labeling. Instead, federal law and regulations provide that the manufacturer bears responsibility for the content of its label at all times. In addition, Wyeth's (D) argument that requiring it to comply with a state-law duty to provide a stronger warning would interfere with Congress's purpose of entrusting an expert agency with drug labeling decisions is meritless because it relies on an untenable interpretation of congressional intent and an overbroad view of an agency's power to pre-empt state law. The history of the Food, Drug, and Cosmetic Act (FDCA) shows that Congress did not intend to preempt state-law failure-to-warn actions. In advancing the argument that the FDA must be presumed to have established a specific labeling standard that leaves no room for different state-law judgments, Wyeth (D) relies not on any statement by Congress but on the preamble to a 2006 FDA regulation declaring that state-law failure-to-warn claims threaten the FDA's statutorily prescribed role. Although an agency regulation with the force of law can preempt conflicting state requirements, this case involves no such regulation but merely an agency's assertion that state law is an obstacle to achieving its statutory objectives. Here, however, the FDA's statement is not entitled to deference, as it is at odds with congressional purposes, and it reverses the FDA's own longstanding position that state law is a complementary form of drug regulation without providing a reasoned explanation for such a change of course. [Affirmed.]

DISSENT: (Alito, J.) Contrary to the majority's assertion that the issue presented is a narrow one, the real issue is whether a state tort jury can countermand the FDA's

Continued on next page.

considered judgment that Phenergan's FDA-mandated warning label renders its intravenous (IV) use "safe." Federal law relies on the FDA to make safety determinations like the one it made here. The FDA has long known about the risks associated with IV push in general and its use to administer Phenergan in particular, but nevertheless concluded that the drug is safe and effective when used in accord with the authorized warning label. Levine's (P) injuries did not come about because the label was too weak—it was because the providers who administered the drug ignored the warning label altogether. Thus, while the case is appropriately one for medical malpractice, permitting it to be a frontal assault on the FDA's regulatory regime for drug labeling upsets the well-settled meaning of the Supremacy Clause and settled conflict preemption jurisprudence. Congress made its "purpose" plain in authorizing the FDA—not state tort juries—to determine when and under what circumstances a drug is "safe." Because the FDA did weigh the costs and benefits associated with IV push, and, given the "balance" that the FDA struck between those costs and benefits, preemption of tort suits that would upset that balance is required by precedent. And, unlike the FDA, juries are ill-equipped to perform the FDA's cost-benefit-balancing function. Juries address actualities, whereas the FDA addresses probabilities and takes a much longer view. Thus, the FDA conveys its warnings with one voice, rather than whipsawing the medical community with 50 (or more) potentially conflicting ones. Under the majority's ruling, however, parochialism may prevail. Because the state's law in this instance cannot coexist peacefully with federal law, it must be preempted.

ANALYSIS

The decision in this case was limited to brand-name drugs, but not generics, which are regulated by a different statutory scheme. In *Pliva, Inc. v. Mensing*, 131 S. Ct. 2567 (2011), the Court held that federal drug regulations applicable to generic drug manufacturers directly conflict with, and thus preempt, state-law tort claims alleging a failure to provide adequate warning labels. Thus, while failure to warn claims against generics manufacturers may no longer be brought under state law, it is not clear that other types of state-law claims, such as design defect claims, against such manufacturers are equally preempted. The distinction between *Pliva* and *Wyeth* turned on the fact that a brand-name manufacturer seeking new drug approval is responsible for the accuracy and adequacy of its label, whereas a manufacturer seeking generic drug approval is responsible for ensuring that its warning label is the same as the label of the brand name drug. In distinguishing the cases, the Court acknowledged that from the plaintiff's perspective it made little difference whether the drug taken was a brand-name drug or a generic, since the drug chemically was the same. The dissent in *Pliva* went further, claiming that the distinction was "absurd" and predicting the decision will make generic drugs a riskier proposition for consumers, and reduce demand for generics, at least among consumers who can afford brand-name drugs.

Quicknotes

GENERIC MEANING A term that encompasses a class of related products and lacks the requisite distinctiveness for federal trademark protection.

PREEMPTION Doctrine holding that matters of national interest take precedence over matters of local interest; the federal law takes precedence over state law.

REGULATORY POWER Power granting authority pursuant to statute to a government agency or body to govern a particular area.

TORT A legal wrong resulting in a breach of duty by the wrongdoer, causing damages as a result of the breach.

CHAPTER 9

Damages

Quick Reference Rules of Law

PAGE

1. *Sullivan v. Old Colony Street Ry.* Damages are awarded to afford monetary equivalent for the actual loss caused by the wrong of another. 166

2. *Zibbell v. Southern Pacific Co.* The amount of damages recoverable is calculated to be commensurate with the injury sustained. 167

3. *McDougald v. Garber.* Some degree of cognitive awareness is a prerequisite to a plaintiff's recovery of damages for the loss of the enjoyment of life, and such damages should be treated as part of the plaintiff's recovery of damages for pain and suffering. 168

4. *O'Shea v. Riverway Towing Co.* Where an adequate means of determining the impact of inflation on the present value of lost wages exists, inflation may be considered in calculating the amount recoverable. 170

5. *Duncan v. Kansas City Southern Railway.* (1) When reviewing whether a trier of fact has abused its discretion in awarding general damages, the reviewing court should determine whether the award is beyond that which a reasonable trier of fact could assess for the effects of the particular injury to the particular plaintiff under the particular circumstances, rather than being guided by awards for similar injuries. (2) Future medical expenses awarded in a tort case must be established with some degree of certainty based on medical testimony that they are indicated and that sets out their cost. 171

6. *Kemezy v. Peters.* The plaintiff does not have the burden of introducing evidence regarding the defendant's net worth for purposes of providing the jury with information necessary to make a proper award of punitive damages. 173

7. *State Farm Mutual Automobile Insurance Co. v. Campbell.* An award of $145 million in punitive damages, where full compensatory damages are $1 million, is excessive and in violation of the Due Process Clause. 174

8. *Harding v. Town of Townshend.* The presence of liability insurance has no bearing on the liability of the defendant for his wrongful acts. 176

Sullivan v. Old Colony Street Ry.

[Parties not identified.]

Mass. Sup. Jud. Ct., 83 N.E. 1091 (1908)

NATURE OF CASE: Action for damages.

FACT SUMMARY: [Facts not included in casebook excerpt.]

RULE OF LAW

Damages are awarded to afford monetary equivalent for the actual loss caused by the wrong of another.

FACTS: [Facts not included in casebook excerpt.]

ISSUE: Are damages awarded to afford monetary equivalent for the actual loss caused by the wrong of another?

HOLDING AND DECISION: (Rugg, C.J.) Yes. Damages are awarded to afford a monetary equivalent for the actual loss caused by the wrongful conduct of another. The rule of damages is a practical instrumentality for doing justice through economic compensation.

ANALYSIS

The fundamental remedial goal in the law of torts is to restore the victim to the state of being he or she enjoyed before the tort was committed. Because it is not physically possible to erase the pain and ramifications of physical or mental injuries, the restoration must come in the form of economic compensation. This is the fundamental theory supporting damage awards.

Quicknotes

DAMAGES Monetary compensation that may be awarded by the court to a party who has sustained injury or loss to his person, property, or rights due to another party's unlawful act, omission, or negligence.

Zibbell v. Southern Pacific Co.

[Parties not identified.]

Cal. Sup. Ct., 116 P. 513 (1911)

NATURE OF CASE: [Nature of case not stated in casebook excerpt.]

FACT SUMMARY: [Facts not stated in casebook excerpt.]

RULE OF LAW

The amount of damages recoverable is calculated to be commensurate with the injury sustained.

FACTS: [Facts not stated in casebook excerpt.]

ISSUE: Is the amount of damages recoverable calculated to be commensurate with the injury sustained?

HOLDING AND DECISION: (Henshaw, J.) Yes. The amount of damages recoverable is calculated to be commensurate with the injury sustained. Although money is an inherently poor substitute for the ability to relieve pain and suffering, it is the only standard of measure available to a court to calculate compensation for tortuously induced injury. As such, the amount of money awarded must be made as closely commensurate with the amount of pain and suffering imposed. It cannot be beyond all proportion to the actual injury.

ANALYSIS

The most unguided area in tort law is the field of estimating the amount of damage due a particular victim. It is relatively clear what types of injuries are recoverable in damages, yet the amount actually due is often very difficult to ascertain. Usually, damage awards must be made by contrasting degrees of injury. Generally, a broken arm will recover less than a severed arm. However, how much less is open for debate.

Quicknotes

ACTUAL DAMAGES Measure of damages necessary to compensate victim for actual injuries suffered.

McDougald v. Garber

Patient injured during surgery (P) v. Doctor (D)

N.Y. Ct. App. 536 N.E.2d 372 (1989)

NATURE OF CASE: Appeal from award of nonpecuniary damages.

FACT SUMMARY: During surgery performed by Garber (D), McDougald (P) suffered oxygen deprivation, resulting in irreversible brain damage and a permanent comatose condition.

RULE OF LAW

Some degree of cognitive awareness is a prerequisite to a plaintiff's recovery of damages for the loss of the enjoyment of life, and such damages should be treated as part of the plaintiff's recovery of damages for pain and suffering.

FACTS: Emma McDougald (P) underwent a Caesarean section and tubal ligation. Garber (D) performed the surgery. During surgery, McDougald (P) suffered oxygen deprivation that resulted in irreversible brain damage and left her in a permanent comatose condition. McDougald (P) sued Garber (D) and the anesthesiologists in a malpractice action. McDougald (P) was awarded approximately $1,000,000 for conscious pain and suffering and approximately $3,500,000 for the loss of the pleasure and pursuits of life. The trial judge reduced McDougald's (P) total award to a single award of $2,000,000 against Garber (D). On cross-appeal, the appellate division affirmed and granted leave for Garber's (D) appeal to the New York Supreme Court. Garber (D) on appeal contended that the trial court erred, both (1) in instructing the jury that McDougald's (P) awareness was irrelevant to its consideration of damages for loss of enjoyment of life; and (2) in directing the jury to consider that aspect of damages separately from pain and suffering.

ISSUE: Must some degree of cognitive awareness be a prerequisite for a plaintiff's recovery of damages for the loss of the enjoyment of life, and should such damages be treated as part of the plaintiff's recovery of damages for pain and suffering?

HOLDING AND DECISION: (Wachtler, C.J.) Yes. Some degree of cognitive awareness is a prerequisite of a plaintiff's recovery of damages for the loss of enjoyment of life, and such damages should be treated as part of the plaintiff's recovery of damages for pain and suffering. Damages for nonpecuniary loss for loss of enjoyment of life are among those that can be awarded to compensate a plaintiff. However, an award of money damages to a person who has no awareness of the loss of such enjoyment serves no compensatory purpose. An award of damages in such circumstances has no meaning or utility to the injured person. The advocates of separate awards contend that because pain and suffering and loss of enjoyment of life can be distinguished conceptually, they must be treated separately if the plaintiff is to be compensated fully for each distinct injury suffered. Such an analytical approach may be warranted when the subject is pecuniary damages that are easily subject to calculation. However, translating human suffering into dollars and cents may not be accomplished by applying a mathematical formula, but rests on a legal fiction. The figure that emerges is unavoidably distorted. If anything, the distortion will be amplified by repetition. New trial granted on issue of nonpecuniary damages.

DISSENT: (Titone, J.) The majority's holding neither comports with the fundamental principles of tort compensation nor furnishes a satisfactory, logically consistent framework for compensating nonpecuniary loss. The loss of enjoyment of life is an objective damage item, conceptually distinct from conscious pain and suffering. An award for loss of enjoyment of life should therefore have been given even in the absence of any awareness of that loss on the part of McDougald (P). Such an award is not altered or rendered punitive by the fact that the unaware injured McDougald (P) cannot experience the pleasure of having it.

ANALYSIS

Pain and suffering, called "general" damages, have been the source of much debate in the legal community. Some commentators have called for their abolition, stating that, at the societal level, they are nothing more than a device for wealth distribution and have nothing to do with compensation. Most accept the need for such damages, however, for reasons cited in the present case. The difficulty with the majority view is that a wrongdoer pays less compensation when his actions turn the victim into a "vegetable" than had the victim retained consciousness.

Quicknotes

COMPENSATORY DAMAGES Measure of damages necessary to compensate victim for actual injuries suffered.

NONPECUNIARY LOSS Damages that cannot be calculated or accurately estimated in monetary terms.

Continued on next page.

PAIN AND SUFFERING DAMAGES In tort law, damages for pain and suffering are compensable only to the extent that some form of physical injury, or at least nominal damages, can be shown.

PUNITIVE DAMAGES Damages exceeding the actual injury suffered for the purposes of punishment, deterrence, and comfort to plaintiff.

O'Shea v. Riverway Towing Co.

Injured ship's cook (P) v. Riverboat company (D)

677 F.2d 1194 (7th Cir. 1982)

NATURE OF CASE: Appeal from an award for damages for lost earnings.

FACT SUMMARY: Riverway Towing Co. (D) contended it was improper for the trial court to take inflation into account in calculating O'Shea's (P) loss of future wages.

RULE OF LAW

Where an adequate means of determining the impact of inflation on the present value of lost wages exists, inflation may be considered in calculating the amount recoverable.

FACTS: Mrs. O'Shea (P) was injured while getting off a harbor boat operated by Riverway Towing Co. (Riverway) (D). She sued for damages, including the loss of future earnings due to her inability to continue working as a ship's cook. The trial court accepted the testimony of O'Shea's (P) economist, who estimated that inflation would continue to rise approximately 5-8 percent between the time of the award and the end of O'Shea's (P) working career. Based on this calculation, he arrived at an overall damage figure for lost wages and then discounted it to reflect the present value of the award. In discounting for present value, he included a large allowance for projected inflationary impact. Riverway (D) appealed the trial court's award based on this testimony, contending it was improper as a matter of law to take inflation into account in projecting future wages.

ISSUE: Where an adequate means of determining the impact of inflation on the present value of lost wages exists, may inflation be considered in calculating the amount recoverable?

HOLDING AND DECISION: (Posner, J.) Yes. Where an adequate means of determining the potential impact of inflation on the present value of lost wages exists, inflation may be considered in calculating the amount recoverable. In this case, the current long-term interest rate provided an adequate gauge of future inflationary impact on the value of money. Therefore, the testimony presented a fair representation of the inflationary impact on the award as it is based on this interest rate. Consequently, the testimony and award were proper. Affirmed.

ANALYSIS

This case illustrates that all awards which are meant to compensate for future losses must be discounted to represent their present value. This involves determining what amount in today's dollars when invested safely will yield the amount of the total award on a future date. Because of the state of the economy over the last 25 years, the impact of inflation must be considered to arrive at an accurate compensation amount.

Quicknotes

COMPENSATORY DAMAGES Measure of damages necessary to compensate victim for actual injuries suffered.

Duncan v. Kansas City Southern Railway

Train collision victims (P) v. Railway company (D)

La. Sup. Ct., 773 So. 2d 670 (2000)

NATURE OF CASE: Appeal from affirmance of damage award in personal injury action.

FACT SUMMARY: One sister, aged 12, was killed, another sister, Rachel, aged 11, was severely injured, and another sister, aged 7, was less seriously injured when the church van in which they were riding collided with a train operated by the Kansas City Southern Railway (KCS) (D). After the jury awarded damages totaling close to $28 million, KCS (D) contended that the damages awarded had to be set aside as excessive.

RULE OF LAW

(1) When reviewing whether a trier of fact has abused its discretion in awarding general damages, the reviewing court should determine whether the award is beyond that which a reasonable trier of fact could assess for the effects of the particular injury to the particular plaintiff under the particular circumstances, rather than being guided by awards for similar injuries.

(2) Future medical expenses awarded in a tort case must be established with some degree of certainty based on medical testimony that they are indicated and that sets out their cost.

FACTS: One sister, aged 12, was killed, another sister, Rachel, aged 11, was severely injured and rendered a quadriplegic, and another sister, aged 7, was less seriously injured when the church van in which they were riding collided at a railroad crossing with a train operated by the Kansas City Southern Railway (KCS) (D). The Duncans (P), the parents of the girls, filed suit against KCS (D) and the church operating the van to recover damages. A jury found the driver of the van and the railroad liable for the accident, apportioned liability between the defendants, and awarded damages totaling $27,876,813.31. Of the total amount, $8 million was for general damages for Rachel for physical pain and suffering, mental anguish, and loss of enjoyment of life, because Rachel's medical diagnosis and impairments included tetraplegia, traumatic brain injury, scoliosis, a tracheostomy, neurogenic bladder, neurogenic bowel, muscle spasms, contractures of upper and lower extremities, pulmonary insufficiency, a non-functioning left lung, left-sided hearing loss, severe headaches, anorexia, severe malnutrition, and depression. She also suffered from recurrent pulmonary infections, recurrent bladder infections, and was in constant danger of developing decubitus ulcers and autonomic dysreflexia. The jury also granted a $17 million award for Rachel's future medical expenses. Although the parties' medical experts presented similar treatment plans, programs, and types of providers that formed the basis of the projected future medical expenses, the jury was presented with differing expert testimony as to Rachel's life expectancy. The Duncans' (P) experts testified that Rachel had a life expectancy of 81 years, whereas KCS's (D) experts opined that her life expectancy was 57 years. The jury used the longer life expectancy period in calculating the award. The state's intermediate appellate court affirmed, and the Louisiana Supreme Court granted certiorari.

ISSUE:

(1) When reviewing whether a trier of fact has abused its discretion in awarding general damages, should the reviewing court determine whether the award is beyond that which a reasonable trier of fact could assess for the effects of the particular injury to the particular plaintiff under the particular circumstances, rather than being guided by awards for similar injuries?

(2) Must future medical expenses awarded in a tort case be established with some degree of certainty based on medical testimony that they are indicated and that sets out their cost?

HOLDING AND DECISION: (Johnson, J.) (1) Yes. When reviewing whether a trier of fact has abused its discretion in awarding general damages, the reviewing court should determine whether the award is beyond that which a reasonable trier of fact could assess for the effects of the particular injury to the particular plaintiff under the particular circumstances, rather than being guided by awards for similar injuries. The $8 million in general damages awarded to Rachel for her physical pain and suffering, mental anguish, and loss of enjoyment of life is beyond that which a reasonable trier of fact could assess for the effects of Rachel's particular injury under the circumstances surrounding her injury. Although the sight of Rachel in her wheelchair may have elicited some sympathetic feelings from the jury, it is abundantly clear that the effects of this accident on Rachel were devastating. Prior to the accident, Rachel was an 11-year-old girl who was enjoying a full life. As a result of the accident, Rachel is unable to function physically in the same manner as before, is severely injured, and has suffered immense mental distress. As a result of the accident, Rachel's whole life has changed. The injuries she sustained when she was thrown from the church van have left her a quadriplegic who is totally dependent on others for all her care needs.

Continued on next page.

In addition to having to cope with her own injuries and challenges, Rachel is also coping with the fact that her older sister was killed in the accident and her younger sister was injured in the accident. She is no longer able to attend school with her friends, she spends the majority of her day in either her bed or her wheelchair, she can no longer go on the family fishing and camping trips she enjoyed before the accident, and she is aware of the effect her injuries have had on her family. Notwithstanding that Rachel suffers immensely, the general damage award of $8 million is excessive and the trial court abused its discretion in accepting and fixing the jury's award. Cases having plaintiffs with similar injuries reveal the highest amount that could reasonably be awarded under the facts of this case is $6 million and, therefore, the award is reduced to that amount.

(2) Yes. Future medical expenses awarded in a tort case must be established with some degree of certainty based on medical testimony that they are indicated and that sets out their cost. The 81-year life expectancy for Rachel was based on her having the same life expectancy as persons her age without spinal cord injuries. However, the more realistic life expectancy is that of a person her age with spinal cord injuries. Not only did her own treating physician postulate the shorter life expectancy, the 57-year life expectancy is also the more scientifically accurate prediction. Accordingly, future medical expenses should have been based on the 57-year life expectancy. Therefore, future medical expenses will be reduced from $17 million to $10,528,722 based on a life expectancy for Rachel of 57 years, based on her treating physician's assessment, and not 81 years, as the Duncans' (P) expert predicted..

ANALYSIS

In reversing the general damages award for Rachel's injuries, the majority emphasized that "[o]nly after a determination that the trier of fact has abused its 'much discretion' is a resort to prior awards appropriate and then only for the purpose of determining the highest or lowest point that is reasonably within that discretion." Yet, here, the majority seems to have determined that the jury abused its discretion by reviewing general damages awards rendered in other cases for what it deemed were similar injuries, rather than on a review of the particular evidence with which the jury was presented. In fact, Justice Knoll, in a concurrence and dissent, faulted the majority for failing to heed that the jury assessed the effects of Rachel's quadriplegic injury on her individually—as "a fantastic, young girl who suffered horrendous injuries"—and based its award for the particular injury for this particular tort victim under circumstances that included a greatly diminished life expectancy and a loss of the ability to bear children. Justice Knoll also pointed out that the majority relied on a case that was "vastly dissimilar" to Rachel's, not only as to the accident victim's age and gender, but also insofar as the victim's injuries did not render them a quadriplegic. Moreover, the quantum recognized in the case was time-dated by approximately six years and failed to consider the diminishing effect of inflation. Justice Knoll's dissent lends force to the argument that a review of a trier of fact's discretion for abuse based on prior awards could become not only the overarching consideration but a rigid preordained scale, rather than guideposts for context, and make facile comparisons to prior awards the primary—if not exclusive—consideration in every step for reviewing juries' quantum determinations.

Quicknotes

DAMAGES Monetary compensation that may be awarded by the court to a party who has sustained injury or loss to his or her person, property, or rights due to another party's unlawful act, omission, or negligence.

Kemezy v. Peters

Individual (P) v. Policeman (D)

79 F.3d 33 (7th Cir. 1996)

NATURE OF CASE: 42 U.S.C. § 1983 action.

FACT SUMMARY: Kemezy (P) sued Peters (D), an off-duty policeman moonlighting as a security guard, for injuries sustained during an altercation at a bowling alley.

RULE OF LAW

The plaintiff does not have the burden of introducing evidence regarding the defendant's net worth for purposes of providing the jury with information necessary to make a proper award of punitive damages.

FACTS: Kemezy (P) brought suit against Peters (D), a policeman, under 42 U.S.C. § 1983, alleging Peters (D) wantonly beat him with a nightstick during an altercation in a bowling alley in which Peters (D) was moonlighting as a security guard. The jury awarded Kemezy (P) $10,000 in compensatory damages and $20,000 in punitive damages. Peters (D) appealed, challenging the punitive damages award on the basis that it was Kemezy's (P) burden to show evidence of Peters's (D) net worth.

ISSUE: Does the plaintiff have the burden of introducing evidence regarding the defendant's net worth for purposes of providing the jury with information necessary to make a proper award of punitive damages?

HOLDING AND DECISION: (Posner, C.J.) No. The plaintiff does not have the burden of introducing evidence regarding the defendant's net worth for purposes of providing the jury with information necessary to make a proper award of punitive damages. This is the law in the majority of jurisdictions. The purpose of punitive damages is to punish the defendant and to deter him and others from engaging in similar, wrongful conduct. This is due to several reasons. First, compensatory damages do not always compensate a victim fully. Where this is the case, punitive damages are necessary in order to ensure that tortious conduct is not underdeterred. This is necessary when the cost of mere compensation for the action is low; thus, the defendant would not be deterred from the action if he derived greater benefit from the conduct than from the loss incurred. Similarly, where the defendant's tortious conduct may be undetected, he may evaluate the risk in term of the likelihood of being caught. Punitive damages also demonstrate society's abhorrence of deliberate or reckless wrongdoing and relieve the criminal justice system of some of the pressure of enforcement. None of these purposes depend upon proof of the defendant's income or wealth. Affirmed.

ANALYSIS

Punitive damages have been a vehicle of the common law for centuries. This presents a difficult issue in the context of products liability. In *Owens-Corning Fiberglass Corp. v. Garrett*, 682 A.2d 1143, 1166-1167 (1996), the court set forth a two-part test for punitive damages in products liability cases, requiring the plaintiff to demonstrate by clear and convincing evidence the defendant's "actual knowledge of the defect and deliberate disregard of the consequences" to its users.

Quicknotes

COMPENSATORY DAMAGES Measure of damages necessary to compensate victim for actual injuries suffered.

PUNITIVE DAMAGES Damages exceeding the actual injury suffered for the purposes of punishment, deterrence and comfort to plaintiff.

State Farm Mutual Automobile Insurance Co. v. Campbell

Insurer (D) v. Insured (P)

538 U.S. 408 (2003)

NATURE OF CASE: Appeal, in action for bad faith, fraud, and intentional infliction of emotional distress, from reinstatement by state's highest court of punitive damages award, on grounds that the award was excessive and violated the Due Process Clause..

FACT SUMMARY: Campbell (P) sued State Farm Mutual Automobile Insurance Co. (State Farm) (D), his automobile insurer, for bad faith, fraud, and intentional infliction of emotional distress action when State Farm (D) refused to settle a claim brought against Campbell (P) by Ospital's estate and by Slusher.

RULE OF LAW

An award of $145 million in punitive damages, where full compensatory damages are $1 million, is excessive and in violation of the Due Process Clause.

FACTS: Campbell (P) caused a collision that killed Ospital and left Slusher permanently disabled. Ospital's estate and Slusher sued Campbell (P) for wrongful death and in tort. Campbell's (P) insurance company, State Farm Mutual Automobile Insurance Co. (State Farm) (D) refused to settle with Ospital and Slusher even though Ospital and Slusher agreed to settle for the policy limit of $25,000 each. State Farm (D) assured Campbell (P) State Farm (D) would represent Campbell's (P) interests, that Campbell's (P) assets were safe, and that Campbell (P) did not need separate counsel. A jury found Campbell (P) to be at fault and awarded $185,849 to Ospital and Slusher. Initially, State Farm (D) refused to cover the $135,849 in excess liability and refused to post a bond so Campbell (P) could appeal. State Farm (D) told Campbell (P) that he may as well put a for sale sign on his house. Campbell (P) obtained his own attorney, filed his appeal, and, in the meantime, agreed to let Slusher and Ospital's attorney represent him (P) in a case against State Farm (D) for bad faith, fraud, and intentional infliction of emotional distress. In exchange, Slusher and Ospital agreed not to seek satisfaction from Campbell (P) but would play a central role in the bad faith action, including receiving 90 percent of any verdict against State Farm (D). The appeals court denied Campbell's (P) appeal in the wrongful death and tort actions and State Farm (D) paid the entire judgment, including the amounts in excess of the policy limits. Despite State Farm's (D) payment, Campbell (P) filed suit against State Farm (D), alleging bad faith, fraud, and intentional infliction of emotional distress. The jury found in favor of Campbell (P) and awarded him $2.6 million in compensatory damages and $145 million in punitive damages. The award was subsequently reduced to $1 million and $25 million, respectively. The state's highest court affirmed the $1 million compensatory damages award and reinstated the $145 million in punitive damages. The United States Supreme Court granted certiorari.

ISSUE: Is an award of $145 million in punitive damages, where full compensatory damages are $1 million, excessive and in violation of the Due Process Clause?

HOLDING AND DECISION: (Kennedy, J.) Yes. An award of $145 million in punitive damages, where full compensatory damages are $1 million, is excessive and in violation of the Due Process Clause. In determining the validity of a punitive damage award, consideration is given to the degree of reprehensibility of the defendant's misconduct; the disparity between the actual or potential harm suffered by the plaintiff and the punitive damages awarded; and the difference between the punitive damages awarded by the jury and the civil penalties authorized or imposed in comparable cases. Here, the reprehensibility of State Farm's (D) misconduct could have been punished in a more modest way and still have satisfied state objectives. The disparity between the actual or potential harm suffered by Campbell (P) and the punitive damages awarded was significant, and the difference between the punitive damages award by the jury and the civil penalties authorized or imposed in comparable cases was great. Although states have discretion over the amount of punitive damages allowed, there are constitutional limitations on these awards. The imposition of grossly excessive or arbitrary punishments on a tortfeasor is prohibited because of fundamental notions of fairness. Moreover, because defendants subjected to punitive damages in civil cases do not have the same protections applicable in criminal proceedings, such awards pose an acute danger of arbitrary deprivation of property. In the present case, it was erroneous for the $145 million to be reinstated. Although State Farm's (D) handling of the claims against Campbell (P) was reprehensible, in that they would probably get a judgment over the policy limits, but still went to trial and then told Campbell (D) to sell his house, a more modest punishment for these actions could have satisfied the state's legitimate objectives. Instead, this case was used to expose State Farm's (D) perceived nationwide deficiencies. However, a state does not have a legitimate concern in imposing punitive damages to punish a defendant for unlawful acts

Continued on next page.

committed outside the state's jurisdiction. A state cannot punish a defendant for conduct that may have been lawful where it occurred. Lawful out-of-state conduct may be probative when it demonstrates the deliberateness and culpability of the defendant's action in the state where it is tortious, but that conduct must have a nexus to the specific harm suffered by the plaintiff. Moreover, the courts erred in awarding punitive damages to punish and deter conduct that bore no relation to Campbell's (P) harm. Due process does not permit courts to adjudicate the merits of other parties' hypothetical claims against a defendant. Furthermore, the disparity between the actual or potential harm suffered by Campbell (P) and the punitive damages award is much too large to be valid. Few awards exceeding a single-digit ratio between punitive and compensatory damages will satisfy due process. Usually, an award of no more than four times the amount of compensatory damages is the maximum. The ratio in the present case is 145 to 1. The measure of punishment in this case was neither reasonable nor proportionate to the amount of harm to Campbell (P) and to the general damages recovered. The harm Campbell (P) suffered was minor economic damage and not physical, and the excess verdict was paid before the complaint was filed. Lastly, the disparity between the punitive damages award and the civil penalties authorized or imposed in comparable cases is great. The civil sanction is a $10,000 fine for an act of fraud. Reversed and remanded.

DISSENT: (Scalia, J.) The Due Process Clause provides no substantive protections against excessive or unreasonable awards of punitive damages.

DISSENT: (Thomas, J.) The Constitution does not constrain the size of punitive damage awards.

DISSENT: (Ginsburg, J.) By entering the punitive damages domain, the Court acts alone without the benefit of federal lower courts' opinions. Punitive damage issues traditionally have been left to the states to superintend, and states' laws governing punitive damages have been accepted as is, and any system-wide changes should be left in the hands of state legislators and judges.

ANALYSIS

As Justice Ginsburg's dissent indicates, the Court's foray into an area traditionally left to the states has not only engendered a debate about states' rights and the appropriate role of the Court in such areas, but it has also given rise to implicit rebukes of the Court's guidelines regarding the determination of constitutional punitive damages by state courts. For example, in the *Campbell* case, the Utah Supreme Court on remand, rejected State Farm's (D) argument that the court had to abide by a 1:1 ratio of punitive damages to compensatory damages. Instead, the Utah Supreme Court, stating that except when punitive damages awards transgress due process guarantees, they are properly the province of the states, not only remitted the punitive damages award to $9 million, i.e., a 9:1 ratio, but also disagreed with the United States Supreme Court on most propositions of Utah law that the United States Supreme Court had addressed in *Campbell*, thus suggesting that the Utah Supreme Court was asserting its right to address matters of state law and to mitigate the effects of federal intrusion into an area of the law traditionally left to the states. Nonetheless, courts' responses to large punitive damage awards have diverged significantly, with some courts strictly adhering to the guideposts set by the Supreme Court, and others, like the Utah Supreme Court, taking the guideposts into account but relying heavily on state precedents in rendering their final decisions.

Quicknotes

BAD FAITH Conduct that is intentionally misleading or deceptive.

DUE PROCESS CLAUSE Clauses, found in the Fifth and Fourteenth Amendments to the United States Constitution, providing that no person shall be deprived of "life, liberty, or property, without due process of law."

FRAUD A false representation of facts with the intent that another will rely on the misrepresentation to his detriment.

INTENTIONAL INFLICTION OF EMOTIONAL DISTRESS Intentional and extreme behavior on the part of the wrongdoer with the intent to cause the victim to suffer from severe emotional distress, or behavior performed with reckless indifference, resulting in the victim's suffering from severe emotional distress.

PUNITIVE DAMAGES Damages exceeding the actual injury suffered for the purposes of punishment, deterrence and comfort to plaintiff.

Harding v. Town of Townshend

Accident victim (P) v. City (D)

Vt. Sup. Ct., 43 Vt. 536 (1871)

NATURE OF CASE: Action on the case for damages sustained by the plaintiff.

FACT SUMMARY: Harding (P) was injured when Townshend (D) failed to maintain a safe highway. Townshend (D) claimed its liability should be diminished by the amount Harding (P) recovered from his insurance.

RULE OF LAW

The presence of liability insurance has no bearing on the liability of the defendant for his wrongful acts.

FACTS: Townshend (D) had a duty to maintain its highways so as not to cause Harding (P) and others similarly situated to be injured thereon. Harding (P) was injured but received some compensation from his insurance. The only issue at trial was damages. Townshend (D) claimed the amount of Harding's (P) recovery from them should be diminished by what he received from his insurer, because Harding (P) is entitled to only one recovery. The trial court reduced the recovery.

ISSUE: Does the presence of liability insurance have bearing on the liability of the defendant for his wrongful acts?

HOLDING AND DECISION: (Peck, J.) No. The presence of liability insurance has no bearing on the liability of the defendant for his wrongful acts. The one who causes the injury should bear the loss. The insurer has no relationship, such as privity or being a joint tortfeasor, with Townshend (D) that should allow it to be subrogated to the rights of the injured party, even though an insurer may be so subrogated. Here, the superior equity is in the insurers who pay the second recovery, not in the wrongdoers. Reversed.

ANALYSIS

The Collateral Benefits Rule has its supporters and detractors in academic circles, although it remains entrenched in American courts. In some jurisdictions, a setoff may be allowed by statute, especially in attempts to keep medical malpractice insurance costs down. In some cases, a governmental agency that provides insurance may be allowed a setoff. The recovery it paid under the insurance may be deducted from what the U.S., as tortfeasor, was held liable for under a judgment. But the principal case states the majority view.

Quicknotes

JOINT TORTFEASORS Two or more parties that either act in concert, or whose individual acts combine to cause a single injury, rendering them jointly and severally liable for damages incurred.

PRIVITY Commonality of rights or interests between parties.

Glossary

Common Latin Words and Phrases Encountered in the Law

A FORTIORI: Because one fact exists or has been proven, therefore a second fact that is related to the first fact must also exist.

A PRIORI: From the cause to the effect. A term of logic used to denote that when one generally accepted truth is shown to be a cause, another particular effect must necessarily follow.

AB INITIO: From the beginning; a condition that has existed throughout, as in a marriage that was void ab initio.

ACTUS REUS: The wrongful act; in criminal law, such action as is sufficient to trigger criminal liability.

AD VALOREM: According to value; an ad valorem tax is imposed upon an item located within the taxing jurisdiction calculated by the value of such item.

AMICUS CURIAE: Friend of the court. Its most common usage takes the form of an amicus curiae brief, filed by a person who is not a party to an action but is nonetheless allowed to offer an argument supporting his or her legal interests.

ARGUENDO: In arguing. A statement, possibly hypothetical, made for the purpose of argument.

BILL QUIA TIMET: A bill to quiet title (establish ownership) to real property.

BONA FIDE: True, honest, or genuine. May refer to a person's legal position based on good faith or lacking notice of fraud (such as a bona fide purchaser for value) or to the authenticity of a particular document (such as a bona fide last will and testament).

CAUSA MORTIS: With approaching death in mind. A gift causa mortis is a gift given by a party who feels certain that death is imminent.

CAVEAT EMPTOR: Let the buyer beware. This maxim is reflected in the rule of law that a buyer purchases at his or her own risk because it is the buyer's responsibility to examine, judge, test, and otherwise inspect what he or she is buying.

CERTIORARI: A writ of review. Petitions for review of a case by the United States Supreme Court are most often done by means of a writ of certiorari.

CONTRA: On the other hand. Opposite. Contrary to.

CORAM NOBIS: Before us; a writ of error directed to the court that originally rendered the judgment.

CORAM VOBIS: Before you; a writ of error directed by an appellate court to a lower court to correct a factual error.

CORPUS DELICTI: The body of the crime; the requisite elements of a crime amounting to objective proof that a crime has been committed.

CUM TESTAMENTO ANNEXO, ADMINISTRATOR (ADMINISTRATOR C.T.A.): With will annexed; an administrator c.t.a. settles an estate pursuant to a will in which he or she is not appointed.

DE BONIS NON, ADMINISTRATOR (ADMINISTRATOR D.B.N.): Of goods not administered; an administrator d.b.n. settles a partially settled estate.

DE FACTO: In fact; in reality; actually. Existing in fact but not officially approved or engendered.

DE JURE: By right; lawful. Describes a condition that is legitimate "as a matter of law," in contrast to the term "de facto," which connotes something existing in fact but not legally sanctioned or authorized. For example, de facto segregation refers to segregation brought about by housing patterns, etc., whereas de jure segregation refers to segregation created by law.

DE MINIMUS: Of minimal importance; insignificant; a trifle; not worth bothering about.

DE NOVO: Anew; a second time; afresh. A trial de novo is a new trial held at the appellate level as if the case originated there and the trial at a lower level had not taken place.

DICTA: Generally used as an abbreviated form of obiter dicta, a term describing those portions of a judicial opinion incidental or not necessary to resolution of the specific question before the court. Such nonessential statements and remarks are not considered to be binding precedent.

DUCES TECUM: Refers to a particular type of writ or subpoena requesting a party or organization to produce certain documents in its possession.

EN BANC: Full bench. Where a court sits with all justices present rather than the usual quorum.

EX PARTE: For one side or one party only. An ex parte proceeding is one undertaken for the benefit of only one party, without notice to, or an appearance by, an adverse party.

EX POST FACTO: After the fact. An ex post facto law is a law that retroactively changes the consequences of a prior act.

EX REL.: Abbreviated form of the term "ex relatione," meaning upon relation or information. When the state brings an action in which it has no interest against an individual at the instigation of one who has a private interest in the matter.

FORUM NON CONVENIENS: Inconvenient forum. Although a court may have jurisdiction over the case, the action should be tried in a more conveniently located court, one to which parties and witnesses may more easily travel, for example.

GUARDIAN AD LITEM: A guardian appointed by the court to represent a minor or incompetent person in a legal action.

HABEAS CORPUS: You have the body. The modern writ of habeas corpus is a writ directing that a person (body) being detained (such as a prisoner) be brought before the court so that the legality of his or her detention can be judicially ascertained.

IN CAMERA: In private, in chambers. When a hearing is held before a judge in his or her chambers or when all spectators are excluded from the courtroom.

IN FORMA PAUPERIS: In the manner of a pauper. A party who proceeds in forma pauperis because of his or her poverty is one who is allowed to bring suit without liability for costs.

INFRA: Below, under. A word referring the reader to a later part of a book. (The opposite of supra.)

IN LOCO PARENTIS: In the place of a parent.

IN PARI DELICTO: Equally wrong; a court of equity will not grant requested relief to an applicant who is in pari delicto, or as much at fault in the transactions giving rise to the controversy as is the opponent of the applicant.

IN PARI MATERIA: On like subject matter or upon the same matter. Statutes relating to the same person or things are said to be in pari materia. It is a general rule of statutory construction that such statutes should be construed together, i.e., looked at as if they together constituted one law.

IN PERSONAM: Against the person. Jurisdiction over the person of an individual.

IN RE: In the matter of. Used to designate a proceeding involving an estate or other property.

IN REM: Signifies an action against the res, or thing. An action in rem is basically one that is taken directly against property, as distinguished from an action in personam, i.e., against the person.

INTER ALIA: Among other things. Used to show that the whole of a statement, pleading, list, statute, etc., has not been set forth in its entirety.

INTER PARTES: Between the parties. May refer to contracts, conveyances, or other transactions having legal significance.

INTER VIVOS: Between the living. An inter vivos gift is a gift made by a living grantor, as distinguished from bequests contained in a will, which pass upon the death of the testator.

IPSO FACTO: By the mere fact itself.

JUS: Law or the entire body of law.

LEX LOCI: The law of the place; the notion that the rights of parties to a legal proceeding are governed by the law of the place where those rights arose.

MALUM IN SE: Evil or wrong in and of itself; inherently wrong. Describes an act that is wrong by its very nature, as opposed to one which would not be wrong but for the fact that there is a specific legal prohibition against it (malum prohibitum).

MALUM PROHIBITUM: Wrong because prohibited, but not inherently evil. Describes something that is wrong because it is expressly forbidden by law but that is not in and of itself evil, e.g., speeding.

MANDAMUS: We command. A writ directing an official to take a certain action.

MENS REA: A guilty mind; a criminal intent. A term used to signify the mental state that accompanies a crime or other prohibited act. Some crimes require only a general mens rea (general intent to do the prohibited act), but others, like assault with intent to murder, require the existence of a specific mens rea.

MODUS OPERANDI: Method of operating; generally refers to the manner or style of a criminal in committing crimes, admissible in appropriate cases as evidence of the identity of a defendant.

NEXUS: A connection to.

NISI PRIUS: A court of first impression. A nisi prius court is one where issues of fact are tried before a judge or jury.

N.O.V. (NON OBSTANTE VEREDICTO): Notwithstanding the verdict. A judgment n.o.v. is a judgment given in favor of one party despite the fact that a verdict was returned in favor of the other party, the justification being that the verdict either had no reasonable support in fact or was contrary to law.

NUNC PRO TUNC: Now for then. This phrase refers to actions that may be taken and will then have full retroactive effect.

PENDENTE LITE: Pending the suit; pending litigation underway.

PER CAPITA: By head; beneficiaries of an estate, if they take in equal shares, take per capita.

PER CURIAM: By the court; signifies an opinion ostensibly written "by the whole court" and with no identified author.

PER SE: By itself, in itself; inherently.

PER STIRPES: By representation. Used primarily in the law of wills to describe the method of distribution where a person, generally because of death, is unable to take that which is left to him or her by the will of another, and therefore his or her heirs divide such property between them rather than take under the will individually.

PRIMA FACIE: On its face, at first sight. A prima facie case is one that is sufficient on its face, meaning that the evidence supporting it is adequate to establish the case until contradicted or overcome by other evidence.

PRO TANTO: For so much; as far as it goes. Often used in eminent domain cases when a property owner receives partial payment for his or her land without prejudice to his or her right to bring suit for the full amount he or she claims the land to be worth.

QUANTUM MERUIT: As much as the party deserves. Refers to recovery based on the doctrine of unjust enrichment in those cases in which a party has rendered valuable services or furnished materials that were accepted and enjoyed by another under circumstances that would reasonably notify the recipient that the rendering party expected to be paid. In essence, the law implies a contract to pay the reasonable value of the services or materials furnished.

QUASI: Almost like; as if; nearly. Essentially used to signify that one subject or thing is almost analogous to another but that material differences between them do exist. For example, a quasi-criminal proceeding is one that is not strictly criminal but shares enough of the same characteristics to require some of the same safeguards (e.g., procedural due process must be followed in a parole hearing).

QUID PRO QUO: Something for something. In contract law, the consideration, something of value, passed between the parties to render the contract binding.

RES GESTAE: Things done. In evidence law, this principle justifies the admission of a statement that would otherwise be hearsay when it is made so closely to the event in question as to be said to be a part of it, or with such spontaneity as not to have the possibility of falsehood.

RES IPSA LOQUITUR: The thing speaks for itself. This doctrine gives rise to a rebuttable presumption of negligence when the instrumentality causing the injury was within the exclusive control of the defendant, and the injury was one that does not normally occur unless a person has been negligent.

RES JUDICATA: A matter adjudged. Doctrine that provides that once a court of competent jurisdiction has rendered a final judgment or decree on the merits, that judgment or decree is conclusive upon the parties to the case and prevents them from engaging in any other litigation on the points and issues determined therein.

RESPONDEAT SUPERIOR: Let the master reply. This doctrine holds the master liable for the wrongful acts of his or her servant (or the principal for his or her agent) in those cases in which the servant (or agent) was acting within the scope of his or her authority at the time of the injury.

STARE DECISIS: To stand by or adhere to that which has been decided. The common-law doctrine of stare decisis attempts to give security and certainty to the law by following the policy that once a principle of law as applicable to a certain set of facts has been set forth in a decision, it forms a precedent that will subsequently be followed, even though a different decision might be made were it the first time the question had arisen. Of course, stare decisis is not an inviolable principle and is departed from in instances where there is good cause (e.g., considerations of public policy led the Supreme Court to disregard prior decisions sanctioning segregation).

SUPRA: Above. A word referring a reader to an earlier part of a book. (The opposite of infra.)

ULTRA VIRES: Beyond the power. This phrase is most commonly used to refer to actions taken by a corporation that are beyond the power or legal authority of the corporation.

Addendum of French Derivatives

CHATTEL: Tangible personal property.

CY PRES: Doctrine permitting courts to apply trust funds to purposes not expressed in the trust but necessary to carry out the settlor's intent.

IN PAIS: Not pursuant to legal proceedings.

PER AUTRE VIE: For another's life; during another's life. In property law, an estate may be granted that will terminate upon the death of someone other than the grantee.

PROFIT A PRENDRE: A license to remove minerals or other produce from land.

VOIR DIRE: Process of questioning jurors as to their predispositions about the case or parties to a proceeding in order to identify those jurors displaying bias or prejudice.